CW00539254

Playing to Lose

Planing to Lose

Playing to Lose

The Memoir of a Jehovah's Witness Turned Submissive BDSM Model

Ariel Anderssen

unbound

First published in 2023

Unbound
c/o TC Group, 6th Floor King's House, 9–10 Haymarket,
London SW1Y 4BP
www.unbound.com
All rights reserved

© Ariel Anderssen, 2023

The right of Ariel Anderssen to be identified as the author
of this work has been asserted in accordance with Section 77 of the Copyright,
Designs and Patents Act, 1988. No part of this publication may be copied,
reproduced, stored in a retrieval system, or transmitted, in any form
or by any means without the prior permission of the publisher, nor be
otherwise circulated in any form of binding or cover other than that in
which it is published and without a similar condition being imposed
on the subsequent purchaser.

This book is a work of non-fiction based on the life,
experience and recollections of the author. In some cases names of
people, places, dates and sequences or the detail of events have been
changed solely to protect the privacy of others. The author has stated
to the publishers that, except in such respects, not affecting the
substantial accuracy of the work, the contents of this book are true.

Text design by Jouve

A CIP record for this book is available from the British Library

ISBN 978-1-80018-260-8 (paperback)
ISBN 978-1-80018-261-5 (ebook)

Printed and bound in Great Britain by Clays Ltd, Elcograf S.p.A.

1 3 5 7 9 8 6 4 2

MIX
Paper from
responsible sources
FSC
www.fsc.org FSC® C018072

To my international kinky family

Contents

Part Three: A Massive Masochistic Moth

Dear Reader

First, you must know that my real name isn't Ariel. It is Joceline. I am telling you this because everything in this book is true, and I'm not going to start it by lying to you about my name.

Prologue

I am screaming. I'm tied almost immobile with tight bands of rope all over my body, a stocking is forced over my face, intensifying the claustrophobic feeling of the big ballgag in my mouth. I struggle hard, trying to find a way to shake the ropes from my body, my peril in stark contrast to the sunny Georgian bedroom of my surroundings. Nothing works; I moan in frustration, then turn my eyes up to my persecutor, who's standing watching me, filming my predicament with a large, professional cine camera. He realises that I'm calling for a cut.

My niece Philippa and her fellow first-year film students lurk unobtrusively around the room, also recording the kidnap on their camera, and making notes as we go. My husband Hywel, who's doubling as my kidnapper and camera operator today, stops recording. Once he's untied my hands, I make quick work of releasing the rest of the ropes. I pull the stocking off my head; it's ruined my makeup, which I'd applied heavy-handedly to give it a chance of showing through the nylon. All seven of us head downstairs to our big kitchen with its sunshine-yellow AGA oven. The students are all staying with us

this week, and the house smells of toast, and is strewn
with sleeping bags and hoodies. On the way down to the
kitchen I give my niece a quick extra hug. I know she's
not distressed by seeing me tied up; it had been her idea
to spend a month doing work experience with us the
year before. But I'd hate to have alarmed her fellow students and embarrassed her. We're still okay, though; I
actually wonder if she finds our middle-aged country-
house-style kinkiness a bit staid and ordinary.

In the kitchen I slice up the chocolate cake I made earlier, feeling impressed by the student director, who keeps
filming as I do so. When my niece and her team eventually send us their finished documentary, I'm happy to see
that my home baking makes the final cut. So does my
account of when Hywel proposed to me. Embarrassingly,
I cried while telling the story. Crying *always* makes the
final cut in everything. I know this, and should probably
control my emotions better, but that is not one of my
gifts. I could probably tell the story of my life by only
recounting scenes in which I'd cried. But perhaps I should
find a cheerier way to share the peculiar series of events
that led me to this day. I could, for example, tell you my
life story by only recounting scenes in which I fantasised
about being tied up or spanked. That does seem a little
more pleasant for you, and the least I can do to thank
you for buying my book. Righty ho, I've got lots to get
through. Come with me, I promise it'll be fun. Well, I
promise it'll be strange, anyway. And personally, I do find
the strangeness of other people endlessly entertaining.
Hopefully, you'll feel the same way.

Part One

An Embryonic Deviant

Part One

Chapter One

Dastardly Captain Hook and My Distressingly Non-Kinky Family

My husband cannot remember his first day at school. I find this inability to recall early childhood inconceivable. I not only remember my first day, I remember what we ate for lunch (pink Angel Delight, two helpings), who I played with (Naomi and Catherine), and the results of the numeracy test our teacher gave us that afternoon (I didn't do well, and cried). I remember detail with a vividness that makes my entire life feel rather recent, and rather tangible. And I remember much further back in my life than my first day of school. I recall being not quite three years old, and running full tilt into a wall at my toddlers' gym class. I remember being too young to recognise my dad when he came home from a business trip and tried to help me get dressed the following morning. He'd been away too long for my toddler's brain to remember what he looked like. I jerked away from him in terror and dislocated my elbow, to his great horror. I can remember being too young to recognise the word for toilet, and asking if I could follow a little boy at nursery school into it;

I believed it must be where the toys were kept. For being able to recall such early (if sometimes unpleasant and embarrassing) bits of my life I feel lucky. And it's certainly most convenient, because I want to give you a really thorough explanation as to why, in 2018, I found myself swearing through a ballgag in a room full of people that included my husband, a close relative, and four people I'd never met before. It's a complicated story, but due to my strangely vivid memory I've got all the details right here.

Which is why I feel fairly qualified to disagree with the popular opinions I hear voiced about people with fetishes. Here are some examples. Please feel free to imagine them all being said with the most annoying voice you've ever heard.

'It's all about early experiences – some people just fixate on something that happened to them when they were young and never get over it.'

Or:

'BDSM is something people get into as a result of trauma – if you're abused when you're young, you'll end up wanting to dominate other people.'

Or this one, which makes me so terribly tired:

'Those men who go to dominatrices are all high-powered judges and lawyers. It's to give themselves a break from all their power; otherwise they can't handle it.'

I am not a dominatrix, for reasons which will become clear. But many of my friends are; they have a broad spectrum of clients, some of whom have to save up for months for an hour's session, while others are wealthy, retired, and consequently see a dominatrix more or less every week. But many kinky people are aware of their sexuality before they even leave school. They don't wait until they've risen to the rank of High Court judge and then suddenly discover that they want to pay hundreds of pounds to be kicked in the balls for an hour at a time.

And while I'm sure that there *are* submissive male judges, and sexual dominants who were mistreated as children, I know that it by no means describes the majority of kinky people. I'm pretty sure I was born this way. And here's why.

I'm lying under a coffee table in my parents' best sitting room. I'm wearing a dress with buttons, but I'm too young either to dress or undress myself: buttons are hard for my two-year-old fingers. I can see the unfinished wood of the table's underside; it interests me that such a highly polished piece of furniture should have secret imperfections. In my head, Captain Hook is tying me to the mast of his pirate ship. The ropes are tight, and are digging into my nightdress-clad body. He's going to make me walk the plank later tonight. He's splendid, vivid in a red coat and high boots. His hair is long and oily and ringleted. He's huge, and scary, and I love him. I'm only two years old, I'm not good at much yet, but my imagination is big, and my imagination is what gives me the gift of being menaced by such a splendid fictional villain. I'll play this story back in my head again, many times. But I have others too, and as I get older, I'll be able to expand my imaginary world, and meet more glorious villains. I yearn to be kidnapped.

So, I don't think there was ever any hope of my being normal. And as far as I can see, my taste for wicked men has nothing to do with my upbringing. My father, for

example, is not a wicked man. He's a nuclear physicist. He works as an expert witness who assesses risks
of radiation on behalf of people suing their govern-
ments or industries after being exposed to dangerous
substances at work. I can't say it's exactly a *wicked* career choice. At home, through my childhood, he was
always quite the opposite of wicked. He was patient,
attentive and kind. He *did* give me some entirely unman-
ageable scientific explanations about the world, which
caused me considerable confusion, but I think he was
genuinely trying to interest me in science. It didn't work.
I just needed my spell checker a minute ago because I'd
forgotten how to spell 'physicist'. Whoops, just got it
wrong again. But my father has never reproached me
for my disappointing lack of love for his favourite
subjects. So I can't lay any blame with him. I don't have
any Daddy issues, as far as I can tell. Although my
husband's original career *was* in particle physics. Maybe
I *do* have a longing to hear more indecipherable explanations of the Large Hadron Collider. Ha. Spelt that
right!

Golly, it's only Chapter One and the story's getting
away from me. But now I'm overexcited, being pulled
back in time to examine whether my family life could
possibly be held responsible for the fact that I was a
very peculiar little girl indeed.

Since I don't want to blame my dad, how about my
mother: could she be to blame? Well, I'm not attracted
to female dominants, so her undoubtedly fiery character
didn't exactly shape my fantasies. She is a determined,
stylish, idiosyncratic lady, whom I loved very much
but was also rather scared of as a child, due to her

propensity to become volcanically angry at the shortest
of notice. Groups of women could do it to her: 'I can't
STAND women!' Messy wardrobes, similarly, made
her incandescent and liable to throw things around the
room: 'This is a SLUM house!' A lady at our church
('She looks like a PROSTITUTE!') made my mother so
angry, with her tight skirts and plastic earrings, that
none of us were allowed to speak to her. But gosh, this
is an uncomfortable thing to be writing. Let's just agree
not to blame my mother for now. She didn't dress me in
latex or anything. Quite the opposite; my elder sister
and I were always dressed the same, in Victorian-style
pinafore dresses that my mother made for us by hand.
You may be thinking that this sounds a little like the
spooky girls in Stanley Kubrick's *The Shining*. You are
correct; that is exactly how we looked. I, parentheti-
cally, loved being dressed like my older sister. Immi,
four years my senior, was a great deal less keen, I expect.

My husband says that I wistfully recite 'I *love* my sister' dozens of times a week. We live at opposite sides of
the country, whereas once we were barely at opposite
sides of our bedroom, mainly because:

Small Me: 'Immi! Immi! Are you awake?'

Small Immi: (sounding about a hundred years old,
reluctant, exhausted and croaky) 'Yes?'

Small Me: 'Can I come into *your* bed?'

Small Immi: (still more reluctant) '. . . yes . . .'

And into her single bed I would hop, all icy-footed
and affectionate. This was repeated regularly throughout our childhood until Immi reached the age of
fourteen and was given her own room. Whereupon
she went in and shut her bedroom door, pulling the

telephone inside with her, for four years. But up until then, I don't know how she found the patience to manage me.

Back to the story at hand, I don't think I can blame Immi for my kinkiness either. She never traumatised me or wore gas masks or pretended to be Captain Hook. So there we are, that's my family, almost definitely not to blame for the fact that I've always wanted to be tied up.

Kidnapping stories in the news electrified me with excitement. Any stories that alluded to spanking made me uncomfortable and fascinated. And when my mother learned to drive and we had to go to Mothercare to pick out seatbelts for the car: glory. I LONGED for a seatbelt. They were fantastically secure, and snuggly, and – well, they were like bondage, though I didn't know the word. I was keen on the five-point one on display in the shop. But at four years old, I was already too tall for it. I had to have a 'grown-up' version with just one strap that zigzagged across waist level and up across one shoulder. It was still tremendous, but I did yearn for the more secure version. I was always a bit baffled by the way adults thought I'd be delighted by anything extra adult. I was always a massively tall child; I already looked extra adult. I didn't need the accoutrements. In fact, I particularly wanted to stay small, for a variety of reasons. But I'll get to them.

First, I'd better give you a bit more background about how I grew up, in case you can spot a reason for all my kinkiness. I was born at the end of the 1970s, and the first home I can remember is the three-storey terraced townhouse in Horsham, West Sussex, in the south of

England, which we moved to when I was two. Immi and I shared a room at the top of the house, rather like the children in *Peter Pan*. But we didn't have any servants, obviously. Or even a dog. We *did* have a cat called Tiger Lily, who terrorised me by being generally nervous and scratchy and liable to bite with no warning, but who never tried to warn our parents that we were about to fly out of the window. Sadly, I've never actually met a cat who *would* try. Despite having a perfectly serviceable bedroom, Immi and I played on the stairs a lot, and I fell downstairs with alarming frequency. I don't *think* this was anything to do with latent masochism, but I can't promise it, I'm afraid. Immi was more sedate and more careful than I was, and sometimes managed to catch me halfway down one of my headlong descents. Quite often, though, she was busy reading, so it'd be my mother who'd rescue me from the heap I'd land in at the bottom. I was never badly hurt; I was a large, rather solid, sturdy child with a big square face, lots of messy blonde curls and fat legs. This last is according to Immi, who introduced me to her friends as 'Fat Legs' when they came to play with her after school. 'Let's all run away from Fat Legs!' they crowed, and I, who had spent the afternoon making gingerbread men with my mother in order to bribe them into liking me ('Come on, friends, ginger boys!'), went waddling after them, wailing with frustration and spraying tears.

I do wonder if perhaps my submissive hunger to be treated disdainfully and cruelly could maybe be traced back to the way in which I've always sought attention from the very people who are least likely to want to give me any. I've forever disliked the feeling of being loved more than I love in return, and would generally prefer things to feel the other way around. The beginnings of that were there in my early behaviour towards my big sister and her friends, but I don't think for a minute that it's the actual *cause* of my submissiveness. Though I do wonder if younger siblings tend to end up submissive more often than older ones. Please send me the answer, if you know. Are you a cruel elder sibling? A needy, submissive younger one? Help me do science, please.

My mother stayed at home with Immi and me; my father left the house every morning and disappeared behind a large bush at the end of our road, returning ten hours later, five days a week. It turns out that he was taking a train to a larger town an hour away where he was working for a nuclear-power organisation. I, however, believed that he sat in the large bush all day, and I once went to look for him there. Disobligingly, he wasn't in there, although it was a really splendid bush, and one in which Immi and I consequently played many times. I began to think that his job must be very dull, and that I'd rather not ever have one. Fortunately, I fully believed I'd never need one.

And that was because, despite looking like a pretty normal (though oddly attired) family, we were not normal.

Chapter Two

An Excess of Piety and a World of Our Own

Rather than embracing normality, my parents had chosen to be Jehovah's Witnesses. Or rather, my mother had chosen it: Jehovah's Witnesses had knocked on our front door when she was home alone, pregnant with me, and looking after a three-year-old Immi. She'd been worrying about nuclear war, and neither Immi nor the unborn version of me were providing her with comfort or advice regarding Cold War hostilities. In contrast, the Jehovah's Witnesses appeared to offer a solution – they confirmed that the world *was* about to end, but that 'true believers' would be saved from destruction, and allowed to live forever, in a world that God (Jehovah) had renewed. If you know much about this faith, you could be forgiven for thinking that their offensively patriarchal worldview might have ended up making me crave dominant men. So we should probably have a look at what I remember from my early days as a (not especially willing) Jehovah's Witness, and see if we can blame religion for my big old kinky brain. Because I would very much like to blame it.

There are many things I could (and may well) say

about this religion, but to begin with, here are some things you'd want to know before becoming a Jehovah's Witness yourself. They don't celebrate Christmas, birthdays or Easter. They don't allow their children to join in any school activities involving these holidays, which makes you dreadfully isolated as a Jehovah's Witness child, standing outside during school assemblies, and not being allowed to draw pictures of Father Christmas. And, horribly, not being permitted to go to classmates' birthday parties. There were theological reasons for all of this, we were told: something to do with paganism, and King Herod, and being No Part of This World. As an adult, I realise that cults routinely do this sort of thing in order to deliberately cut their followers off from opportunities to relate to the rest of the population. It was very effective. Furthermore, Jehovah's Witnesses have to attend three church meetings a week: one on Tuesday evening, one on Thursday evening, and one on Sunday morning. Obviously, we didn't call it 'church'. That would have been too normal. Jehovah's Witness churches were called Kingdom Halls, and they were much uglier, because they were often built by members of the congregation, who generally weren't up to much in the way of gothic archways or flying buttresses. The Kingdom Hall meetings were extraordinarily boring. There was barely any singing, but there was a lot of talking, much of it on egregiously non-child-friendly topics. Particular highlights of impropriety I recall include: a sermon about how much crucifixion would hurt (the answer, friends, is a *lot*); how to solve marital arguments (read Jehovah's Word with your wife and help her see that Jehovah's will is the same as yours, cos he is also male); what the Song of Solomon is about (I never figured this out, but to be honest I stopped listening); and which member of a married couple should be allowed to invite friends to their home for dinner (THE MAN, apparently. But the woman should do the cooking). As Jehovah's Witnesses we were also compelled to spend several hours a month evangelising: knocking on people's doors, preaching on street corners, or visiting people in their houses to study with them. None of this is optional, even if you're a child. Consequently, being a Jehovah's Witness child is not very entertaining, unless you really love keeping rules, wearing formal clothes and sitting still. I did not enjoy these things. Neither did Immi. Neither, in fact, did my father, who decided at the last minute not to get baptised as a Jehovah's Witness. My mother took the literal plunge alone, and so although we were in reality a two-parent family, we became a single-parent family within the religion. We were allowed to live with my father as normal, but it did largely separate his life from ours.

Despite my sturdy limbs, my emotional sturdiness was somewhat less impressive, and I worried about my father, being left alone at home on Sunday mornings when we all went off to the Kingdom Hall. Furthermore, the end of the world was nigh and he was in danger. Back then, in the early 1980s, the Jehovah's Witness head office was predicting Armageddon by the end of the decade, which meant that everyone except Jehovah's Witnesses would die, and very soon. So my father, suffering the terminal disease of Unbelief, wouldn't get to come with us when we entered Paradise after Armageddon. We were going to have to live forever, on earth, without him. This was of course all nonsense, but I believed it entirely, and I grieved for my father, who was so kindly, so inclined to read extra chapters of books to me if I implored him, and so very patient with letting me ride on his back when I was far too big to do so. I didn't feel as though he deserved to be murdered by God.

While I can't say that being a Jehovah's Witness was a positive thing for me, neither do I think it is responsible for my sexual identity. Even as a young child I found the ingrained sexism of the religion irritating, and didn't agree that men should automatically be in charge. Jehovah's Witness boys as young as ten were allowed to stand at the lectern and lecture the congregation, but even adult women were banned from doing so. Men were 'the head of the household' and only men were permitted to become leaders of the congregation. I quite fancied lecturing the congregation, and I didn't feel as though women should be treated as 'the weaker vessel', the way Jehovah's Witnesses taught us. I liked the idea of being submissive on an individual basis (to Captain Hook, specifically), but the wholesale 'men-are-in-charge-of-everything' belief always made me feel cross. It still makes me feel cross. I, personally, am sexually submissive, and, by chance, I'm female. But I don't think female submission is the natural order of things, and I believe that submissive men should be as free to explore their identity as I am. Ditto dominant women. Ditto people who aren't kinky at all.

But I do wonder whether the very *boringness* of the religion has something to answer for when it comes to my kink. Perhaps it was the fact of having to sit still listening to child-unfriendly adults talking for at least six hours a week that forced me to train my imagination into providing stimulation and excitement from nowhere. Maybe it was doing too much of this that led to me coming up with kinky stories. But honestly, my earliest kinky memories come from before the time that we started going to Jehovah's Witness meetings, so much as I'd love to blame them for more, I don't think it's a very credible argument. I really would like to blame them. And I *am* going to hold them accountable for the fact that I *didn't believe I was ever going to grow up*. Because Armageddon was apparently so imminent, I believed it was almost bound to fall before I became a fully-fledged adult. I didn't expect to ever have to work for a living; I'm still more or less in shock about it now. I expected to spend eternity cuddling tame lions, having picnics and building log cabins in Paradise, not to spend my adult life trying to earn actual money. We were shown numerous pictures that promised exactly this. Where is Armageddon, friends? Where is my pet lion? I already checked the garden and the post box, and there is NOTHING.

Possibly I shouldn't give credit to the Jehovah's Witnesses for this, but my sister and I did somehow end up with vast, useful imaginations with which to envelop ourselves at will. Quite separately, and in strictly enforced silence, Immi and I devised entertainments for ourselves to keep our minds occupied during the endless hours at the Kingdom Hall. I, for example, had a wonderful long-running game about mountain climbers. The climbers (played exquisitely by my fingers) had to navigate the treacherous terrain of whatever dress I happened to be wearing as I sat in my plastic chair, failing to listen to a series of men telling me about Satan. The finger-climbers made light work of the gentle foot-hills formed by the skirts of my dress, but then came the hazards of my more-or-less vertical bodice. Sometimes I helped them by forming pleats and creases up one of my sleeves, giving them something to hang on to; although they fell frequently and thrillingly nevertheless. I was capable of being entirely swept up in this game – my plucky finger-climbers were immensely enthralling. So much so, in fact, that eventually they made their way onto the dress of the elderly lady sitting next to me, quite without my realising. She took this weirdness with remarkably good grace, but I was mortified by my fin-gers' act of trespass and never played the game again. I had lots of others to fall back on. For example, I took great pleasure in a game that involved timing myself on my watch after taking a deep breath and holding it. I can only assume that I looked very odd indeed, gulping in air and staring rigidly at my wrist as the seconds ticked by. I could happily play this game for an hour at a time, although it did leave me a little light-headed.

Meanwhile, my sister, sitting next to me in an identi-cal (spooky) dress, was entertaining herself elsewhere within her own mind. She had developed a fascination for the textured polystyrene ceiling tiles above our heads. While trying to keep her head rigidly still, she would attempt to count as many rows of tiles as possible, by means of only moving her eyes. She discovered that, although her vision would start to blur, she was capable after much practice of rolling her eyes so far back in her head that she could look up through her eyelashes at the tiles right above her. An achievement indeed.

We always sat at the front of the Kingdom Hall, and I like to imagine that between us Immi and I formed quite an intimidating sight to whoever was on the platform speaking, with me looking increasingly catatonic as I held my breath, and Immi slowly, determinedly, rolling her eyes back in her head. I wonder if they thought we were possessed – Jehovah's Witnesses had extraordinary faith in the ability of demons to jump inside people at will if someone's belief in God wasn't strong enough, and we heard about people becoming possessed on a regular basis.

I don't honestly know whether I'd have been such a fearful child if we'd not been Jehovah's Witnesses. They loved to emphasise the danger of everyday life because they saw every disaster as evidence that Armageddon was almost upon us. And there's no doubt that I ended up constantly afraid for my own safety and for that of my family – Jehovah's Witness textbooks were full of the most hideously vivid, violent pictures and I found them hard to shrug off at the end of each study period. By the time I was six, my nightly prayer ritual had become quite a remarkable list of fears. It went something like this:

'Dear Jehovah, thank you for the lovely day and for all the lovely things. Thank you for Mummy and Daddy and Immi and Granny. Dear Jehovah, please don't let the house fall down in the night. And don't let the house catch fire in the night. Or in the early morning. And don't let the house fall down in the early morning either. And please don't let a bad man break into the house. And please don't let any of us die in the night. And please protect Daddy at work tomorrow. And please protect Mummy tomorrow. And please protect Daddy on his way to work. And please protect him on his way home from work. And please don't let me get ill in the night. And please don't let any of us get ill. And please don't let any of us go blind or deaf. And please don't let anything horrible happen. And please let me be a ballerina. In Jesus's name, Amen.'

As you can see, I regarded God as a rather slippery character, who'd look for loopholes in my prayer and possibly let the house burn down at 12.01 a.m. if I wasn't specific enough in my prayer request. In addition to my nightly praying, I felt it necessary to augment my prayer schedule by checking in with God several times an hour while I was at school, separated from my parents. I worried very much about my mother being murdered or being in a car accident while she was away from us each day, and having had the likelihood of being murdered by a stranger vastly exaggerated by Jehovah's Witness literature, it seemed like an ever-present threat.

I'd hate to give you the impression, though, that my childhood wasn't happy. In many ways it was, it's just that I worried constantly about it all ending in Armageddon. My parents actually went a little further than typical Jehovah's Witnesses in ensuring that we were segregated from secular life, by not allowing us to have a television. This was a social disaster for Immi and me, because it meant that we couldn't watch all the TV shows that all our peers were absorbing on a daily basis, and which they consequently wanted to talk about and play games about at school. But it forced us to be imaginative with creating entertainments on our own. Being able to do this in perfect silence and stillness while at the Kingdom Hall meant our creativity was enormous when we were free to roam around and be noisy. I was very lucky in having Immi as my big sister; as an adult she would be a successful novelist, and even as an eight-year-old she was capable of structuring wonderful, complex stories for us to act out with each other. Some of our games were long running like soap operas; we played them on a regular basis for years, advancing the story a little further each time.

For example, we had Barbie dolls just like almost every other girl in the country. But our game with them was an ongoing family saga played out in real time; in our version, they were our daughters. Immi's was called Cindy. Mine, more originally and far more weirdly, was called Gling. I was aware that this wasn't a real name, but I prized originality as much then as I do now, and didn't want my doll to have to tolerate a name that had been sullied by previous owners. And so, she was Gling. In our saga, Immi and I played sisters, which made our dolls cousins to each other. Our husbands were permanently away on business and our dolls were always the same age that we were in real life. This game was so fantastically believable to us that we were more than capable of playing it for hours without our dolls even being *present*. I remember a lengthy country walk made vividly pleasurable by my being able to pour out my anxiety to Immi that my daughter (back at home) was behaving badly at school. I worried that she was missing her father's influence. Immi was full of kind aunt-like advice as to how I should handle her niece, and the long hours of the walk rolled by unnoticed.

When we went on holiday, our 'daughters' came with

us, packed into their own little suitcases. Once at our hotel, we'd quickly fashion a drawer into their bedroom, building them beds from handkerchiefs and towels, and making them eat the disgusting instant coffee from the hospitality tray because of the medicinal properties we claimed it had.

This was my idea, and this is an area in which Immi and I tended to differ. Immi, being older, normally took control of what we played, but I did exert my influence whenever I was able to, being drawn towards storylines in which someone got punished. I chewed the foot off my first Barbie doll when I was five while deeply engrossed in a game in which my doll was kidnapped and tortured. Her foot, in my imagination, was destroyed by a machine, and I don't think I realised what I'd done until it was too late. I know I'm making myself sound like a psychopath at this point – I won't do that to you if we meet. I promise I've never chewed an actual person's foot off. Not realising yet that I was kinky, or indeed that being kinky was a thing at all, I often found myself doing things that I didn't feel fully in control of, and that I later regretted. One day, when Immi wasn't home and I was playing alone with our Barbies, all of them ended up getting punished for some minor misdeed. Immi's doll Cindy was imprisoned between floors in our three-storey Barbie house's elevator. Gling was balanced precariously on a semi-inflated beachball, which in turn teetered on the house's roof terrace parapet. Happily, none of this was based on the ways in which our parents punished us: this was coming entirely from my own confused, latently kinky brain. And much as I enjoyed the game, I also realised somehow that it had got away from me, that I wasn't behaving like a good mother or aunt to my Barbie dolls, and that I wished it hadn't got so out of control. I felt guilty, and wanted to pretend that I'd never been so cruel. Although I sometimes felt frustrated by the lack of conflict, kidnap and punishment in games orchestrated by my sister, I also felt safer with them, knowing she'd never steer us into tragedy or disaster.

She did lead us into some tremendous adventures, though. Quite often, our games didn't involve any dolls or equipment at all. One of my favourites was 'Second World War', in which we played civilians on the home front, dealing primarily with air raids and rationing. Immi had learned about it at school and somehow fashioned a soap opera for us from what she'd learned, in which endlessly discussing how to cook with powdered egg and diving for occasional cover in an imaginary air-raid shelter kept us happily occupied for hours at a time.

'Boarding School for Witches' was another favourite. We discovered the joy of learning magic at school well before Harry Potter did, and it was a fantastically flexible game that we played everywhere. My parents, in between Jehovah's Witness commitments, tried very hard to take us on entertaining, informative outings at weekends. Their ideas for doing this involved lots of country walks, cycle rides and visits to stately homes. Immi and I weren't especially grateful for these outings, and would have been relatively bored if we hadn't taken such enthusiastic refuge in playing imaginary characters. The witches at boarding school, for example, went on a lot of school trips. So when we went to stately homes, Immi and I took great delight in spending the entire day talking as though we were witches visiting a famous witch or wizard's house. 'Look at all these people she's turned to stone!' we would exclaim if there were statues on display. We were suspicious that one of our classmates was actually a fairy in disguise, and would question her, trying to trap her into admitting her lack of credentials. This, of course, in real life just involved us talking to the air, as we didn't have anyone to play our supporting cast. We really must have been two very baffling girls to observe when out and about. Dressed identically in vaguely Victorian fashions, muttering at the air, occasionally talking about our sadly absent husbands and wilful daughters, and sometimes diving for cover from imaginary bombs. Reciting spells, waving invisible wands, darting disquietingly around while hiding from foes that only we could see. We didn't do a great job of appearing normal, and it didn't occur to either of us to care.

Even when I was playing with Immi, there was plenty within our games from which I could get a frisson of what I now recognise as kinky excitement. Our house was set in large communal gardens, where we were allowed to play without supervision as long as we stayed together. Which wasn't a problem: I wanted to stay with Immi *always*. One of our oft-repeated games involved one of us being tied to a lamppost with a skipping rope by the other. The lamppost ticked, presumably because the light within was on a timer, but we enjoyed pretending that it was a time-bomb, and that if we didn't manage to escape quickly enough, we'd be blown up. This game was one which we sometimes played with other neighbourhood children, and I, being the youngest, was the one who was most likely to be last to get tied up. Often, it seemed that the others would tire of the game before I got my chance, which I found hugely annoying. Immi and I tied *ourselves* to a road sign once, playing suffragettes. And an old lady who lived opposite took it upon herself to come out and tell us not to. It was *dangerous*, she claimed. Had we considered what would happen if the housing estate burned down? We had not. We were surrounded by damp grass and concrete. It seemed unlikely. I suspected this old lady must also have believed in a Jehovah's Witness-style God who capriciously sent unlikely disasters down from heaven if the correct prayers had not been said. Anyway, we didn't play suffragettes in front of her house again. I sensed that maybe we shouldn't have done it, for some reason I couldn't explain. Being tied up felt somehow private to me, and being confronted over doing it felt like an unpleasant exposure which I didn't want to repeat.

It's probably worth saying at this point that of course when I was this young, being tied up or playing games about kidnap wasn't a sexual experience. I wasn't yet a sexual being; I wasn't capable of responding to anything sexually yet. I just knew that it made any game far more fascinating to me, and that I always wanted more of it. And all kinkiness aside, playing with my sister was still one of the very best and most enjoyable things in my life. I *love* my sister. Did you know? I've never dared to ask whether Immi found my frequent desire to make our games a little more tragic a bit annoying. I imagine that taking part in any collaborative activity with a monomaniac is something of a trial.

The world of our own, created mainly by Immi and entered into wholeheartedly by me, was a joyful refuge from the limits of our Jehovah's Witness existence. And the large and rambling communal gardens of our home formed a perfect canvas on which we could create. Sadly, we lost access to this particular playground when I was seven, Immi eleven, when our parents cruelly decided to move house. Why do parents do this? Let's jolly well race to Chapter Three and find out.

Chapter Three

The Sexy School Library

While I was falling down stairs, tying myself to things and agonising over my imaginary daughter's perform-ance at school, my father had continued to go to work in his bush, day after day, week after week. He did such a good job in there that he was headhunted to work for a big international scientific organisation. My father was to be their scientific secretary, and confusingly, he was also going to *have* a secretary for the first time in his career.

This, excitingly, meant that our family was going to have more money, for two reasons. Firstly, my father's salary would increase. Secondly, my mother was worried about him having a secretary, because she thought that whoever this secretary might be, she'd probably fancy my dad. As a result, my mother, in a determined and impulsive move, took a course in shorthand and typing, qualified, and then applied to be his secretary herself. She got the job. So instead of having one parent at work, we suddenly had two. We would be more affluent, and that meant we could move to a bigger house.

I remember our first house as enormous, because it

was on three floors, and because you could run round and round endlessly between the connecting sitting room and study. Our second house was nowhere near as grand in my eyes. It was in a long, narrow village a few miles away from where we'd lived before, and we lived at one end of it, in a two-storey, 1960s detached house with extraordinary white-plastic cladding on the front. Its front drive sloped steeply down, which made it splendid for skateboarding on, and its back garden was full of spiders, the smallish, jumping kind. I'd never seen so many in my life; it was terrifying.

When we first had a visitor, a friend of my mother's from the congregation, she asked me whether I liked the new house. 'No, because it's smaller than our old one,' I replied. When she'd left, my mother was very cross. I'd made my parents sound as though they were downsizing through poverty, she explained. My mother was sensitive about such things, and must have been proud of my father's success. She did not want me giving the impression that we'd fallen upon hard times.

But we *had*. At least, Immi and I had. We started a new school in the middle of the summer term. We'd both been happy at our original schools, despite a bit of bullying from kids who thought we were weird because of our religion. Starting at Southwater Primary School was a nasty shock.

The first sign that we were at a school with bullying problems came for me on my first day. One girl in my class, Laura, was a warm, good-natured person who befriended me immediately. This was a brave and kind-hearted thing to do, and I appreciated her very much. She wasn't skinny like the rest of the class who persisted in a pretence that she had fleas because of this. None of them would touch her, and none of them would stand on the top step of our classroom stairs because, apparently, it was 'her' step and if you stepped on it you'd catch her fleas too.

All of this, I suppose, is pretty standard unpleasant behaviour of a sort that's repeated all over the country among children who are too young to have learned empathy. But the organised nature of it shocked me – the fact that they were willing to work together to make another child's life unpleasant struck me as sinister.

Quickly, the word went round that Laura and I were lesbians. We'd been seen holding hands, which was all the evidence they needed. Jehovah's Witnesses took an anti-homosexuality stance, so I'd sadly grown up with the idea that it was wrong. But even so, it seemed vicious to me to use it as an insult, especially for such an innocent thing as holding hands with another seven-year-old. I started to feel nervous going to school with these children, who behaved in a way I found unpleasantly tribal and hostile. Once people discovered that Immi and I were Jehovah's Witnesses, the bullying started in earnest. Immi was more stoic than me, so I didn't realise till years later how bad it had been for her. At the time, I only knew that I was getting scared of going to school.

In my second week, a group of girls surrounded me on the school field at playtime. One of them pulled up the skirt of my red-and-white-gingham summer uniform. I was used to this kind of behaviour. At my old school, boys took plenty of delight in playing 'knicker chase' with girls who ran shrieking away from them at the horror of having their panties shown to the rest of the school. As a fast runner, it had never actually happened to me, but I was aware it was a normal thing for kids to do. However, these girls went further. One of them grabbed hold of my panties and pulled them right down, while the others crowed in triumph. Despite their religious conservatism, my family was not shy about nudity, and at seven I didn't have any particular shame about my body. But even so, I was aware that this conduct crossed a line. I felt that people who could pull someone's panties down for fun could not be trusted. I wonder if they ruined any potential I might have had to enjoy being dominated by women? I *shall* blame those grubby-minded little girls. They also liked to pick the locks on the toilet stalls by using the buttons on their cardigans as screwdrivers. It seemed to me at the time (and still seems now) that wanting to humiliate people like that was pretty mean, but also crude, and stupid. I did not relish being in a classroom with these individuals for six hours a day. I was not altogether sorry that they'd all die in Armageddon.

I was, as I've said, a tall child. For the first time in my life I wanted to be shorter, less visible, less likely to be picked out in a crowd. Everything about me seemed to attract unkind attention, and I became less and less willing to go to school. Fortunately for me, either my parents were unusually gullible or I was a better than average actress for my age. I like the sound of the latter.

'Mummy, I don't *feel* well.' I would subside, droopily, against my mother as we got ready for school in the mornings. My mother was always worried about catching viruses, so her fear of illness probably stopped her from being as suspicious as she should have been. 'Please can I stay at home today?' Staying at home, in

fact, normally meant being transported to my determinedly non-Jehovah's Witness grandmother's house.
This excellent lady had a house with a television in it.
She let me watch a programme called *Super Gran,*
which I assume she picked out for purposes of propa-
ganda. She also had an excessively sweet tooth; her
biscuit tin was always bountifully full, and she'd take
me to the local shops to buy chocolate at lunchtime.
Really, in this regard I had a family with the most
extraordinarily relaxed attitude towards school attendance. I suppose that's what not believing that I'd ever
have to actually work for a living did to them. At my
granny's house, we had eggs and oven chips for lunch,
and I was allowed to loll around in front of her electric
fire. This was far preferable to going to school.

And when forced to attend school, if I managed to
ignore the meanest kids, there was also joy to be found.
With few ways to express my latent kinkiness, I found a
position that felt spectacular. At playtime, all the boys
(predictably; what a shame) played football. And the
girls played Humiliate Whoever's Alone. Which is, I
hope, a little less traditional.

I did not wish to gang up on people with the other
girls; neither did I wish to play football. However, I
found a better role. The boys did not have proper goalposts to aim at. They had to make do with piles of
school jumpers, which did an inadequate job and led to
much uncertainty as to whether a goal had actually
been scored or not. This is where your author and her
friend Laura came in. I offered our services as goalposts.
I was tall and thin: exceptionally goalpost-shaped.
Laura was not, but was good-natured and willing.

It's hard to express how briefly proud, joyful and satisfied being the boys' goalpost made me. I know that this is ludicrous, and it certainly wouldn't be arousing for me now, but it felt marvellous at the time. I liked being useful to the boys. I liked being needed. And I liked the objectification, though I didn't know the word yet. Sadly, this lovely role did not last; eventually a football-to-the-head incident occurred, I cried, and the boys realised that aiming footballs at girls' heads probably wasn't the wisest thing to do. A boy in my class called Stephen was particularly chivalrous and kind, and made me feel special and brave for having been hurt so grievously in the line of duty. And thus, friends, I discovered the double pleasure of being a submissive masochist. You get the sensation of being hurt in the first place, plus all the lovely attention if anyone thinks they've maybe pushed you too far. It is heaven. I fell in love with Stephen, and the crush lasted for the rest of my school career.

I'm afraid I wasn't altogether faithful to him in my heart, though, because when I moved up a year group, I also fell in love with my teacher. Mr Bryce was the first male teacher I'd ever had, and there I began my tradition of falling in love with every single one. He was far more scary-looking than the softer, older female teachers I'd had up to this point, and was capable of putting on the most spectacular rages when he thought it necessary. But for the first time in my school career I found myself really caring about whether my teacher liked me or not. As I look back, I realise how kind he was. He must have noticed that my religion isolated me. After all, it was he who had to look after me during school assemblies when I had to stay in the classroom, and he was the person who had to make up alternative activities for me to do at Christmas time. He regularly made sure that I felt special, not just an outsider, by inviting me to talk about my religion's traditions when festivals came up, and by making sure that general-knowledge quizzes always contained at least one question that only I, with my freakishly in-depth biblical knowledge, would be able to answer. I doubt anyone has ever made anyone else fall in love with them by displaying superior biblical knowledge, but I think that in my muddled, childish brain, that's what I tried to do. He, obviously, didn't fall in love with me, because he was a proper actual grown-up man who probably wasn't as impressed with my memorised list of the books of the Bible as he pretended to be. But he was kind, and didn't let people bully each other in his class, which I appreciated.

I also appreciated the school library. It was there that I discovered the fascinating world of Victorian England. In *The Victorians*, a book I found on my first visit, there were detailed depictions of judicial floggings in the crime-and-punishment section, and descriptions of corporal punishment in the chapter on education. I *loved* the Victorians. I borrowed and read every book in the school library before moving on to borrowing more from our local town's library, which was much bigger and had a book about the history of education. It was glorious; the main thing that happened in history, in schools, seemed to be a plethora of beatings.

'Shall we play Victorians?' I asked Immi, hopefully, one afternoon. Immi hadn't fixated on that era as I had, so was short on inspiration. I, with *all* the knowledge, was too diffident to suggest that we could set the game in a prison. When we did manage to get a game afloat, it developed into being mostly about dressing up. We experimented with putting our dressing gowns on back to front, which we thought looked very historical indeed.

Privately, I went one step further – I'd been interested in the restriction-themed possibilities of corsets, but hadn't figured out how to approximate one. Then it occurred to me that I could create a tiny waist for myself by wrapping my dressing gown cord around it, and tying it off as tightly as possible. The result looked wonderful, I thought. But best of all was the feeling; it hurt and it made me short of breath, but for reasons I couldn't begin to understand, both of these sensations were appealing to me. I'd read that Victorian ladies even slept in corsets in order to maintain their figures. Extreme as this seemed, I did try, and consequently found that my masochism does have limits.

It wasn't until years later, at twenty-five, that I was finally laced into a proper corset in an expensive shop in Kensington. It was every bit as splendid as I'd imagined. But we'll get to that. First I have to tell you about ballet, exhibitionism and looking in the mirror. It'll be just as delightful as it sounds. Come along, everyone!

Chapter Four

Early Episodes of Exhibitionism

'Joceline,' read my form tutor's report, describing my fourteen-year-old self, 'is a quiet girl who rarely makes herself heard in class.' This was, broadly speaking, true of my at-school personality throughout my school life. At Southwater Primary School I'd learned that children were capable of grotesque cruelty towards each other, so I absented myself as much as possible. I continued to be 'ill' as much as I could get away with. Which was a lot. I aimed for a four-day school week throughout my high-school years, but when forced to attend school physically, I took myself elsewhere internally. My high-school biology notes, for example, took the form of a gaily coloured, comprehensive series of drawings of gymnasts. I did not enjoy biology, so I treated myself to rhythmic gymnastics instead. I was convinced that I'd never need biology notes anyway. It turns out that I was correct.

My parents found the frequent messages about my supposed 'quietness' and inability to make myself heard puzzling. Despite my unhappiness at school, I still managed to be extraordinarily bumptious and annoying with my family. In fact, I probably saved up the most precocious and wearing aspects of myself to express in the safety of my home, in front of people who were trapped with me, and therefore had to absorb it. My parents took this with good grace. Immi began to avoid inviting her friends back home so as not to expose them to her little sister's increasingly show-off behaviour. Most irksome of all to her was my new experimental way of talking. At around eight years old, I became aware that I was far too big. I was no longer small enough to wear any clothes from Mothercare, and had to wear black, grown-up-looking wellington boots instead of the little short red ones that normal-sized children enjoyed. At least, I assume they enjoyed them. Perhaps they just took them for granted in a nasty, smug, under-sized way. I did not want to be a big girl. I wanted to be a *small* girl, because small girls were cuter. Since I couldn't do anything about my physical size, I decided to modify my voice. I would have a small, cute, *sweet* little girl's speaking voice. 'Am I SWEET?' I enquired of Immi, in a high-pitched cutesy way. I pronounced 'sweet' as 'shweet', deciding that speech impediments were more childishly alluring. I sounded like a sinister falsetto Sean Connery impersonator. Immi informed me that I was not, in fact, sweet.

'I'm feeling shhhhleeepy!' I insisted, subsiding against Immi in the back of the car on the way home from a Jehovah's Witness meeting. Immi retreated into her book, plastering herself against the car window to get away from her cloyingly weird little sister. 'I love shhhaushhages!' I exclaimed over dinner. My mother smiled indulgently. Immi looked slightly sick. Finally, I went too far. 'Can I shhhhit on you?' I implored Immi, sidling over to her on the sofa and trying to perch on her knee. 'WHAT did you say?' she exploded, hearing the forbidden word that I, in my attempt at being shhhhhweet, hadn't realised I'd said. In my horror that Immi might tell our parents that I'd started using obscene language, I decided that talking like a small child wasn't bringing me a sufficient return on my investment, so I started seeking attention through more physical means.

By this point, I had lost all interest in ever trying to look normal in a single picture anyone ever took of me. I'm not sure why – maybe it was the beginning of my desire to prioritise originality over propriety. It may have started with my first school photo, taken when I was six. Most children seem to become quite bashful when confronted by a school photographer. I, on the other hand, responded by pulling an extremely odd face, out of the sheer delight of being able to exercise my own choice in the matter. Subsequently my school photos became increasingly disquieting to look at, as I experimented with faces (chin pushed right in against neck, weird cutesy Shirley Temple smirks, brows lowered while glaring up through eyelashes). Doing a normal face became entirely uninteresting to me. It is still of only limited interest, to be honest with you.

Once I discovered ballet, I became more ambitious, and involved my entire body in this glut of creativity. Balletic arm positions while out on country walks, striking angular poses while half-hidden by tree trunks, 'casual' stances while balanced precariously on narrow walls. A particular low point is captured in a family photo posed by a farmer's fence. My sister is standing, looking normal. My father is standing next to her, also looking normal, except for a perm that my mother had made him have. I, aged ten, am wearing a bright yellow parka. My hood is up, so that I look both bald and like an alien. One parka-clad arm is pointing out at a right angle to my body, resting on the top of the fence post. Both my hand and fingers are rigidly splayed out. I am smiling like a maniac, head tipped determinedly to one side. It was an excellent preparation for my future career. Now, doing this sort of thing is a way of life. The only difference is that quite often I don't wear clothes, and as a result, I usually no longer look bald.

It didn't occur to me as a ten-year-old that I could ever be a model, since I fully expected Armageddon to arrive long before I reached adulthood. Also, I'm certain that modelling wouldn't have been seen by anyone as an acceptable job for a Jehovah's Witness. Most of them seemed to be window cleaners. So I just enjoyed doing peculiar things on camera with no expectation that I'd one day earn a living doing exactly that.

There was a large mirror on our living-room wall, and I spent happy hours in front of it perfecting my next poses. By this, I genuinely mean hours. With no television, by far the most interesting thing in our house to watch was me, at least in my own estimation. I tried to bring my family around to this way of thinking too. 'Watch me, Mummy! I'm doing the splits!' 'Watch me, Daddy! I'm standing on one leg!' 'Watch me, Immi! Oh. You've gone.' And once my father had bought a video camera, I began making 'advertisements', including wafting around in lace underwear talking about perfume. My parents were remarkably relaxed in allowing this bizarrely sexualised behaviour, and it gave me the confidence as an adult to eventually explain to them what my job involved. I don't know why I even *had* lace underwear at the age of thirteen. I have a suspicion that my grandmother might have let Immi and me choose whatever we liked from a catalogue. As a result, I had some stunningly inappropriate sheer lingerie. And it seemed not at all unnatural to spend afternoons reclining on our sofa, filming myself as I rubbed a bottle of perfume over my body and murmured in what I fondly believed to be a seductive voice, 'A rose, is a rose, is a *rose*,' and, 'Parfum de Parfait, a fine fragrance for her . . .' Obviously, none of it made any sense. Having been denied access to TV adverts, I only had the shakiest idea of how to actually make one. But it does strike me as odd that I was doing almost the exact thing that I now earn my living from when I make custom fetish videos for clients. I love it as much now as I did then. I'm just grateful that the internet didn't exist back in the 1980s, because if it had, my 'adverts' would be all over it. Unless YouTube banned them for being in abysmally bad taste. In which case they'd be right.

I also very much enjoyed being naked in public. My naive, liberal parents had gone to some lengths to stop Immi and me feeling any sense of inhibition or shame about our bodies. Both my mother and father were casually naked around the house, steadfastly avoided euphemisms for body parts, and wandered in and out of the family bathroom irrespective of who else was using it. These efforts should really have conspired to make me similarly unaware of, and disinterested in, nudity, and I can't think why it failed. I *was* perfectly comfortable naked. On the other hand, I was aware that other people weren't, and got huge enjoyment from the power this gave me. One summer, on a country walk with members of the Jehovah's Witness congregation, my family, and Immi's (secret) boyfriend, I decided to take off my top. At eleven years old I didn't have even the beginnings of breasts, so my torso might as well have been a boy's. However, the connotations are different, and Immi was mortified. 'Mummy, make her *put her clothes back on*!' she whispered, horror-struck, to our mother. 'No, no; we shouldn't be ashamed of our bodies!' admonished Mummy, completely missing the point that I wasn't casually undressing for comfort. I was undressing for my *audience*, even though most of them were steadfastly looking the other way in case Jehovah suspected them of actually *wanting* to look at a ridiculous topless child. 'She's showing off!' argued Immi. Immi was right. Semi-naked, I felt superior to the more inhibited members of the group. I felt interesting, bold, original and rather naughty. I was insufferable. But thirty years later, I realise that it was this ghastly character trait that's allowed me to work so happily as a nude model, and with maturity I've learned to make other people (like new, shy photographers) feel comfortable around me when I'm naked. Dear Immi, I'm so sorry that the eleven-year-old me lacked any compassion. I've never really put my clothes properly on again since.

Chapter Five

A Great Divide

A few years before, when I was eight years old, my dad had given up being a non-Jehovah's Witness, and had joined us at the meetings, then in knocking on people's doors to evangelise to them at weekends, and was eventually baptised, just like my mum. It was an immense relief. The world, we were assured on a weekly basis, was surely about to end in Armageddon, and now my entire family would be safe. Unless we were murdered by apostates, of course, which was another threat we were regularly warned about. The closer we got to Armageddon, the more murderers there'd be, and the more likely they were to specifically target Jehovah's Witnesses. *If* we were murdered, God would resurrect us immediately after Armageddon, we were promised. But I'd retained a degree of suspicion regarding God's promises, and it seemed vastly preferable to me to just stay alive until God established Paradise On Earth for us, straight after all the murderers/Muslims/Catholics/other Christians were killed during Armageddon itself. To this end, I became hyper-vigilant, repeatedly checking that men in the street weren't following us with

predatory intent. I'd developed the impression from
reading the literature that roughly 50 per cent of non-
Jehovah's Witnesses were likely to be dangerous
criminals, and that everyone else probably had HIV. I
became anxious in multi-storey car parks, where I felt
murders were more likely, and I didn't like it when my
parents answered the front door, in case the person
who'd rung the doorbell had come to kill us. By the
time I was ten years old, I was scared most of the time,
but in part, I think, that's because I felt we had something worth protecting: an entire family unit of Jehovah's
Witnesses, destined for eternal life if only we could survive the next five years.

But it was not to be. One Saturday, when I was eleven
and Immi fifteen, we were getting into the car, ready to
be driven to our regular Saturday morning Bible study
in preparation for spending the rest of the morning
evangelising at people's front doors. I wasn't delighted;
it was always boring and I wanted to practise ballet.
But when our father unexpectedly opened the back
door of the car and told us to get back indoors, bore-
dom seemed suddenly to be a very small and aspirational
problem. Daddy hardly ever told us what to do, and
when he did, it was always in a nice voice, and mostly
phrased as a question. 'Would you like to help lay the
table?' 'Would you like to change into your pyjamas?'
'Would you like to stop throwing yourself repeatedly
over the sofa in that exceptionally noisy way while I'm
trying to read *Nature* magazine?' Today, Daddy didn't
have a nice voice. He sounded angry, or worse, scared.
But he couldn't be scared; he was never scared.

Indoors, my mother gathered Immi and me either

side of her on the sofa. My dad sat at the far end of the room. This was increasingly weird and frightening. My parents always sat next to each other, and if they were about to tell us off (which seemed the least alarming of the frightening possibilities pouring into my mind) they'd surely want to present a united front. Were they about to announce a divorce? Unlikely; it was banned by the Jehovah's Witnesses. Was one of them dying? Had Immi and I somehow done something so awful that they were sending us to a children's home?

It was worse. My dad was talking, and he was telling us he couldn't be a Jehovah's Witness anymore. They'd recently published a book about the 'false science' of evolution, and my dad, as a scientist, had spotted a multitude of errors and deliberate misrepresentations within the text. He wouldn't try to stop us from continuing as Jehovah's Witnesses, he said, but he couldn't take part in the meetings anymore. Men in the congregation were expected to take it in turns to address the rest of us on subjects chosen for them by the governing body, and now that we were studying the evolution book page by page in our weekly meetings, my dad couldn't bear to stand up and lie; he was the only scientist there, and perhaps the only person who could be sure that we were being deceived on this subject. And if they had lied about this, what else had they lied about? 'I don't know,' said my dad, 'and I'm so tired. I am *so tired.*' And with that, he began to cry.

I'd never seen my dad cry. My dad was always happy. And he was *never* tired. I'd never even seen him take a nap. He was awake and cheery when I went to bed, and the first I saw of him in the mornings was when he brought me tea in bed, just as cheerful as the night before. I was horrified, scared for him, but scared for us too. My mum leaned across to me and whispered furiously into my ear, 'He's a *bloody* liar.'

The room felt like it had tipped upside down; my dad was crying, which never happened. My mum was swearing, which happened plenty, but she'd never called him a *bloody liar* before. And they were separated by a no-man's land of impractical white carpet and pale blue rugs. The gulf between them – Jehovah's Witness and scientist – seemed to be stretching into an uncrossable chasm, with my dad on the side of the murderers, Muslims, Catholics and all. Except worse: he'd been a Jehovah's Witness now, so if he left, no one would be allowed to talk to him anymore. He'd be not just an unbeliever but an *apostate*; we'd have a dangerous enemy in the house. So when my mum leaned over to me again and whispered, 'Go and hug him,' I didn't want to. He was on the condemned list. He was an enemy. He was a *bloody liar*. Obediently, I crossed no-man's land and hugged him. 'Oh, poor Daddy!' I said, ineffectually, patting uselessly at the new, dangerous apostate in our family. I had nothing helpful to add; I was eleven and what I knew about God and religion was from my parents. If they no longer agreed, I didn't know what I should believe. Though Immi and I were not being given a choice; we wouldn't have been allowed to be apostates even if we had been brave enough to say 'We'll die in Armageddon, please!' We were not going to die in Armageddon; we were going to go and live in Paradise On Earth with our mum and the other Jehovah's Witnesses. Our dad was going to die alone. But before that, we were all going to collude in a giant lie.

Across the carpet, my parents were brokering a deal. We wouldn't tell anyone about my dad's desertion. We would make excuses about his absence at the meetings; he travelled a lot for work, so we could just pretend he had to do more of that. He'd still come to occasional meetings so that our Jehovah's Witness friends would still speak to him and would continue to visit our house. My mum wouldn't have to field the pity of other ladies with proper Jehovah's Witness husbands. No one would treat my dad like a traitor.

Inconveniently, the stakes were raised further by the fact that Immi had a Jehovah's Witness boyfriend. She spent most of her free time in her bedroom talking to him, having dragged the phone on its cord from the landing and under her door. Assiduously, I curled up on the other side of her door, listening eagerly to their conversation. It sounded hideously boring, but its very secrecy imbued it with romance. Peter seemed infinitely sophisticated to me.

He was a year older than Immi, and I'd always wanted a big brother. He had a computer, and he didn't seem keen to acknowledge my existence. This fascinated me; how could he possibly be more interested in my sister than in me? I thought the solution was probably to demonstrate my physical prowess. I showed him how I could do the splits. I skateboarded winsomely at him and showcased how fast I could go. I demonstrated my handstands. 'I can see her KNICKERS,' complained Peter to Immi, apparently appalled rather than impressed.

Peter, it appeared, was a very serious Jehovah's Witness. He told us that we shouldn't listen to Rick Astley because his song about dancing was actually about *sex*. He told Immi that our parents shouldn't let me go to a residential ballet summer school because I'd probably lose my virginity. Peter, I can now conclude, was a tedious religious zealot. But neither Immi nor I recognised this.

And now Immi was supposed to lie to him about our dad, and because he was visiting our house a lot, Peter couldn't fail to notice that our father was at home more than we pretended at the meetings. Naturally he became suspicious. And having correctly sensed the weakness of my character from my willingness to turn upside down while wearing a skirt, it was me that he decided to approach for answers.

One Saturday we were out evangelising. Immi and I were often paired up to knock on doors together, but this time I was paired with Peter. I was rather proud to be seen socialising (if you could call it that) with a boy an entire five years older than me, and was feeling especially sophisticated myself, wearing a long red double-breasted coat with black velvet collar that my mother had made for me. I probably looked like his girlfriend, I thought, as we walked between houses. Then Peter stopped on a street corner. 'There's something weird about your dad, isn't there?' he asked, suddenly and accusingly.

I was stunned. This is what we'd been afraid of: someone had noticed that my dad was all but absent from Jehovah's Witness activities. And we weren't allowed to lie, but I absolutely had to. 'No!' I replied. But my emotions betrayed me, and tears welled up in my eyes and splashed down onto my red coat. I wasn't a sophisticated teenager with an older boyfriend at all. I was a scared eleven-year-old with a responsibility to lie and protect my dad. Somehow, in my confused and worried mind, I'd hoped that if no one found out, it wouldn't become real, and that Daddy would change his mind again and survive Armageddon after all. If Peter found out, he'd tell everyone, and my dad would definitely be Disfellowshipped, meaning that no Jehovah's Witnesses would be allowed to speak to him anymore. And then he'd certainly die. I looked up miserably at Peter, who looked back, equally frightened and guilty. He'd been alone with me a mere ten minutes and he'd made me cry. He'd be in massive trouble if anyone saw us; Jehovah's Witnesses were meant to be happy. Silently, we conspired to pretend our horrible street-corner conversation hadn't happened. We approached the next house and knocked on the door. 'I'll do the talking,' said Peter; I was still sniffing and red-eyed. I expect we made an admirable impression of spiritual joy, between us. We failed to convert anyone that morning.

Altogether, things had begun to feel precarious at home, like an only semi-successful role play. My father disappeared into work, my mother read the Bible and had weekly meetings with a Christian minister who'd studied Ancient Greek and was trying to convert her to his faith, while she tried to do the same to him. Immi hid in her room and claimed to be revising for her GCSEs. And I, in front of the big mirror in our sitting room, aided by a library book, began trying to teach myself backward walkovers. I'd not been allowed gymnastics classes, so I was figuring it out by myself, using the green velvet chesterfield sofa as a sort of inanimate gymnastics coach that I hoped would stop me falling on my head.

Upstairs, the phone rang. It wasn't for me; it was never for me. I kicked up into a handstand, and let my feet continue onwards over my head, to finish up on the sofa seat behind me. I lifted one leg straight up and prepared to kick back up, off the sofa and back to my feet. Curiously, I couldn't hear anyone talking on the landing where the phone lived. It must have been a short conversation. I kicked up into a handstand again, and over onto the sofa cushions.

Above me, the house was quiet. Immi's bedroom door opened and shut, then the bathroom door opened, and shut. I felt a little light-headed and stopped practising walkovers, to let my body recover its equilibrium. I looked in the mirror and wondered if putting my hair in a higher bun would be more flattering. I decided it would. I restyled it, and posed in the mirror. That was better; I looked much more like a gymnast. I resumed my walkovers. Then I heard sobbing from the bathroom. I crawled upstairs silently, and hovered just below the level of the landing like a crocodile lurking under the surface of the water, so that no one on the top floor would see me. Who was crying? Why? There were voices, too, from the bathroom. *Multiple* voices. My entire family were shut in the bathroom without me. And it was *Immi* who was crying.

While I'd been coached in the art of walkovers by the amenable couch, Immi had answered the phone. It had been Peter, whose mother had found a letter Immi had written to him. Relationships among Jehovah's Witnesses were forbidden until the age of eighteen, and she'd insisted Peter break up with my sister. To this end, she'd enlisted the help of a Jehovah's Witness Elder (a senior, and always male, member of the congregation), who, having learned of the illicit romance, had deemed it ineligible and ordered its demise. So Peter, like a mindless guided missile, had phoned up my sister and broken her heart in the shortest conversation they'd ever had. And Immi, speedy, resourceful and fuelled by much reading of *Romeo and Juliet*, had collected a full bottle of paracetamol and locked herself in the bathroom with it.

My mum, who'd managed to miss the extraordinary and fascinating achievements of her younger daughter on the ground floor all afternoon, *had* noticed the unnaturally short conversation and the ominous silence from Immi that had followed. She had gained access to the bathroom, confiscated the pill bottle, and ascertained what had happened. She had then invited my dad into the bathroom for a briefing session.

From my crocodile's-eye view on the stairs, I saw the bathroom door was opening. I scuttled back down to the hall and hid behind a corner. My dad erupted onto the half-landing and picked up the phone. Then he was *yelling* into it, at the Elder who'd spoken to Peter. I gathered that the man had tried to put my dad off until he could escape to a more private room for a conversation that he probably immediately sensed would be uncomfortable, because, 'You'll stay RIGHT WHERE YOU ARE, YOU BASTARD!' roared my dad at the top of his voice.

I was very impressed; I'd never heard my dad swear and now in one year he was exhibiting *all* the emotions. But this was bad – this meant the end for us, at our congregation at least. Swearing at Elders was not the sort of thing that could be brushed under any kind of carpet. Especially since the last thing Peter had said to Immi was, ominously, 'Beware of your dad.' Despite my denials, Peter knew my dad wasn't a real Jehovah's Witness anymore. And why would he keep our secret now?

What followed was several strange months. Immi desponded, and my mum made her come with us to my ballet lessons and all other activities, afraid to leave her alone in case she found another paracetamol supply. My mother, in fact, seemed altogether far too interested in Immi for my tastes, but no amount of showing off (and I promise you, I tried) seemed able to distract her. And we suddenly had a lot of free time. Jehovah's Witnessing had taken up at least ten hours of my week on a regular basis. After a few dispirited visits to a neighbouring congregation, we stopped going to Jehovah's Witness meetings at all. It was disconcerting (Armageddon) but it was heaven. On Sunday mornings, I played on the street with my friends and our skateboards. There were no Bible studies, no knocking on doors, no rushing dinner on Thursday evenings to get to the Kingdom Hall on time. Gradually, the Jehovah's Witness grip on our family relaxed. The Ancient-Greek-reading Baptist minister who'd been doing Bible studies with my mother proved so convincing that she stopped trying to convert him, and began to consider letting him convert her instead. My parents visited a local evangelical church one Sunday, and invited me to go with them the following week. At this church, you were allowed to wear casual clothes and the singing (and dancing) took up the entire first half hour of the service. There was a Sunday School for children and teenagers where we could talk about age-appropriate topics and play games, so we didn't have to stay and listen to the sermon. And tea and biscuits were served afterwards. It seemed very much like a party.

Gradually, I began to let go of the fear of Armageddon. And slowly, with difficulty, I began to come to terms with the likelihood that I would grow up on earth as it was, support myself somehow, and eventually die. It wasn't easy, but it was freedom. I wondered what kind of job someone like me, who mostly liked pretending to be other people and turning upside down, could possibly enjoy. I found out in the very next chapter. Well, I didn't. I found out something else, and it was terrible.

Chapter Six

A Teenage Sexual Deviant

After leaving the Jehovah's Witnesses, several things happened, and while they were naturally absolutely *fascinating*, they're not especially relevant to the story I'm trying to tell you. So here's a little list, from which I implore you to choose your favourites and write your own chapters. I'm sure they'll be splendid.

- I auditioned for the Royal Ballet School aged thirteen, and was told that I was *already* too tall to be a ballerina.
- I went off to a (less choosy) ballet school in Wales and lost a huge amount of weight because they didn't feed us enough. I was invalided out.
- By age fifteen, I reached the massive height of six foot two. That's roughly the height of two normal-sized ballerinas standing on top of each other.
- I slunk through my exams at sixteen without doing any revision whatsoever.

- I started gymnastics classes. I became completely obsessed, bought a full-size trampoline and nearly lived on it in the garden.
- Immi got married to a lovely Christian man who worked for a homeless charity, and moved to London, whereupon she became the entirely perfect big sister and invited me to visit her often. She let me eat toasted Battenberg cake for breakfast. I recommend it.

So as we pick up the story, I'm sixteen years old, doing ballet and gymnastics in every spare waking moment, and about to go off to sixth-form college because I now realise that I'm very likely going to reach adulthood and need a real job. I have no idea what this might be, since my only interests are ballet, for which I'm too tall; gymnastics, for which I'm both too tall and too old; and vaguely wondering whether one day my gymnastics coach might make me stay behind after class and whip me with his belt (he doesn't wear a belt).

I chose sixteenth-century history as one of my four A levels, in the belief that less had happened back then than during the twentieth century, which was my other option. I truly believed that this would make the course easier. In this, I was mistaken. I also chose English literature because I quite liked reading, sociology because I thought it sounded grown-up, and media studies because... well, I wasn't quite sure. In fact, it was an excellent choice because it meant that, for the first time in my life, I could insist that we needed to have a television and that I needed to be able to watch it because it was 'my homework, Mummy!' Since we no longer had a religious reason to avoid TV, my mother, who hated television the way she hated groups of women, messy wardrobes and plastic earrings, had to relent. My father began to use it to furtively watch rugby matches on occasion, and mostly got away with it even though he didn't have any study-related excuse.

Naturally, as I started my A levels, I had no intention of actually *doing* any homework. I fully intended to spend my two years at sixth form planning gymnastics classes (by this time, I was a part-time gymnastics coach) and making lesson plans for my Sunday School class. Why, yes. I was a Sunday School teacher. For this, I liked to dress like Anne of Green Gables in absurd frilly pet-ticoats and long skirts. I cannot explain this, and yet I still find myself approaching my life as though every-thing I do – hospital appointments, meeting accountants, dinner with friends – is actually a theatre production.

My attitude to study changed entirely on my first day of college. My history teacher was a supremely attract-ive, tweed-jacketed twenty-seven-year-old man who had, it was rumoured, dated Helena Bonham Carter while at university. My sociology teacher, who was twenty-six, was a tall, thin gentleman in his first year of teaching. My English teacher, I'm now convinced, was a sexual sadist, though I think his interests lay in being unkind to other men. Nevertheless, he was disquieting and fascinating to observe, and I very much did observe him. And my media studies teacher. . . well. His name was James, and I fell in love with him. He was only twenty-three, also in his first year of teaching. He had little round spectacles, a dark blue three-piece suit, and a rather anxious, shy demeanour. I don't know why I found this so appealing, but I felt immensely protective of him. Especially since the rest of the class, a rather hip, laconic crowd, were inclined not to take him terribly seriously, as a result of his youth, earnestness, and willingness to let us use his first name. I did not use his first name; this would have felt immensely inappropriate. But when he set our first piece of homework, an essay on semiotics, I was determined to actually write it, to show him that he really was a bona fide teacher.

And I did. I found it more interesting than I was expecting, and wrote more than the minimum word count for the first time in my life. I handed it in, enjoying the feeling of, for once, not having to worry about trying to make myself invisible. And when he handed our work back to us a few days later, he'd given me my first ever 'A' grade.

I'd never thought of myself as academic. There'd been no point in it when we were waiting for Armageddon, and I'd been too preoccupied turning somersaults on my trampoline ever since that threat had been removed. I wondered if I could get another 'A'. I wondered if I might be able to repeat the success with my other subjects. It turned out that I could. I started actually working hard on non-physical tasks for the first time in my entire life. And once I started, it became addictive. People began asking me for help with their media studies homework. My grades were the best in the class. Craving attention in general, and from my exciting new teachers in particular, I became unwilling to let my grades drop below the standard I'd set. I felt like a whole new person; it was exhilarating. And my gratitude focused itself entirely upon James, my media studies teacher. At the end of my first term, I gave him a hideous homemade bottle of white wine as a Christmas present, and for the first time felt something other than profound relief that school was over for a couple of weeks. I went home for Christmas, with no inkling whatsoever that the greatest personal crisis of my life up to that point was hovering only a few days away in my future. That my vague fantasies about being punished and mistreated were about to turn into a nightmare that came closer than anything else ever has to making me want to end my own life.

Over Christmas, on our new television, I'd watched *The Nun's Story* (it's my homework, Mummy!), an old movie starring Audrey Hepburn. I was still new to watching movies, and was uncritically fascinated by them all. Audrey looked so beautiful in her wimple. It was so romantic and sad. And suddenly, my goodness, she was being instructed in self-flagellation. Which was, it seemed, a perfectly normal thing in religious orders.

I was transfixed. And suddenly, all my concerns about what to do for a career were over. *I* was a Christian; I could be a nun! Giddily forgetting that I was, in fact, a Protestant, and that I liked looking in the mirror, jumping on trampolines, being naked, and flirting ineffectually with my teachers via A grades, I suddenly felt sure that I'd found my place in the world. Terrific. I thought I should probably start praying more. Perhaps kneeling more. And definitely, I thought, I should try out this self-flagellation. It looked like an important part of being a nun. I had turned into someone who did my homework. And this was very important homework indeed.

The next morning, 2 January 1994, my family went to church. Oddly, for someone who was about to become a nun, I stayed at home. I think my rationale was that the cheery, evangelical church was no longer my spiritual home. I needed to create the atmosphere from the movie. I prayed the Lord's Prayer for a while. That was great; really joyless and formal and nunnery-like. I was definitely going to be an amazing (though not, obviously, excessively proud) nun. I read the Bible. It felt no more interesting than normal, but doing it kneeling down felt very much more pious and excellent. And then it was time to do the self-flagellation. This was going to be wonderful. I had found my vocation. I was going to pay penance, though I had no idea what for. In the movie, they used a leather strap, whipping themselves over first one shoulder, then the other. I had a leather belt that would be just perfect. I wondered how many strokes I should do. Probably quite a lot. I thought maybe ten.

I went to my dressing table and got out the belt. I could almost see myself in my nun's habit, looking romantic and beautiful and penitent like Audrey. I looked at myself in the mirror, just to check that I appeared suitably movie-star like. Then I wondered if that maybe counted as vanity. Maybe I should add more strokes. I doubled the belt over, and flung it over my right shoulder. Wow. That really hurt. It felt fantastic. I was an amazing Christian. I threw the belt over my left shoulder. Even better; that was even more painful. I'd never felt more wonderfully, fabulously pious and holy. I should probably do it even harder, I thought. I repeated myself, delivering all ten strokes in a dreamy haze of wonder, feeling that everything in the world was finally,

absolutely right. This was a profoundly beautiful spiritual experience.

This was . . .

This was a turn-on.

What on earth had I just done?

I knew what I'd just done. I'd turned my faith into
some kind of sexual experiment. I hadn't meant to. Had
I meant to? Is that why I'd been so looking forward to
trying out being a nun? There was something horribly
wrong with me. I'd committed a form of blasphemy
that God himself hadn't thought to warn us about in
the Bible. Or was this like worshipping false idols? Had
I broken one of the actual Ten Commandments? Or
maybe this was fornication?

Horribly shaken, I stood up, trying to fight back the
rising feelings of panic and self-disgust. I put the Bible
back on my bookshelf. I pushed the belt right to the back
of my drawer. I'd never felt more lonely or frightened in
my entire life. And for truly the first time ever, the idea of
seeking company held no comfort. For the first time, I'd
done something so awful that I'd never be able to tell
anyone. Not even the people who loved me the most.
I was sixteen, and I'd always been able to tell *someone*
if I felt guilty or afraid. And afterwards, I'd always felt
better. But this was something I was going to have to deal
with alone, because no one I told about this would love
me anymore. And if I tried to explain it to anyone who
didn't love me, they'd see me for the pervert that I was.

I left my bedroom, and walked slowly, shakily downstairs. In the sitting room, I put on the TV and flicked
through the channels. All the faces that appeared on the
screen seemed to judge me; they were normal, clean,

mentally healthy people. I'd thought I was one of them but I was not. I was sick. And then a word, an awful word that I'd been introduced to in sociology class came to me. *Deviant.* That's what I was. Sexually deviant. And I couldn't stand it. I sat on the sofa, rigid with misery. I barely took in the re-run of *Little House on the Prairie* which was moving on the screen in front of me, except to notice that the two children in front of me were what I wanted to be. Clean. Healthy. Normal. It occurred to me, briefly and hopelessly, that this was a dream. Perhaps I'd wake up in a minute and I'd still be yesterday's me. An A-grade student with a family who weren't wrong to love her. A teenage Sunday School teacher in ridiculous clothes with her group of three- and four-year-olds who liked her. A gymnastics coach people trusted their children with. She was gone, and this wasn't a dream. I couldn't erase what I'd just done and I couldn't climb back into being the old me. I'd destroyed her.

I don't know how long I sat there, stunned and wretched; eventually my family arrived home from church. Any hope that I'd feel better surrounded by their familiar company died. I wasn't like them anymore. I was on the other side of an invisible divide, and it couldn't be crossed. But I couldn't explain. I must have been quiet. I didn't go out to my trampoline. I didn't look in the mirror; I was too ashamed to see my new self, staring back.

The rest of the Christmas holiday was taken up with my miserable, guilty internal monologue. Maybe I could make it better by never doing anything like this again. Maybe God would help me to forget what I'd done. In church the following week (I was never going to stay home alone again) the pastor preached a sermon about Jesus washing away our sins, and he illustrated it with some kind of baffling chemistry experiment – turning a glass jar filled with ink-stained water clear. I wanted to believe that it could happen to me, but I felt so grubby, so tainted. And I started to wonder, with what felt like perfect rationality, whether I should kill myself for the good of a society that didn't need people like me polluting it. The word 'deviant' echoed and ricocheted in my mind.

When the Easter term started and I was back in college, I found myself feeling quite lost, attempting to do an impression of the person I'd been in my first term. I kept working hard and getting As for my essays. I taught my gym and Sunday School classes. I entered gymnastics competitions and won some medals. And all the time, the thoughts of being a danger to society, a pollutant, a risk to children, echoed in my conscience. I felt like a fraud, hiding behind a false, decent exterior which concealed the deviant that I really was.

And then, a story arrived in the news. A British MP, Stephen Milligan, had been found dead at his home, apparently the victim of an autoerotic asphyxiation episode that had gone wrong. The coverage wasn't especially kind, but the story told me two important things. Firstly, that there was a thing called a 'sadomasochist', who derived pleasure from pain. Secondly, although he was now dead, there had been, in this very country, a person who was somewhat like me, who had been experimenting on his own, like me, with the pleasure of inflicting physical pain upon himself.

It is extraordinary to me now, looking back, that this revelation didn't serve to help me see that I wasn't alone.

After all, there was an actual word for what I was. Which implied that there were at least several of us. However, in my poor emotional state, all I could read from the situation was that there had been two of us, but one of us was now dead and I was alone. If people found out about me, they'd be no kinder than the papers had been to him. And it reiterated my feeling that engineering my own death was the best course of action.

However, though waking up each day felt an intolerable burden and my sense of guilt was no less crushing than it had been when it arrived on 2 January, I did know that I couldn't kill myself. At least not without explaining why to my parents. It would be unconscionably cruel to do so, and I knew they'd never stop wondering what they could have done to help. So somehow, I had to find another way out of my crisis. My college, being large, well funded and forward-thinking, had a professional counsellor on site, working from an office that I walked past every day on my way between classes. But, desperately unhappy though I was, I didn't consider making an appointment. I was far too ashamed, and certain that she'd be both disgusted and incapable of helping me.

'Do you,' I asked my friend Caroline, while we were waiting for our respective buses at the end of our college day, 'ever feel really disgusted with yourself, and as though nothing will ever be okay again?' Caroline, a calm, reasonable mathematics student, looked puzzled. 'Well. . . no,' she replied eventually, 'I don't.'

Scared though I was, I was also overwhelmed with sadness for everything I'd lost: my pride in having begun to be a functional, almost-adult human being, my optimism about the future, my belief that I was fundamentally sane and good. So I decided to try to talk to someone who loved me, and who was maybe smart enough to have some insight.

'Immi,' I asked my sister on the phone that night, 'did you hear about Stephen Milligan?' Immi hadn't. I continued, dreading making her think less of me, but desperately hopeful she might be able to help. 'The papers are saying that he's a sadomasochist and I'm scared that I'm one too. What do you think people should do about it if they realise that they are? It's a sin, so I don't want to be one but I don't know how not to be.'

Immi and I have talked about this since, and she feels as though she said the wrong thing. She didn't. She said the very kindest, wisest and most comforting thing she could have said, given that we were members of a religion which, at the time, was still excommunicating gay people. She said that people couldn't help their inclinations, and that it wasn't a sin to have deviant sexual tastes. The only sin, she said, was indulging in it. If you put it to the back of your mind and didn't act on your desires, then it was okay. At the time it brought me considerable comfort. I wasn't afraid of hard work. If I could get top grades in my A levels, I could suppress my desires. I could make myself clean again. And I could maybe get back enough self-esteem to want to stay alive.

I've been thinking about it, writing this book, and wondering what the current me would say to the sixteen-year-old me, if I could only phone back through time. This is what I wish I could say to her. And to you, dear reader, if you're going through even the palest shadow of the guilt and anxiety that I was experiencing.

You're right, you aren't normal. Neither is anyone else. We're all a minority of one when it comes to our sexual identities. And many of the people you love and respect will have aspects of their sexualities that they have struggled with as much as you are struggling now. But what's more important for you to realise right now is that you're also far from alone when it comes to an interest in sadism and masochism. There's a whole community of people who share your interests. And they're not depraved, they're not dysfunctional, and they're not dangers to society. They're just people, some of whom you'll like and some you won't. You're too young to go and meet any of them now, so keep learning about yourself, and appreciating the things that give you pleasure. Take note of the things that turn you on: your knowledge about yourself will make you a more enjoyable, emotionally literate partner when you're ready for that. And bear in mind that, just like your A levels and your gymnastics, we get more pleasure out of things that we work hard at and engage with thoroughly. If you're going to be kinky (and you are), aim for wholehearted, A-grade kinkiness. And never, never be ashamed of what you are. Which is, for the record, a submissive masochist. You're going to win awards for it, babe.

But naturally, I didn't have the benefit of finding a mentor in her forties with twenty years' worth of professional BDSM experience. Immi had done her absolute best, but she was only twenty herself, and though I considered her to be a vastly sexually experienced woman of the world, she'd been married for less than a year and had only had one sexual partner. But armed with her wisdom and kindness, I was determined to make myself a better, cleaner person. I would suppress whatever had been wrong with me. I would not be an enemy of society; I would help *fix* society. I would . . .

. . . join the Campaign Against Pornography.

I don't suppose you saw that coming. Especially since, friends, at that point in my life I had not seen a *single* piece of pornography. Unless perhaps you counted the topless photographs of glamour models in newspapers. Which I did. The Campaign Against Pornography saw porn as a deliberate attack by the patriarchy (which I knew all about from sociology classes) upon women. The Campaign sent out generous quantities of literature to educate their members on just how degrading the acts that women were being forced to participate in were. The answer was: *extremely degrading*. It opened my eyes. I'd joined, fully intending to fight the good fight against bare breasts in newspapers, but discovered that actually there were entire movies, with *actual sex in them*, that were even more dangerous to society than glamour models in bikini bottoms.

Some of the films, I learned, included *tying women up*. And deliberately hurting them. Well, this was perfect. What better way to make amends for being into S&M than to campaign against its representation in art? It was irrational, but at the time it seemed to help me make sense of my confusingly strong feelings about pain, bondage and humiliation. Far from being turned on by it, I said to myself, I was actually passionately committed to *stopping* it. I told myself this over and over again, as the months went by, and my despair and depression slowly started to lift.

'I'm a Marxist feminist,' I announced proudly over

dinner to my parents. I had a stack of Campaign Against Pornography pamphlets on the table next to me; I'd started carrying them around with me everywhere, like some sort of talisman. 'It is iniquitous,' I continued, 'that women are required to be the sex slaves of the wage slaves.'

My mother, the wage slave's sex slave with whom I was sharing a dining table, did not appear to recognise my accusation. She has not, to the best of my knowledge, ever felt remotely like anyone's sex slave, least of all my father's. My father was more complicated, according to my new-found sociological wisdom. I suspected him of being a wage slave, but also sometimes wondered if perhaps he was a capitalist. A *fat cat* capitalist in the words of my neo-Marxist sociology teacher. At the time, my dad was earning the equivalent of perhaps £60,000 a year; back then he was still an employee of a company, having not yet launched his consultancy business. On this salary, he was supporting all of us; my mother didn't have a job. And naturally, I didn't. I was busy doing somersaults and essays, and disapproving of men. Of course, I now see that my father's salary was far from capitalist riches, fat cat or otherwise. But he did seem to earn more than most of my friends' fathers did. So I leaned towards thinking he was a cat rather than a slave, even if he wasn't, perhaps, a particularly fat one.

'Don't you think,' I began, looking at my father accusingly, 'that capitalism is absolutely wrong, and evil, and pervasive?' My dad is a socialist. Furthermore, he is a gentleman. 'Yes, Jossy, I do,' he said agreeably.

This was not what I wanted to hear from him. It was

profoundly unsatisfactory. He was a man, and therefore must be part of the patriarchy intent on degrading women. 'And what do you think of pornography?' I asked bullishly. 'Well, I don't actually *own* any,' replied my dad, who, I now suspect, may have been rather enjoying himself. This did appear to be true. He had an awful lot of copies of *Nature* magazine, and bought *Classic CD* magazine for himself sometimes. This did not stand for Cross Dresser, but for Compact Disc. And for the next two years, my father stoically failed to behave as though he believed in doing anything other than respecting, listening to and being kind to women. As well as paying for all their goddamn clothes so that they could teach Sunday School classes while dressed like Anne of Green Gables. The bastard.

Eventually conceding that perhaps my father wasn't actually the main problem with society, I cast my net a little wider. Our college's Christian Union, for example. It was mostly led by a male student; it was clearly patriarchal. I stopped going to it. And I devoured more Campaign Against Pornography literature. One of their newsletters included a long, prurient description of a porn film in which they suspected the female participants had been non-consenting. At the time, I was entirely convinced that this was likely. I read the newsletter over and over again, until I almost had the piece memorised. How *dreadful* for the poor women. How *humiliating*. How *degrading*. I told many people about it. I read the article a couple more times in order to be sure of the facts. And I looked forward to my next newsletter.

Indeed, friends, I had managed to turn Campaign

Against Pornography literature into my very own porn magazine subscription. Which, in its way, is at least as shameful as having turned an attempt at a religious experience into a sex game the way I had the previous year. This entire chapter has been excruciating to write. But it does illustrate my belief that when we, as individuals or as a society, try to suppress aspects of what we are, we end up doing more harm to ourselves and each other than we ever could have done by being honest about our desires.

I wish I could say that I got over this phase of my life by the end of my A-level courses, but I graduated with my authoritarian version of Marxist feminism intact. And with three As and one B, thank you for asking. My history teacher let me down by being so sexually attractive to the entire student body that I lost interest in him; as a result, my B was in sixteenth-century history. Naturally, I got an A in Marxist feminism/ sociology. My extended essay was on sexism in sport, where I cited my (perfectly lovely) gymnastic coach's behaviour as evidence. I think I still bore him a grudge for not wearing a belt. And I got an A in media studies, where my extended essay was about sexism in Disney films. As you can see, I was an extremely well-balanced individual by the age of eighteen. Well done to me. And I'd decided on a career path for myself. I was going to go to drama school, and then make feminist action movies. I was also going to write a lot of God-awful poems about rape, but I didn't know that yet.

Chapter Seven

A School Full of Drama

I got into drama school largely on the strength of my dancing ability, and was given a place on the musical theatre course. But a back injury during the summer before starting my course ended my ambitions in the dance department. Damned trampolines. My college, the Academy of Live and Recorded Arts in Wandsworth, south London, offered to allow me to transfer to the actors' course instead. I was happy to try it. I'd been in a couple of plays at sixth-form college, and I'd always offered to read aloud when we were studying plays in English literature. I thought I'd probably be okay at acting.

In case you've not been to drama school, allow me to explain a couple of things. Firstly, the students are quite terrifying, if you happen to be a shy suburbanite: highly physically attractive, projecting gargantuan levels of confidence, and often from relatively wealthy families. The vision of my fellow students on my first day at drama school was almost enough to make me turn around and go back to my student bedsit and hide for the next three years. Of course, once I'd got to know a few people, everything was okay. They *were* quite an intimidating group – a lot of them were older than me and had already worked professionally or been through university. Having been mocked all through my school career for being 'posh', it was a little disorienting to find myself among *actual* posh and privileged people. One of my classmates had come straight from a Swiss finishing school. One of them had a beautiful three-storey house her parents had bought her as a starting-drama-school gift. One lived with her parents in a mansion apartment in Bayswater. One was an ex-pop star. All of them also appeared to be wildly promiscuous. During our first week of studying, one girl in my class slept with two different boys, also in our class, and no one seemed to find this either surprising or awkward. I was fascinated; it was like watching a TV drama.

Secondly, the teachers at drama school aren't actual teachers. At least, they weren't back in the late 1990s. Most of them were working actors. Which makes sense, doesn't it? And probably sounds quite good. It *was* quite good: it meant that they had actual, current experience of the industry we were trying to enter. On the other hand, it meant that they didn't feel any great duty of care towards their students. My new back injury was giving me trouble during my first term, and I was feeling overwhelmed by the pain it was causing me to join in with our basic compulsory dance classes. I arrived at my voice class looking tear-stained. The teacher, an ex-TV star with a rumoured cocaine addiction (though really, I had no idea whether that was true. She might have just been naturally red-eyed and angry all the time), asked me to stay behind after class. I, used to professional teachers, expected words of advice and comfort. I was surprised. 'Darling,' she began, in a deep, resonant voice, 'you can't just come to class crying. It's not professional.' I was rather staggered. I'd assumed that going around emoting constantly would be totally okay in a school dedicated to drama. I explained that I'd recently acquired a back injury and was feeling awful about not being able to show what I could, until recently, have done easily in our dance classes. Which, I thought, would be enough to make her stop being beastly. 'MY back aches CONSTANTLY!' she rejoined, abruptly bringing the conversation around to herself, as though she'd bafflingly forgotten she was a teacher at all. 'I was in a car crash. My back muscles literally *crossed over* from the impact. Hellish!'

'I'm so sorry!' I stammered. 'How awful for you!' *Really?* I wondered. *Could back muscles actually do that?* I had none of the skills associated with bringing the conversation back to how she, my teacher, could help me to figure out training through an injury. She told me more about the car crash. I asked her questions, feeling as though I was interviewing her for the *Radio Times* or similar. We parted on good terms, and I decided never to ask one of my teachers for help again. They were merely actors pretending to be teachers, and they weren't even pretending very hard.

This became particularly clear in our improvisation classes. Which, for the record, were taught by a man I consider to be exemplary as a technical performer and acting coach. Everything I really learned about how to act came from him. However, in our first term, he also achieved the following:

- Groping a female student's ample bosom during an improvisation exercise. Her job was to respond as if surprised. She was, in fact, surprised. As were we all.
- Taking off all of his clothes in front of the class, before encouraging us to do the same. We did. We'd quickly learned that the worst thing of all to be accused of at drama school was being inhibited. Being accused of being a sexual predator seemed less worrisome.
- Creating an exercise in which the students were each assigned an animal to play, and then asked to roam the room until we found a student who was playing the same animal. At which point we were supposed to simulate having sex. I was a deer. My classmates Rob and Helen were *lizards*.

We often left classes, en masse, stunned and a little traumatised. It helped us to bond as a group, and discovering that even my more sexually sophisticated, experienced new friends found the teacher's methods a little difficult to cope with made me feel like less of an outsider than I'd initially expected.

After our first term, I left my student bedsit and moved in with three of my classmates. Being a Christian virgin who was determined that 'True Love Waits' wasn't the easiest choice for a drama-school student. After some initial interest, everyone discovered that I wasn't offering sex, and started ignoring me from a romantic point of view. But nevertheless I started to feel as though I belonged there. Though I couldn't participate in all the sex that was happening, apparently, between most of the students, most of the time, I could certainly try to help when the inevitable dramatic breakups occurred.

Year two was an even greater adventure. Our first year had been dedicated to learning the basics of acting: voice projection, articulation, phonetics, movement and improvisation technique, alongside working on scripts. In our second year, we took up several new subjects. Two of them quickly became my favourites.

Firstly, physical theatre (a type of performance art in which aspects of movement like mime and dance are the primary method of storytelling). If I'm honest, I'm not a big fan of watching physical theatre. It can be hard to follow, self-indulgent and pretentious. I'd rather watch a proper scripted play with the actors speaking lines in such a way as to resemble how real people talk, while wearing actual costumes to give me a clue as to who they're meant to be. But goodness, I adored *performing* physical theatre. With my damaged back, I couldn't do classical ballet or gymnastics anymore. Physical theatre was less demanding, owing to the fact that we could make up our own moves. It gave me an opportunity to wave my arms, fling myself around, and do the dramatic faces I'd so enjoyed performing in school photos. And because it wasn't scripted, we were encouraged to write pieces of our own for the class to interpret through our bodies.

Almost no one wanted to write anything; most of the actors on my course weren't interested in doing so. But I stepped nobly into the breach, with all the confidence of a nineteen-year-old with almost no life experience and an A in English literature. And, crucially, a deeply suppressed obsession with sexual violence. As a result, my peers were subjected to the following:

- Many, many angry poems about rape. I had not been raped. I didn't know anyone who'd been raped. I wasn't, actually, especially angry about rape. It sounded quite appealing to my muddled, kinky brain. But, knowing that I obviously couldn't write anything overtly about my fantasies, I resorted to fake anger as an excuse to approach the subject matter. I'm so grateful that I don't have any copies of my absurd poetry from this period. If I did, I'd feel compelled to share them with you in the interests of honesty. So use your imagination, and add an extra 25 per cent of pent-up sexual frustration. That'll be about right.

- I also wrote a goddam nightmare of a piece about intimate partner violence. Had I been a victim of intimate partner violence? I had not. Had I heard any first-hand accounts? Nope. Did I have fantasies about it? Well, yes, shamefully, I did. This is part of the problem with trying to suppress an interest in BDSM: you end up sexualising some utterly abominable events, and in the process, exploiting actual victims' experiences. If there's anything I'm ashamed of in my past, it is this. And it's one of the reasons that my present self is so keen on trying to make the production and consumption of BDSM porn more socially acceptable. It feels much better, and more honest, to sexualise

scenes that were designed to be sexualised,
rather than turning someone else's trauma into
your own fantasy.

- Also, I created a series, friends, an actual *series*
on the seven deadly sins. I wrote a poem (sort
of) for each one. Lust was my favourite –
because of course it was. And my class had to
act each of these ridiculous pieces out. I
sometimes wonder if they resented me by the
end of the physical-theatre course. Or maybe
they were just grateful that none of them had to
write anything because of Joceline and her
relentless, never-ending supply of fantasies. I
mean, her social commentaries. Jeez.

Until I started writing this book, I'd not actually
thought about my physical-theatre classes for years.
And that's because, though I loved it, its impact on me
was nothing in comparison to the subject that became
my favourite, and my greatest pleasure through the next
two years of study.

Back in sixth form, I'd had a tiny part in a production of Edward Bond's *Lear*, a modern adaptation of
Shakespeare's *King Lear*. It was a hideously, luridly violent piece, with people's eyes being plucked out, people's
tongues being cut out, and lots of fighting, rape and
torture. When I watched rehearsals, I was both fascinated and distressed by how realistic one of the fight
scenes was. I didn't know how they were making fake
unarmed combat look so real, and the boys in the scene,
who had leading roles and who I'd never spoken to,
were too intimidating for me to ask. I assumed they

were some kind of highly trained martial artists, and it certainly never occurred to me that I might be able to learn similar skills. As a first-year at drama school, I'd noticed the second-years practising sword fighting in the great hall at lunchtimes. I'd not paid much attention, knowing that I'd get my chance to try it the following year. And I never saw the teacher, until our first stage-combat class of the year.

Scott, our fight master, was a short, stocky, muscular man, probably somewhere in his late forties at the time. In our first class he walked down the line of students before him, shaking hands with each of us. It was his first teaching point, it turned out. Making eye contact is both confrontational and also important for safety in dramatic combat. I mainly noticed, as he briefly looked into my eyes, that this cheerful middle-aged man was giving off an energy that felt. . . well, it felt quite dangerous. He was smiling, but he looked as though he could quite happily kill me. How *interesting*.

In our first term, we were going to devote our classes to learning sixteenth-century rapier and dagger fighting. I had no great confidence that I'd be good at it; remembering the sixth formers practising their fake fist fight in *Lear*, I suspected that this was the sort of skill that only people who actually liked fighting in real life would be able to acquire. However, I hadn't reckoned on sword fighting's similarity with learning dance choreography. And although I couldn't dance anymore, I *did* have ten years' experience of picking up choreography fast.

In our first class, we paired up to learn the opening moves of a rapier and dagger fight. Scott came around the class, stepping in to help us stay out of range of the sword tips, correcting stance and taking turns partnering us. This way we could benefit from working opposite someone who knew the choreography, was using his sword correctly, and could put enough realism behind each attack to force us into parrying properly. It's very easy to just clash swords around without making it look dangerous at all, but we needed to learn to make every move look as though it was intended to be deadly, and to rely upon our partner to *really* move out of the way of our blades. When my time came to work opposite Scott, I looked into his eyes again and felt the same sense of confrontational, dangerous energy. It made me want to make him like me.

We went through the moves, with everything feeling more real with his expert technique behind each action. He parried my thrust with a circular movement that was meant to beat my sword aside. Practising with my student partner, it'd had no power behind it and been entirely ineffective. Scott parried, and suddenly my sword was flying away from me, landing several metres out of my reach. It was funny, and it was embarrassing, and it was a great teaching point about not relaxing your grip on your weapon. But it was also rather electrifying, I thought, as he raised his sword to point directly at my chest, with his bright eyes no less friendly, but somehow still deadly all the same. I stood opposite him, disarmed, and rather delighted to have been so.

And just like that, I found the thing that was going to become the closest approximation of BDSM in my life up to that point. Blessedly, I didn't have to feel guilty about it; it was part of my course. I could claim that I liked it because it was a bit like dancing, and that claim was true. At the end of the first class, Scott came up to me. 'I think you will be good at this,' he said quietly. For all I know, he took the opportunity to say that to everyone. He was really a superb teacher. But as an ex-dancer who was still privately devastated about not being able to use my body like a dancer anymore, this feeling of a second chance to excel at an elegant, beautiful physical pursuit meant an awful lot to me. And his approval did too. I decided that I'd work extra hard in his classes.

I'm nothing if not predictable. I'd just developed a new crush on a male authority figure. And my response was to – SURPRISE! – try to get top grades. Which is what I did. Soon, *I* could disarm unsuspecting people with my own sword. I could help my fellow students with the choreography. And in the second term, we started learning unarmed combat.

With most stage fight with weapons involved, there's not much physical contact. And with unarmed combat that's often the same – you can't punch someone in the face night after night in a stage production. You have to fake it for safety and sustainability. The same applies to most fight moves. But there are exceptions: face slapping, for example. With good technique, it's safe enough to do for real, and gives you, as a fight choreographer, the advantage of not having to hide the lack of contact from the audience. So naturally, we learned how to slap each other in the face. I didn't like doing it much; inevitably it hurts your partner, however much you try to relax your wrist, get your distance correct, and avoid hitting them in the eye or over the ear. But *being* slapped. That was a different matter. I liked that very, *very* much. Once we got advanced enough to choreograph our own fights, there was a lot of full-contact face slapping in my routines. Also hair pulling. As I'm sure you can imagine.

By the time we were ready to choose partners and to start putting together two fights for our external exam, there was no doubt in my mind that I would do the best I could, with the hope of taking my advanced exam the following year. I'd already discovered that I didn't like fighting with girls, just as I'd discovered that I didn't fancy girls. In the sexually charged environment of drama school, stage fight was my one displacement activity for sex, and I had every intention of only doing it with boys I fancied. My friend Joseph and I partnered up for our exam. Need you ask? Of course I fancied him. I really was thoroughly sexually predatory in my own elliptical way, and I used the fact that I was good at stage fight to attract the fight partner I wanted. Possibly you think I'm being too harsh on myself. That's because you don't know (yet) what I made poor Joseph do to me in our exam.

Although I couldn't script two scenes where I lost the fight without getting dangerously close to sharing my kink with the world, I got as close to it as possible. For our sword fight, I scripted a piece in (not especially excellent) iambic pentameter. To make one of the lines fit the rhythm, I had to make up a new word, just like Shakespeare did. The word, friends, was 'degredating'. Yes, that's right. Instead of 'degrading', which didn't have enough syllables. And yes, that's also right, I was still obsessing about degrading women. Or degredating them. Like a hybrid of degrading and dating. Which was more or less my fantasy, now I come to think of it. Poor Joseph. Anyway, the sword fight was set in a tavern and he groped me, whereupon I challenged him to a duel. And eventually lost, whereupon *he* lost interest in *me*. By all means, psychoanalyse that. I can't bear to.

Our unarmed combat piece was also, naturally, scripted by me. It was a quite ludicrous story about an escort (played by me) and her GUESS WHAT? Yes. Her abusive pimp. Because that is both original and sexy. I'm afraid that it seemed so to me, anyway. He tried to rape me; I stabbed him at the end of the piece, but not until a lot of face slapping had occurred.

I passed my exam with the highest available grade. And the following year, I took my advanced exam. My original fight partner didn't want to continue, due to the emotional trauma I'd caused him. At least, I hope that wasn't the reason. So, looking around for another potential partner, and not finding my classmates sufficiently exciting, I partnered with a student who'd already graduated a couple of years before, but who hadn't taken his fight exam, so was still eligible to do so. By this point, I'd befriended Scott's assistant Jon, as well as Scott himself, and it was Jon who introduced me to Bradley. I'd noticed him from afar when I was a new first-year and he was a third-year; he was an excellent actor who moved beautifully, and was possessed of what I considered to be dramatically Bohemian good looks. He had long, black curly hair, like Captain Hook. He picked up choreography quickly and projected vicious emotional intensity during fight scenes. And how do you think I felt about him? You're quite right. Having imported him into our fight classes, I also decided to make him my boyfriend, which seemed a natural extension of our fighting together. Because fighting, to me at that point in my life, was sex.

Naturally, we didn't have *actual* sex. True Love Waits, obviously. Sorry, Bradley. So all of our combined sexual frustration went into our choreography. For our advanced exam, we needed four scenes, all with different weapon systems. For our sword fight, I chose to play someone accused of being a witch during the Spanish Inquisition. Bradley played my interrogator. For the love of God. Although, naturally, I preferred playing to lose, I didn't feel as though the Spanish Inquisition actually deserved to win. So I killed him (grudgingly) at the end of the scene. Our second scene, with quarterstaffs, was about a woman being forced into marriage. Honestly, no historical abuse of power escaped my monomaniacal trawling. Our knife fight incorporated a length of rope binding my left wrist to Bradley's. And my pièce de résistance was a long unarmed combat scene, a James Bond parody in which I abandoned all pretence and choreographed a fight of which approximately 50 per cent was made up of sexual positions. I'm not even exaggerating.

'Ahhhh,' said Bradley, as James Bond, 'from this position you remind me of your sister.'

'You dog!' I replied, elbowing him in the groin. 'The neutron trigger is mine!' And so forth.

By the time we took our exam, our relationship was over. He was a lovely man but we had nothing in common other than our desire to qualify in advanced stage fight. Which we did, with top grades. I can only assume that the examiner enjoyed watching thinly disguised BDSM porn.

I graduated from drama school with an invitation to come back and assist Scott in teaching stage fight to the

new students, and I started looking for professional acting work. Immi and her husband Philip had generously
invited me to live with them in their house near London
while I found my feet, and I hoped to start earning a living
as an actor as quickly as possible. Of course, I hoped that
I'd be able to find roles that'd utilise my stage-combat
experience and give me continued access to my proxy sex
life, but I was prepared to take any work I could get,
knowing that I was in an overcrowded professional field,
and that London was flooded with young actors who
were prepared to work for low wages.

Looking back, I do find it extraordinary that I was
able to get so much pleasure from something that
involved my having to act out so much violence. Now,
as a BDSM model, I refuse to play dominant, sadistic or
violent characters, unless it's a piece to camera with no
human being to play the recipient of my aggression. I
suppose that when we can't find what we're really looking for, our minds can be astoundingly resourceful in
finding us approximations of what our hearts desire. I'm
grateful to have found stage fight because it gave me an
outlet for what was in my mind, and helped me to
reclaim my old fantasies and turn them into something
acceptable in the specific context of fight-exam scripts. I
think, with hindsight, it gave me some peace, something
that I'd not really found since my highly disturbing sexual awakening on 2 January 1994.

Chapter Eight

Playing at Slavery

Being a young actor in my first summer out of drama school was predictably hard. I auditioned, and auditioned, and carried my CV and headshots around London for castings. And at the end of the summer, just as I was beginning to lose hope, I was cast in a low-budget fringe production of Shakespeare's *Much Ado About Nothing*. It was a play I adored, and I was cast in the role of Hero, the second romantic lead. She's not an especially vivid character. *Much Ado* is a comedy and she is one of the few straight characters. However, she does get jilted at the altar during her own wedding, her bridegroom having been tricked into believing she'd cheated on him and was no longer a virgin. So although it was nowhere near as satisfying as my stage-fight roles, I did at least get to play a victim of sorts. As well as an actual virgin; probably I was the only fully qualified young actor in the whole of London for that particular role. Being on stage, in London, even in a tiny theatre above a pub, felt fantastic. I got my first non-drama-school CV credit. And at the end of the show's run, the director who was putting on the next production at the theatre invited me to audition for her version of *The Tempest*.

I knew *The Tempest*. It wasn't one of my favourite Shakespeare plays, and most of the characters were of limited interest to me, since many of them are old men. However, Prospero, the dubious hero of the piece, who controls the island on which *The Tempest* is set, has a slave. A slave called Ariel. And that was a part that *definitely* interested me. The idea of playing a slave had immense appeal. Many productions choose to portray Ariel as a cheery, willing servant; whimsical, breezy and uncomplicated. My idea was to play Ariel like a long-term prisoner of war; resentful, terrorised and yearning for freedom. At the audition, I watched the other actresses who were interested in playing Ariel. None of them seemed to see the role in the way that I did, and I hoped that this would be an advantage. Prospero had already been cast, so was reading Act I Scene II with each of us in turn.

Prospero called, 'Approach, my Ariel, come!' and by the time my chance came, I knew the first lines by heart:

> All hail, great master! Grave sir, hail! I come
> To answer thy best pleasure, be 't to fly,
> To swim, to dive into the fire, to ride
> On the curled clouds. To thy strong bidding, task
> Ariel and all his quality.

Perhaps that sounds like Shakespeare to you. To me, it sounded like sex talk.

All through my early life I had a collection of words that fascinated me, but that I was strangely reluctant to say aloud. They felt special, private, and as though, by my saying them, everyone would be able to see that they meant something extra to me. Which, obviously, was to be avoided at all costs. These words included, but were not limited to the following. Discipline. Submission. Punishment. Surrender. Compliant. Capitulate. (We'd had no TV for years, remember. Consequently I read a lot and had a big vocabulary.) Insubordinate. Insurrection. Bound. Tied. Gagged. Blindfold. Master. Slave. Captive. Humiliation. Domination. This is beginning to sound like a stream-of-consciousness poem, isn't it? The sort of poem a monomaniacal drama student might write, for example. But I couldn't have put those words in my poems, since I couldn't even write them without feeling dreadfully uncomfortable. I certainly couldn't have said them.

Most of the time, I managed to avoid all of these words. Occasionally, though, this could be challenging. Here's an especially memorable example.

I was fifteen years old, in high school, and was failing basketball. How could someone who was already six foot two be anything but good at basketball? And how, in any case, can you fail at it? It's a team sport. Well, let me tell you. Firstly, with very little wisdom, I had chosen to take physical education GCSE, which is why I needed to be assessed as a basketball player. It, along with seven other sports, would form part of my final grade. GCSE PE was a ridiculous choice, but at that age, the thing that gave me the most joy was being upside down and balancing on things. And since part of the GCSE PE syllabus was gymnastics, I chose it. Unfortunately, I hadn't considered what kind of other kids would choose this option. In case you can't guess, I'll tell you. The motherfucking popular ones. The loud, overconfident boys. The sexy, miniskirt-wearing, cigarette-smoking girls. I was none of these things.

Most of the time, I did fine in PE. I represented the school in sprint hurdles, long jump and the 200 metres. But I hated basketball. The boys had been playing it longer than the girls, and were much better. We'd not had the rules explained to us, which meant that students with access to TV had a clear advantage. And being tall, people's assumptions were that I'd be naturally awesome at it. I was not awesome. I was hesitant, easily disoriented, and psyched out by being shouted at by my team. At the end of a particularly miserable class, my teacher, Mr Lewis, asked me to stay behind, and invited a (ghastly, popular) boy to remain as well.

Mr Lewis was quite a small man. Not especially athletic himself, he resorted to being shouty and overbearing in his style of teaching. I did not enjoy being in his class. I found him noisy, and hyperbolic, and a bit of a bully. He explained to me that he thought I was falling behind on this part of the course. He spoke at some length about this. I looked back at him mulishly and wondered why he'd invited Mr Popular from my class to hang around and listen to him criticising me. I felt aggrieved and irritated.

Eventually, Mr Lewis turned to The Popular One and asked if he'd be willing to give me extra coaching. Fucking hell. One-to-one coaching in a team sport. I'd never heard of anything so spectacularly unappealing.

The Popular One might as well have saluted. 'Yes, sir!' he replied.

Urgh. In my school, none of the other teachers insisted on this antiquated formality. Mr Lewis was the exception. Maybe it was because he didn't get to wear a suit like the rest of the teachers. Perhaps he needed to compensate for having to wear shorts. As a result of his desire to be addressed this way, I'd managed to avoid speaking to him directly at all for over a year. Because, you see, calling someone 'sir' sounded to me like the language of sex. It would have felt as inappropriate as calling a teacher 'darling' or 'my love'. And now here I was, trapped in an intimate conversation with someone who wanted to be called something that I was saving up for my future sex life. Bloody, bloody hell.

Mr Lewis turned his head back to me. 'And will you be willing to work with [Mr Popular] here?'

I would not be willing. Mr Popular was an arse. He bullied the girls, was mean to fat kids, and referred to himself and his friends as 'The Dream Team'. Like a dick. But obviously, I was trapped. I'd have to agree and then figure out a way to avoid it later. I was good at being invisible.

So. 'Yes,' I replied, warily.

Mr Lewis looked at me with his pale blue watery eyes. 'Yes, what?' he asked. Just as though he were playing a teacher in a spanking movie.

I was not prepared to call my least favourite teacher this most painfully exciting of titles. My sense of propriety demanded that I shouldn't. I was not going to have an experience that, for me, would be not only sexual but romantic, with this annoying man in nylon shorts.

'Yes, I would be willing to,' I expanded, more firmly.

For several horrific seconds, Mr Lewis just looked at

me, waiting. But for some reason, it was he who gave up first. Maybe he just felt too ridiculous to keep insisting. Maybe he was intimidated by the fact that I was six inches taller than him. So he let me go.

Afterwards, I felt guilty. As a rule, I avoided openly defying teachers. And I recognised that he'd probably been trying to help, albeit in an emotionally illiterate way. So, dear reader, I made him a card.

'Dear Mr Lewis, I'm sorry I'm awful at basketball. Joceline.' And, because I've never really been capable of just being normal, I drew a picture of a gymnast on the front. Which strikes me as both quite clever and rather passive aggressive, now. What I was really saying, I think, was, 'Dear Mr Lewis, I'm awful at basketball but – remember – the best in the class at gymnastics. Joceline.'

He never checked up as to whether Mr Popular and I had met up to do any remedial basketball. We hadn't. I never spoke to Mr Popular again. Sorry, Mr Lewis. I was not interested. I still passed the exam. And you're welcome regarding all the sprint hurdle races. It was a pleasure.

Okay, where were we? Auditioning for *The Tempest*. 'Approach, my Ariel, come!' called Prospero.

I ran in from the wings, and positioned myself, kneeling before him. 'All hail, great master, great sir, hail!' I recited. I wanted to play Ariel as outwardly respectful, while inwardly desperate to escape, even as I agreed to Prospero's plans and sought his approval for work I'd just completed. I'd been reading about Stockholm Syndrome, and wanted to play Ariel as though her feelings towards Prospero were coloured by this condition;

wanting approval, fearful but dependent. From the inside, this interpretation felt perfect, as though, even in the audition, there was some complexity to the relationship between captor and captive; a dynamic that flowed between the words, unspoken but real.

From the outside it probably just looked like a reasonable audition. From the inside it felt like everything I wanted to experience in a real relationship, but was sure I never actually would. But whatever it looked like, it was enough for the director to cast me as Ariel, and I was overjoyed. There was even sword fighting – Ariel acts as Prospero's assassin. I absorbed myself in the role.

During rehearsals it was decided that Ariel should wear a white bikini throughout the show. I was fine with that, though my character research had taken the form of reading military memoirs about Special Forces soldiers incarcerated and tortured on overseas missions. So in my mind, Ariel was dressed in tattered, filthy combat gear. But, used to the disconnect between what I looked like and how I felt inside, I didn't worry about not *looking* much like Andy McNab. That wasn't the point.

At our dress rehearsal, a press photographer from the *Evening Standard* came to take pictures of us. Afterwards, he approached me, and asked if I'd ever tried modelling. I was very flattered by this. Up until about the age of ten, I'd thought myself rather marvellous-looking. Subsequently, a combination of growing so tall so young, experiencing bullying through secondary school and not finding a long-term boyfriend yet had left me feeling anything but gorgeous. But since the cast of *The Tempest* were all female, and I was the only one the photographer had invited to model for him, I felt that I must, somehow, look okay in my white bikini. So he suggested I come to his house the following Sunday, with a selection of clothing, to do some pictures with him.

Naturally, I said yes, though when I'd had actor's headshots taken during my third year at drama school, I'd put it off until the very last minute because I was so sure I'd look horrible in them. As an adult, I now realise that many people go through this sort of thing, but of course, when it's happening to you, you don't realise that you're being irrationally critical of yourself. I sometimes thought that I was so ugly that I was on the brink of looking genuinely deformed. I had hated having my headshots taken. When they'd arrived in the post, I'd opened the envelope and cried. I thought I looked awful. Looking back, I realise that a large part of this anxiety was due to feeling as though I was rotten inside; the strain of being kinky and feeling guilty about it had pervaded my sense of self in multiple ways. I thought it showed.

A kind word from a professional photographer couldn't fix all of that internal anxiety in one go, of course, but it helped tremendously. He was giving up his Sunday to photograph me, and he didn't even want any money for it. My headshots had taken half an hour and cost me £175. It wasn't until I was back at Immi's house, ironing clothes to take to my shoot, that his real motive suddenly suggested itself to me. He was probably a murderer.

Consider, if you will, the full irrationality of that statement. He'd given me his home address, in front of at least ten people. He was a professional photographer, and all of us knew which paper he worked for. His picture, which had me in it, was about to be published *in* that paper. Even if he *had* been a murderer, I'd have been a poor choice of victim. But the fact that it seemed more likely to me that he was a serial killer than that he might have honestly thought I looked nice and that he'd like to photograph me, perhaps illustrates the depth of my anxiety when it came to what I looked like.

Nevertheless, I have always been optimistic. I thought it was fairly likely that he'd try to kill me, but I was taller than him, with fast reactions and a wealth of (fake) fight experience. He'd photographed me with my swords during the rehearsal; maybe he wouldn't realise that I was only trained in *pretending* to hurt people. So it still seemed worth taking the risk of going to shoot with him. If by some miracle he *wasn't* a murderer, it meant that he thought I was pretty. And that, friends, seemed worth risking my life for.

He wasn't a murderer. He photographed me posing with his Sten gun and wearing a white summer dress. He took some pictures in dubious taste of me wearing a rollneck and satin panties, stroking his cat. (It was between my legs at the time, and I didn't notice that it might look a bit suggestive.) He tried to persuade me to pose topless. I said no because, though I was no longer a member of the Campaign Against Pornography, I didn't want to be a traitor to them. A couple of weeks after the shoot, he posted me some prints; I loved them, and discovered as a result that being photographed was much more comfortable for me when I could absorb myself in a character. The actor's headshots I'd posed for had been meant to represent the real me. I wasn't comfortable with the real me yet, and didn't like my face enough to enjoy seeing pictures of it. Full-length shots of me looking vaguely unhinged and menacing while holding a Sten gun were another matter. I was playing a character, and I loved it. I wished that there was a way to do more modelling for photographers.

At the end of *The Tempest*'s run, I regretted leaving Ariel behind, but was excited to have an audition for a touring production of *The Taming of the Shrew*. My excitement was two-fold. Firstly, I really wanted to tour. It seemed vastly more exciting than staying in the same theatre for weeks at a time, and being paid to travel seemed like an unbelievable privilege. Secondly, I had a confused fascination with the play itself.

For those of you who don't know the piece, here's a very simple summary. There's an old rich man with two daughters. Everyone wants to marry the younger one, but no one wants the elder – she's got a dreadful temper and is rather wild and unruly. The old rich man needs to marry her off so that the younger daughter can have her chance. A young, slightly less rich man hears about this situation and the dowry, and decides to marry the older daughter, believing that he can tame her through sheer force of personality. The wild daughter doesn't want him, but is forced into marriage with him anyway, whereupon he is so unreasonable and determined that she eventually breaks down and does what he says. Then they fall in love and everyone thinks the young man is amazing for having turned her into a good wife.

It is an awful, sexist plot by modern standards, made all the more so by the fact it's meant to be a comedy. Joceline the sixth-former was infuriated and scandalised by it. Joceline the young actor, however, very much wanted to play the role of Kate, the wild older daughter. My reasoning for this was complicated. I believed that the whole problematic plot could be updated for a modern audience, by simply turning the two protagonists into people who liked power exchange from a sexual point of view. At this point, I only dimly understood that sadomasochism existed, and believed that it was a thing only a very few, very sick people dabbled in on their own. But fiction wasn't bound by the rules of real life, and to my way of thinking, the whole plot made sense if you looked at it with that dynamic in mind.

The older daughter (Kate) doesn't like any of her suitors, since they can't give her what she wants in terms of dominance. She doesn't realise that is what she's looking for, but she recognises its absence in the men asking for her hand in marriage. Petruchio (the hero) comes along, knowing himself to be dominant, and therefore confident that he can handle her. Once they're married, he makes a whole load of unreasonable demands, but in doing so introduces Kate to the fact that power exchange is fantastically hot. At which point, she's so turned on by the whole dynamic that she's more than happy to go along with appearing to have been 'tamed' in public, because she knows that in private, it's all just a violent, joyful sex game and that they're wonderfully compatible.

Do you like my interpretation? *I* liked it. Of course I did. I liked this reading of the play *so much* that I was sure that, once I'd been cast as Kate, I'd be able to persuade the director to see the story my way. This was a huge and ridiculously arrogant gamble, because theatre directors quite like to be allowed to direct. They don't tend to want first-year graduates telling them what the whole play is about. And they certainly don't want members of the cast fulfilling their own complicated sexual fantasies through the text.

I neither knew nor cared. I needed to play Kate, and an audition had come up for just that opportunity. I took a National Express bus to Newcastle, and walked three miles to the audition venue. Whereupon I discovered that in place of a normal audition in which everyone would perform their prepared pieces, we were doing a group audition with all the people who hoped to be cast. Ever since playing Victorians with Immi, I've loved improvisation, and although I liked performing my audition pieces, I saw this type of audition as an opportunity to develop and demonstrate some on-stage chemistry with the actors who could potentially be cast opposite me. I just hoped that we'd get to do our audition speeches too at some point.

We were ten minutes into the audition and had been just been directed to choose partners when the door opened.

And I stared at the doorway. A man had stepped through the door into the room. He was well over six feet tall, with broad shoulders, long, glossy black hair, and the musclebound build of a professional athlete. He was strikingly handsome, with a straight nose, wide cheekbones and a beautiful mouth. Tattoos spiralled up his arms, only subtly visible across his smooth dark skin. He looked older than me – perhaps twenty-seven or twenty-eight. He looked exactly like my idea of a romantic hero. He looked like my Petruchio.

To be fair, I want you to know that I always, then and now, offer assistance to anyone who is, however temporarily, an outsider. My years of being excluded from social events as a result of my family's religion would have counted for nothing if I hadn't learned never to leave anyone out of anything when it's in my power to include them. Whoever had walked through that door, I'd have offered to partner with them, given that the rest of us had all at least already met, talked a bit and were on first-name terms. But his staggering, unnaturally good looks made it feel like the absolute opposite of a sacrifice.

'I'm Joceline – would you like to be my partner?' I asked prophetically. And there we were, Lawrence (for this was his name) and I, teamed up for the first part of the audition.

And imagine what the first exercise was? Sword fighting. We weren't given actual swords – we had to use our index fingers instead, and fight as *though* they were swords, trying to score hits by evading each other's parries. This was exactly the sort of thing that I loved. And Lawrence, it turned out, was excellent at it. He was agile, taller than me, so with a similar reach, and (as I discovered in between bouts) also equipped with his advanced stage-fight qualification. We were evenly matched, and he was gracious whenever I scored a point. I stared at his muscles and liked him immensely. And it felt like a great activity for mirroring the verbal sparring between Petruchio and Kate in the play. I hoped the director was watching us. And I wondered hopefully if perhaps the next audition game would be face slapping and hair pulling. I was sure we could do an *excellent* job of that together. I smiled at Lawrence.

He smiled back, and lunged towards me. I parried, and wondered what he looked like naked.

Too soon, we were directed to find different partners for the next exercise. And over the next couple of hours I didn't get to work with Lawrence again, though I watched him acquisitively throughout. Looking around the room, I couldn't see another man who could compete with Lawrence's physical presence – he, surely, was bound to be cast as Petruchio. We hadn't had much opportunity to do dialogue, but from the little I'd heard of him, his text work was as impressive as his appearance.

The female casting seemed far less certain. There were, as always, more women than men at the audition, and fewer roles for us to fight for. Certainly, *I* thought that, given our respective heights, it'd make sense to cast me opposite Lawrence if they chose him, but I was in a room full of pretty, qualified, classical actresses. And the last exercise of the audition involved not reciting our audition pieces, but singing a nursery rhyme with actions in a group. *Why?*

Standing in a circle with the other actors, Lawrence and I made brief, horrified eye contact. The frustration of travelling all the way across the country at my own expense and not getting to do any actual Shakespeare in an audition for a Shakespeare play was considerable, and I sensed that perhaps Lawrence was feeling similarly irritated. Because the hot man would be on the same wavelength as me, obviously. The audition finished in confusion, and I had to rush back across Newcastle to get to my bus. I didn't even exchange phone numbers with Lawrence. And really, what was the point? I asked myself as I travelled home. He was bound to get the

part. If I did too, I'd get to see him again. If I didn't, there
was nothing I could do about it. And he probably had a
girlfriend anyway. You couldn't, I was sure, just waltz
through life looking like some kind of movie star/Chip-
pendale hybrid without some single girl predatorily
asking if you wanted to be her partner, and capturing
your heart.

Days, and then weeks went by. I didn't hear from the
producers of *The Taming of the Shrew*. My faint hopes
for being cast weakened and died. I tried not to think
about Lawrence starring in my BDSM Shakespeare fantasy with some other woman. I auditioned for another
Shakespeare production: *A Midsummer Night's Dream*.
It was being produced by a professional company pre-
senting a series of plays in Cardiff over the summer. *A
Midsummer Night's Dream* had a perfect role for me:
Helena, one of the romantic leads, who's described as
'tall' multiple times in the text. I was tall. It didn't seem
like a particularly compelling reason to get a part, but
since I couldn't change my height, and since it often got
in the way of my being cast in other roles, I thought it'd
be nice if it worked to my advantage for once.

And I *did* get the part. I was delighted to have been
cast in a production that actually came with housing too.
The casts of all six productions were going to be staying
in Cardiff University accommodation, together, for the
entire summer. This sounded perfect to me, especially
since I'd already been offered a role in a national tour for
a Christian theatre company starting that September. I
suddenly had over a year's worth of work and accommodation lined up. I felt as though I was properly on my
way to becoming a real, grown-up actor.

On the first day of rehearsals for the Shakespeare season, the artistic director held a drinks party in his garden to help all the arriving actors get acquainted with each other. I'm shy, but normally do fairly well at being friendly in situations like that; again I think it's because of my childhood experiences of being forced to be an outsider. Now that I don't *have* to be one, I find it comforting to concentrate on not letting anyone else feel left out either. It's tiring in the long term and I tend to burn out after an hour or so of partying, but it helps me to make a strong start, at least. Which is what I was trying to do, when:

'Joceline!'

I spun around, and screamed. Lawrence. He was standing not two metres away from me, smiling a broad, beautiful smile, his perfectly white teeth dazzling against his dark skin. I flew into his arms. Two hours later we were still talking; he said he'd regretted not getting my number after the audition, and that he'd thought of asking the producer for my details, before realising that they wouldn't have been allowed to hand them out. He, like me, had heard nothing back from *The Taming of the Shrew*, and he, like me, had been cast in a production for this company. Sadly, he wasn't in *A Midsummer Night's Dream* with me, but when we were shown to our accommodation, his room was opposite mine. The first night, I dropped my key into my radiator by mistake, and knocked on his door.

'You don't happen to have a long poking device of some sort, do you?' I enquired innocently.

Lawrence, bare-chested, dressed in nothing but olive-green shorts, smiled the lazy, confident smile of a man who knew exactly what effect he was having on the women around him.

'I'll see what I can do,' he said, opening his door wider.

And thus began a ridiculous courtship. Lawrence did not want a girlfriend, but was more than happy to fuck. I was determined not to do so unless we were in a committed relationship. Though I was beginning to see that waiting until marriage was entirely unfeasible in the community of actors that I was part of, I didn't feel capable of having casual sex. He told me that he wasn't good boyfriend material. Naturally, this just made him more irresistible. He just needed the love of a good woman; I would save him from himself, I thought.

I set out to make him fall in love with me. In the process, the actor playing opposite me in *A Midsummer Night's Dream* asked me out. Several girls tried to get Lawrence into bed. In the melting pot of sexually active young actors, it seemed miraculous that he didn't entirely lose interest in me in favour of a woman who wasn't trying to stay a virgin. Instead of sex, we played a lot of chess. It seemed quite hot: I liked losing, and hearing him announce 'checkmate'. In his deep actor's voice, it sounded like a threat. Sometimes I lost on purpose. I wondered about gambling my virginity on the result of a chess game. By which I mean I fantasised extensively about this possibility. We kissed in the dark. We played Scrabble. He knew a lot of words; it turned me on. We talked about Shakespeare. We listened to opera, we read sonnets, we undressed each other. He was the most beautiful man I'd ever seen in my life. I wondered how to make him love me, the chess, Scrabble, opera and

kissing having not yet succeeded. I certainly didn't consider the possibility of talking about my fantasies. Surely
a man so much bigger, stronger and more confident than
me *must* be dominant too, I hoped.

Because it was all I had in terms of seduction technique, I offered to choreograph the fight scene for the
production Lawrence was in. I hoped that he'd understand what I was trying to communicate, as we worked
through the moves together with our épées. But though
stage fight may have been sex for me, to everyone else, it
was just choreography. Then time was running out, the
season was nearly over, and tempted though I was, I
couldn't have sex with him in the hope that it'd make
him love me. I did at least have that much sense. And I
was about to go away on tour for a year; the timing was
not on our side. I was scared to lose him – if we weren't
together by the end of the season, he'd be someone else's
boyfriend by the time I finished my year-long tour. I
stayed with him at his house for one night, once the season had finished, and I set off for the north of England
the next day to begin rehearsals. We kissed one more
time. He said he'd write to me, and I promised to do the
same. And I cycled off to the station, my vision blurred
with tears. All my life I'd wanted to fall in love, and now
I had. And, like so many people before me, I discovered
it was much more complicated than I'd envisaged.

Chapter Nine

The Christian Tour of Hell

Devoting a year to being a full-time Christian, just like Immi had done when she first left home, was absolutely certain to help me find a husband. That's what I'd thought when I accepted the job. Surely God would notice my loneliness and reward my piety? I was only going to earn £67 per week, for heaven's sake. I definitely deserved a husband in return.

I'd been a little concerned to hear that in our cast of four, only one of us was male, so we wouldn't all be able to marry him. But on arrival in Yorkshire, that was the last thing I was worried about. I was having a lot of trouble leaving my Lawrence-related hopes behind. He was off to appear in another Shakespeare play, opposite an actress who fancied him. Although we'd spent the last night of our tour together, I knew he didn't want a relationship, so I was aware that the best thing I could do for myself was to find someone else. But I loved him. Hopefully the Christian tour would be so much fun that I'd stop thinking about it.

The Christian tour was horrific.

To be fair to them, I had not done my research

thoroughly. I was just excited to be offered an entire year of employment as an actor, and knowing how well it had worked out for Immi to sacrifice a year of her life for God had made me optimistic that I'd benefit too. When already under contract, however, and reading through the scripts for our sketch show, I realised the disparity between my own worldview and the message that the company expected me to preach in schools. I didn't *want* to tell people not to take drugs. I'd never taken any, I didn't know what I was talking about and I had no medical qualifications. Similarly, I wasn't comfortable with telling teenagers not to have sex before marriage. It didn't feel like any of my business. And I certainly didn't want to do a sketch about the evils of advertising. There was nothing in the Bible about that. I didn't feel as though it was our place to criticise, especially since any member of our cast would have been delighted to take a part in a commercial, just like any other struggling young actor.

I should have looked further into their work before signing my contract. There were some nasty surprises. I'd known that we'd be putting on productions in churches, schools and prisons, for example, but not how we'd need to be dressed. As an actor, naturally you'd expect to wear costumes. The Christian theatre company had, bafflingly, gone a step further. Not content with making us dress up for being on stage, their idea was that we should turn up at the venue already *in* costume. In order, to their way of thinking, to act as an icebreaker and facilitate conversation. Naively, their expectation went something like this:

Four attractive young actors pull up to a high school in their van. They get out, dressed outlandishly in an array of Doc Martens, tutus, combat trousers and tailored jackets.

IMPRESSED TEEN: Hey, you guys look crazy! Why are you dressed like that? I'm fascinated, man!

CHRISTIAN ACTOR: Well, we're from a theatre company; we're here to tell you about Jesus. But we're going to have a *crazy good time* while we do it. We're going to put on a comedy sketch show that'll have you rolling in the aisles while we tell you how Jesus is actually a *really cool guy* who you'll want to know more about. Okay?

IMPRESSED TEEN: Wow, thanks! That sounds incredible; can't wait! I'll go and tell all my friends; they're *definitely* gonna to want to know more about Jesus!

Naturally, this is the opposite of what happened. We turned up at high schools, certainly, but the students met our arrival with looks of a sort of disgusted pity. Being from a Christian theatre company already marks you out as a weirdo; they probably assumed that we dressed like this all the time. They'd file in to their assembly halls because they had to, and would sit, steadfastly unentertained through our sketch show. At this time, our theatre company was all about rap. Rightly, realising that teenagers *liked* rap, they thought that if they wrote some sketches in this form, our audience would be hooked. It had not apparently occurred to them that one of the reasons that teenagers liked rap is because of the subject matter. Also the swearing. Four young white adults earnestly reciting poetry about God with no backing track did not have the same effect as Jay-Z.

So, we performed the following:

- A rap about not having sex before marriage. 'The stains on sheets/the empty bed/the clinic, the panic, the wishing I was dead.'
- A mime routine about ecstasy being really, really bad for you, guys!
- Another rap about Zacchaeus, the tax collector who climbed up a tree to see Jesus – it was very much like N.W.A.
- A sketch about advertisers selling *sex*, guys!
- A mime about deforestation.
- A dramatisation of the foolishness of blasphemy.
- And, as a finale, another goddamn rap about Jesus: 'God is doing something new/Watch out!/ Listen up!/It could be you!'

In case you're finding this hard to visualise, allow me to enlighten you as to our teenage audiences' response. They stared at the floor. They gazed at the ceiling. They glanced at our ridiculous clothing and whispered to each other. They snorted laughter during our moving whole-cast attempt to die from ecstasy. To the best of my knowledge, none of them wanted to know more about Jesus as a result of our show. At the end of each performance, we invited questions from the audience.

'Why are you all wearing the same shoes?' was what we were asked most often.

'Cos our company bought them for us; they're actually

really comfortable,' we replied, like hostages with Stockholm syndrome.

'Have any of you had sex?' they asked. We weren't allowed to answer that; the truth was that two of us had, two of us hadn't. But the ones who'd had sex felt like they shouldn't have, and we were meant to be preaching abstinence.

'No, but I've choreographed a lot of pornographic stage-combat pieces,' I replied helpfully. 'And I've decided blowjobs don't count as sex!' Okay, I didn't. No one was really listening to our answers anyway.

'Why's she so tall?' asked a smirking thirteen-year-old. Oh, for fuck's sake. I'd thought that maybe going back into schools as an adult would be good for me in that I'd see that teenagers were nothing to be afraid of. I was wrong. Teenagers were still terrifying. I felt no less scared of them than I'd been when I *was* one, but I was a lot more irritated. And I'd have been grateful to be back in one of my mother's Victorian pinafore dresses instead of my stupid suit jacket/tutu/glittery braids combination.

I felt tired. I was not enjoying feeling trapped into sending out a message of social conservatism along with our message about Jesus. And I wasn't a good fit. We shot our promotional poster for the touring show, all four of us posed against a wall. I was wearing a man's white shirt, black trousers and flat boots. When the pictures came back from the printer, the company decided that they couldn't include me on the poster. I looked 'too sexual'. I didn't know what they meant. I was fully, baggily clothed, for heaven's sake. I wasn't wearing heavy makeup. I was just leaning against a wall, looking at the camera, like everyone else was. But now, I rejoice. They couldn't make me something I wasn't. I *am* sexual. Ha ha ha.

We worked six-day weeks (over £11 per day!) visiting schools during the daytimes, and putting on our show in churches in the evenings. Occasionally, we went into prisons. This was, surprisingly, my favourite bit of the tour. Firstly, that was because getting through security took forever, so we normally couldn't fit in a school performance on the same day that we were in a prison. Secondly, three of us were young women. The prisons we visited were all-male environments. To say that our reception was warm would be a considerable understatement. I felt like Dame Vera Lynn. 'You're GORGEOUS! Will you marry me? My mate loves your tits! Show us your legs!' Perhaps this doesn't sound especially pleasant, but honestly, compared to the apathetic, sniggering teenagers, it was. The inmates were even happy to talk about Jesus, given that they were so bored. I'm not sure they particularly enjoyed the show; we were banned from doing the anti-sex rap, for example, when performing to inmates, on the grounds that it might be too inflammatory. So we mainly performed our sketch about the thief on the cross who died next to Jesus. Because, you see, we were all about targeting our demographic. We were insufferable.

Our performances in churches, on the other hand, were met with a completely different but no less disquieting reception. We were preaching to the converted, who didn't need to be convinced of the truth of our sketches. They simply enjoyed the confirmation that what we were saying matched their own beliefs. Consequently, they bellowed with generous laughter. Including during the sketch in which we died from taking ecstasy. They were so determined to respond appropriately to our show, which was billed as comedy, that they also laughed uproariously through our sketch about a man with a terminal illness. It was most disconcerting, with our teenage audiences steadfastly refusing to laugh at all, our Christian audiences determinedly laughing at *everything* and our prison audiences treating the whole thing like a peep show. I started to feel quite disoriented by the experience, and also quite irritated with God.

Because, in between all the questions about whether any of the cast members were fucking each other, people *did* sometimes ask questions about Christianity. Like: 'What about Muslims? What happens when they die?' I fielded that question more often than not. I responded that I believed the God of the Bible to be a God of Love, and that all you had to do to be welcomed by him was to *want* him to welcome you. This was not an acceptable answer to the more fundamentalist members of our cast, who complained that I was watering down God's message. I probably was, but I was becoming uncomfortable with God's message. It didn't seem fair to me that your country of birth was so likely to influence your choice of religion. And if God truly only accepted people who were members of just *one* of the world's religions, that didn't feel like a level playing field. It felt racist. I'd thought this as a Jehovah's Witness, and I felt the same as a Christian. Also: 'Why does God allow bad things to happen to good people?' I started to realise that I didn't even have an answer that satisfied *me*. God had let me be born with a gift for dancing, and had allowed me to sustain a career-ending injury when I was just on the brink of beginning my professional dancing career. My back was becoming increasingly painful during the tour, as a result of having to set up and take down heavy pieces of stage scenery multiple times a day. God was allowing me to be hurt further, as a direct result of trying to do his work.

And that was just me. There were far worse stories than that all around me, and on the news every night. 'Why did God let Adam and Eve sin?' I didn't know. But I became certain that if *I* was God, I wouldn't have kicked them out of the Garden of Eden and punished them *and* all their descendants forever, after one mistake. I wouldn't do that to a friend, let alone a member of my family. I'd been convinced by the idea that God was Love, but I felt as though any half-decent human being would be kinder than he was when people disappointed him. I couldn't even bear to see insects struggling and drowning in outdoor swimming pools, and was compelled to rescue them. How could God look down and see the human equivalent over and over again, and *not* intervene?

My year of trying to persuade others to become Christians was enough to shake the foundations of my own faith, as did the way in which the theatre company treated its cast. As did the fact that God didn't see fit to find me a husband. I'd given him a year, and he'd not come through. It seemed possible to me that rather than just being really bad at being God, perhaps he didn't actually exist. In which case, I reasoned, maybe I shouldn't keep looking, uselessly, for a Christian husband. I phoned Lawrence, and arranged to meet up at the end of my tour. I had plans, and they didn't include God.

Part Two

A Sexual Caterpillar

Chapter Ten

Total Poverty and a Lack of Chastity

I was done with trying to find a Christian husband. I'd dated several potential ones, and they hadn't worked out for a multitude of compelling reasons. One of them, a vicar's son training to be a police officer, was so bad at kissing he gave me a nosebleed, and then wouldn't speak to me the next day. I was no longer sure if God even existed, and I was anxious from worrying that Lawrence would find a girlfriend who wasn't me. *I* wanted to be his girlfriend, and I was tired of being a virgin; it felt, at twenty-three, like an intolerable burden. I went to London and visited Lawrence at the flat he was borrowing from a friend. Liberated from the Christian tour, I felt young, irresponsible and achingly sexually frustrated. I explained to Lawrence that I didn't need him to commit to a long-term relationship before we slept together, I just needed him to promise to give it a go. By the time we got to this point in the conversation, we were both naked, impatient and aroused.

'All right,' murmured Lawrence, lowering himself over me in the semi-darkness, his beautiful muscular arms either side of my head, his gorgeous, patrician face close to mine. 'I'll be your boyfriend . . .'

The next day, I was certain that I was pregnant, feeling this was the least of what I deserved for my extramarital sin, but I wanted to do it all again with him, immediately. I might not have waited for marriage, but I promised myself I'd commit to the relationship as though it was one. Perhaps, I thought, having only one sexual partner for life was almost as good in God's eyes as having a husband. I loved Lawrence, and since I'd managed to convince him to be my boyfriend, maybe I could inspire him to love me back, forever. I knew *I* wouldn't leave *him*.

It was an uncertain beginning to a relationship. But as far as I could tell, the sex was marvellous. I finally had a real, proper grown-up boyfriend to have a genuine carnal relationship with, and although I'd not succeeded in discussing my sexual fantasies with him, because I didn't want him to think I was weird, losing my virginity to an experienced, older man who was so much bigger and stronger than me felt, in my own head, like a dominant/submissive act in itself. And of course, no one knows what you're *thinking* about while you're having sex with them. My thoughts were my own, and they were not vanilla. Possibly some of my preferences did start to become dimly apparent to Lawrence, though – a few weeks into our relationship he said, in rather a puzzled voice, 'It's amazing. I can do *anything* to you, and you like it!'

I did. And I liked it that he thought so. He didn't pick up on the depth or complexity of my submissive instincts; I believe that he just thought I was more than usually amenable in bed. But it seemed like a hopeful beginning.

After a few months of rushed meetings in friends' London flats, and continued delightful carnality, the next step in our relationship seemed to be to move in together. I loved living with Immi, Phil and my baby niece, but I needed to be in London, since that was where most of the acting work was. And Lawrence also needed to be there; he'd been commuting from the north of England for auditions and jobs. I had nearly no savings, having struggled to squirrel much away during my £67 per week Christian tour job. Lawrence, being a more established actor, was in a better situation, but had already got a job touring with a theatre production, so didn't want to sink unnecessary money into accommodation he wouldn't be in much. So we looked at the cheapest possible options for flats within the London Underground area.

What we found was quite extraordinary. I didn't see it until the day we moved in, but honestly, it *was* the best of the places that we'd viewed. Its plus points were as follows. It was two minutes' walk from a tube station. It was in the northwest of the city, which made escaping London easy. And it had its own front door.

I'm afraid that's pretty much it. The negatives? It was literally one room. And there were two of us, both over six feet tall, living in it. It had a miniature kitchen in one corner, a sofa opposite it, a kids-sized wardrobe, and a bed crammed into another corner. There was also a bathroom, tucked into a corner opposite the bed. Another negative: it was on one of the biggest road junctions in London. On our first night, we lay sleepless, looking up at the ceiling, which was bathed in orange light from the powerful street lamps outside. The traffic roared ceaselessly. When lorries passed, the building shook. We had no double glazing, so the noise was impossible to shut out. And when autumn came, we discovered that there was no functioning way to heat the place. The one elderly storage heater was secreted behind the bed, and so couldn't be used safely. We resorted to using a cheap electric heater, pointing it in our direction as we moved around the flat. It was, I thought, rather romantic. I bought blackout fabric and lined the curtains to shut out the night-long sodium glow of the outdoors. I bought heart-shaped cushions from Ikea. I baked cakes. And I auditioned for the role of a lap-dancer, captured and tortured by gangsters in a low-budget thriller.

'You're very good at screaming!' complimented the casting director. 'You make a great damsel-in-distress. Are you okay with nudity?' And I got the part.

I was happy, I thought. I didn't have to dress up in a tutu and Doc Martens and be stared at by hostile school kids on a daily basis anymore. I was in an actual movie. I had an absolutely beautiful boyfriend who I even got to go to bed with. And yet, living with Lawrence soon started to become a little disquieting.

I'm going to have to say some unpleasant things about Lawrence, in order to explain what happened to us over the next few years. I'm going to be as quick as I can with it, because it's a bit miserable and I'm not sure that he could help all of it. So before I do, I want you to know some genuinely good, admirable things about him. He was a hard worker, and exceptionally self-disciplined. In order to maintain his physique, he trained every day, and ate a horrible diet of porridge, salmon, pasta, turkey, red peppers, rice and raw eggs. He never deviated from this regime, and it was impressive to see

how dedicated he was to it. He was clever, well educated, knowledgeable in our field, and constantly
educated himself further by reading plays, working on
his accents and languages, and taking courses to add to
his professional skills. He worked, between acting jobs,
in the profession which had been his original choice
before he became an actor. On occasion, he could be
perceptive, funny and charming.

And vulnerable. When I'd first met him, he'd seemed
very alone in the world. He was estranged from most of
his family, and the ones he still spoke to lived on the
other side of the globe. He had very few friends, and
although people seemed initially drawn to him as a
result of his exceptional looks, he didn't seem to be
good at maintaining relationships. I saw this as very
sad, very romantic, and very definitely fixable by me. I
would be his friend. I would share my friends with him.
I would save him, just like Jesus.

But once I was living with him, other, more worrying
aspects of his character became apparent, and perhaps
explained his lack of friends. He could be unkind, seem-
ingly for purely recreational reasons.

'You're actually quite fat. I'm only joking.' 'Your
teeth are awful. Only joking.' 'And you smell bad. I'm
joking.'

And he didn't compromise. I was learning to play the
guitar for my CV. Once we'd moved in together, he flatly
refused to let me practise. At first, I carried on when he
was out, but felt guilty about the amount of space that
the guitar took up in our tiny home, and I abandoned it.
I tried telling myself that this was what I'd wanted. He
was dominant, I supposed; this was, perhaps, how he

expressed it. Maybe it was just the preamble for all the kinky sex we'd eventually end up having. But sometimes it felt as though, whatever preference I expressed, he would deliberately do the opposite.

He was also vile to my friends, and he didn't like my family. Immi and Phil were warm and welcoming to him; he responded by saying that Phil didn't have enough muscles ('He's just a pencil-neck!'), and that Immi was 'pear-shaped' (she is beautiful). My wonderful actress friend Beth met him only once. He invited her to join us for a threesome. I was embarrassed, and puzzled. I'm heterosexual. Threesomes with my hot female friends had never been on the cards. Beth and I, from then on, only met when he was away, or when we could meet up in central London without him.

On that first day when he'd walked into my *Taming of the Shrew* audition, I'd wanted him to be my Petruchio – now he was. And he was wearing me down in a way that appeared to be fun for him, though definitely not for me. Preventing me from doing things I wanted to do (like playing the guitar, or going to the theatre with him); criticising things I *was* doing (like taking on a new theatrical agent, and learning to drive); behaving inappropriately towards the people I loved; and, from time to time, with what felt like staged cruelty, talking about his attraction towards other women.

As months went by, I nevertheless continued to be in love, and radiantly happy for long periods. But it gradually dawned on me that the happy periods coincided with the times when Lawrence was away working, either on theatre tours or on location movie sets. When he wasn't there, I could sustain myself by replaying my edited highlights of life with Lawrence. The sex. Our shared enjoyment of reading plays. His moments of humour and affection. Then when he returned, I remembered over and over again that he often acted as though he didn't like me very much.

But I'd chosen him. He'd tried to warn me that he might not be good boyfriend material. I wondered sometimes if he was deliberately testing me, to see if I'd leave him, but I was determined to make it work somehow. Maybe one day he'd realise that he'd never be able to push me away, however hard he tried, and that might make him finally relax and be nicer. I came from a family of people who'd all married their first sexual partners; nothing else was acceptable to me. I felt that you couldn't just try people on for size, and then dump them again.

My personal morality dictated that there were only two justifications for leaving a relationship. The first was adultery, which even the Bible agreed with. The second was violence. Which might sound odd, given my proclivities. But, even as a (slightly wobbly) Christian, I believed that your first duty was always to yourself. And if you were in danger from your partner, you had to leave the relationship. I repeated this to myself, because I knew that I was at risk of romanticising violence. But nothing else felt like enough of a reason for leaving my partner – something that the Bible was clearly against.

We'd been together for a couple of years when I reached a crisis point. I was feeling increasingly undermined by his jokes about my fatness, ugliness and career failures. And I didn't think I could make him happy enough to justify my own unhappiness. I'd taken him on a weekend away to Stratford-upon-Avon to see the Royal Shakespeare Company and to stay in a hotel. I was terrifically excited to see *Julius Caesar*, with my real-life actor boyfriend, at the ultimate Shakespearean venue. It seemed wonderfully romantic, not to mention sophisticated and grown-up, to be staying at a lovely hotel within walking distance of the theatre. I could barely afford it, but I'd been working hard as a medical secretary and receptionist between acting jobs, and was proud of being able to pay for it myself.

Lawrence, however, didn't like the production. I was crestfallen. I thought he was bound to enjoy the actual RSC, performing Shakespeare. He then announced that, rather than spending the rest of the afternoon with me (I'd booked us afternoon tea at our hotel), he'd accepted a short-notice job. I went back to our hotel alone, very lonely and extremely confused. As I sat in the lounge, eating scones and drinking tea by myself, I looked around at the other guests. There was a group of older women having their own tea at a table near me. They were talking animatedly and happily, and I wished that I could join them. Even more, I wished that I'd come with a friend and not tried to share the experience with Lawrence. Even a friend who didn't like Shakespeare much would have been *polite* about it.

This feeling became a very familiar one, as Lawrence rarely wanted to do anything sociable with me. He tolerated cinema visits because they were tax-deductible expenses for professional actors, but he refused to go there in time to buy snacks, or to watch the trailers. I got used to leaving home for the cinema on my own, and meeting up with Lawrence in the auditorium just in time for the main film to start. Those cinema visits didn't feel like dates. They felt wretched. And he was highly unwilling to eat out, due to his regimented diet. When occasionally I did persuade him to, I had to bribe him by offering to pay for both of us, and he'd repeatedly shut down any attempts to converse over the meal. I became more and more used to looking around restaurants, as I'd done during my lonely tea party at Stratford-upon-Avon, and wishing that I could be transported to any table other than the one I was sitting at with my boyfriend. I'd never expected to feel so lonely when I wasn't alone.

I felt used and demoralised, and I eventually broached the subject of breaking up. Whereupon he told me something horrifying. A previous girlfriend had broken up with him, he said. He'd attempted suicide, and had ended up hospitalised. Clearly, I realised, I couldn't break up with him without endangering his life. I felt trapped, but I loved him, and wanted to do the right thing by him. I wondered if there was another way to make it work. And when he was away, my optimism always returned. He was beautiful, and talented, and we had our careers in common. I was, at least on some level, lucky to have him.

And I learned a sad truth. In a relationship where you don't feel especially safe, respected or cared for, the desire to be honest about your sexual tastes starts to atrophy. My fantasies were still all about being tied up, spanked, dominated, hurt and humiliated. But the real-life humiliation of being treated disrespectfully by my boyfriend as a matter of course stopped me from wanting to talk about it with him. Lawrence knew some of the things I liked, at least, and since it was the bit of our relationship that worked the best, I was grateful that he sometimes put his hands around my throat when we fucked, occasionally held me down, and liked to tell me what to do. There was time, I thought, to explore more when the rest of our relationship matured.

But the difference between my fantasies and the reality of my life with Lawrence was illuminated for me one day in a way that cooled my desire to explore any potential dominant/submissive dynamic between us. I'd been prescribed antibiotics by my doctor, and had been warned that they'd make my contraceptive pill ineffective until my next period. I, of course, warned Lawrence.

Strangely, this information appeared to interest him. We were at home, in our vibrating, noisy, orange-lit studio flat. I was sitting on the bed, going through *The Stage* newspaper, looking at the job advertisements. He joined me on the bed. And then rolled on top of me, pulling up my skirt.

'Lawrence, we can't have sex. At least, not unless you have a condom? Like I explained, I could get pregnant.'

I said it calmly. Clearly, he'd forgotten what I'd told him. I was sorry to disappoint him, but there was a pharmacy across the giant road junction from our flat. We could get condoms if he wanted to carry on.

He did want to carry on. This much was evident.

I pushed him away, gently at first, and then harder. It made no impact. He was much heavier than me, much bigger, and far stronger.

'Lawrence! Stop it. You're being an arse. Let me up.'

I was still calm. He wasn't going to hurt me, and

surely he wasn't going to actually fuck me when I had a clearly stated, serious reason for not wanting to.

But he was going to. And the fact that I didn't want to appeared to be the reason that he *did*. I was trapped underneath him, and talking to him was making no difference. It was ridiculous. I liked sex with him; I'd never said 'no' before. And I'd only said it this time out of medical necessity. Furthermore, a quick trip to the pharmacy would make it perfectly possible for us to spend the entire afternoon making love, if that's what he wanted. But I hadn't consented to *this*.

I tried to struggle out of his grip again. It was pointless. And there was nothing else I could do.

Though that's not true. If I'd been choreographing it, my character would have bitten his neck as hard as she could. Surely, that would have hurt plenty, and would have been enough to stop him for a minute so that I could get through to him that what he was doing was unacceptable. I could reach; he was right on top of me. It would have been easy.

But, I couldn't. I loved him. I couldn't deliberately hurt my partner, however absurdly he was behaving. And I couldn't risk damaging his gym-sculpted, depilated body. He'd be furious.

And wasn't this, also, what I'd wanted on some level? No, it wasn't. I wasn't sure *what* it was, but it certainly wasn't sexy in any way whatsoever. It was horrible, and made me feel dirty, disrespected and angry. It wasn't until years later that it occurred to me exactly what behaviour like this is called.

It's called rape, isn't it?

All those drama school poems about rape, and I'd

not understood what it really was at all. In my fantasies, it'd been all melodramatic, with scary, gorgeous, menacing strangers, and me, a breathless damsel. What an idiot I'd been.

I didn't behave like a breathless victim, and I didn't pretend that it was all okay, either. I just waited for him to stop. Then I got dressed, and I crossed the dual carriageway to our local pharmacy. I asked to purchase the morning-after pill. It was painfully expensive – a day's worth of my medical-secretary wages. The pharmacist looked apologetic.

'It's a pricy option; I recommend using condoms next time,' he advised. Yeah. Well, that's what I'd advised too. And I couldn't explain to this friendly, courteous man that I hadn't had the choice. So I went home again. And what I should have done is to have broken up with Lawrence then. But I couldn't. He'd not physically hurt me, he'd just been incredibly selfish, and stronger than me. And he'd not cheated on me. The Bible, as far as I could remember, was silent on the issue of forcing yourself upon your partner. So, in my mind, this wasn't an excuse to leave him, though it was definitely a reason not to share any more of my fantasies with him. Clearly, he did not respect me or my opinions. I was not inclined to make that lack of respect any worse.

If I could go back and visit twenty-four-year-old me, this is what I'd say.

Leave him. Don't wait until he does something worse, because if you do, he will. Violence and cheating are not the only two reasons to leave a relationship. Rape is another really good reason.

PS You'll still get to enjoy all the rape fantasies you

want, later, with someone who respects you. And it won't be like this. So don't worry about it; you're still kinky. You just think consent is important. In this, you are correct.

PPS If there's ever a next time, bite him as hard as you want, babe.

I'm sorry this chapter has been miserable. Many, many people have worse relationships than this, especially when they're young and inexperienced. And I'm entirely fine now. Being in a badly executed relationship like this one, though, helped me to form some of my personal morality, attitudes to other people and my priorities. The way I stayed happy while I was Lawrence's girlfriend was to learn to enjoy being alone, to appreciate my friendships and to prioritise spending time with my family. All of these things have contributed to the fact that, as I write this book, all is well.

And to be fair to Lawrence, he wrote to me a few years later to apologise for what he came to see as his unkind behaviour. I accepted his apology without reservation. Unfortunately, things between us were about to get worse. But before that happened, my life got a great deal more exciting, and I'm going to tell you all about it. Follow me to the next chapter! It will include an awful lot of unexpected nudity. Unexpected for me, at the time, that is. Not for you, cos I literally just warned you.

Chapter Eleven

A Magical Career from the Internet

Lawrence aside, my life as a just-turned twenty-five-year-old professional actress was a delight. I worked as a medical secretary to help me pay my rent, and although I only had two office-appropriate outfits, and no money to buy more, since I only earned £210 after tax each week, I still enjoyed taking the Underground to work every day, applying for acting jobs at lunchtime, and meeting my friend Helen for coffee before going to our weekly yoga classes. And, just as I was beginning to worry that no acting work was on my horizon, I was cast as the lead in my first feature film. It was low budget – I didn't get paid at all – but it involved an entire month staying in a big, beautiful farmhouse in Norfolk with the rest of the cast and crew. And I got to play a character that I loved. A twenty-one-year-old with autism, coming to terms with the death of her brother. It wasn't a sexy role, quite the opposite, and the script was wonderful. It was shot at lonely, beautiful outdoor locations all around Norfolk. I loved every bit of it, adored working with the same people all month, and made friends with a local farmer and his horses too.

I came back to London feeling very hopeful indeed about my career, but totally broke. I immediately got another day job, working in the office of an art college, and started looking for acting work again. The problem was, I couldn't afford to do anything else that wasn't paid. I simply couldn't earn enough to live in London and put money aside too. And applying for acting work wasn't free; I had to pay for casting services, and I had to send out CVs and headshot photographs each week. I'd had a new haircut for the feature film, too, so my old headshots didn't look sufficiently like me anymore; I needed new ones.

Getting professional headshots taken and reproduced would cost me more than my weekly earnings in my office job, and I didn't have any money to spare. I thought back to the photographer who'd photographed me for free back when I was playing Ariel in *The Tempest* a few years before. Probably, I realised, he'd have been happy to take some shots of my face if I'd asked him. We'd not stayed in touch, but now that I was living in London, photographers were approaching me in the street fairly regularly to ask if I'd like to model for them. So far, I'd said no, since I continued to believe that they were all probably murderers on the hunt for their next victim. I blame the Jehovah's Witnesses and the garish illustrations of murder in their literature. Though to be fair, I do not believe that they had anything specifically against photographers, so perhaps that particular prejudice came from me alone.

But I thought, instead of trusting a random man on the street who *said* he was a photographer, what if I approached someone who was *definitely* a photographer – someone with an actual website? I had a lot of free time in my office job; no one had sorted out security clearance for me yet, so some afternoons there was nothing that I was officially allowed to do. So during that time, I started looking for photographers online. I needed someone who had a studio, did good portraits, but who also looked as though he'd have need of young females who were happy posing partially clothed. Like me.

I found someone who looked perfect. His name was David Linaker, he was based a short train journey west of London, and his work was beautiful. He shot products and commercial pictures, but also appeared to photograph lots of models. Hoping that I wouldn't come across as horribly arrogant and offensive, I decided to email him.

Rather tentatively, I explained that I was looking to have my actor's headshots retaken, and since I couldn't afford it, I was looking for someone who'd be happy to trade in return for my posing for them. I can't imagine how I had the nerve to ask. I certainly wouldn't these days. He was a professional photographer who deserved to be paid for his skill. But having no money meant that I couldn't afford to be cowardly.

Amazingly, he wrote back. He'd be happy to do my headshots, he said. And he'd book a makeup artist to ensure that we'd get the best result. All he was looking for in return was for me to pose for some art nude images on the new set he'd just built in his studio. I had never heard of art nude, but I assumed it couldn't be anything obscene, since it hard the word 'art' in it. And I was fine with being nude. At that point in my career,

I'd done nudity classes at drama school, shot a fully nude sex scene in a short movie, and another for a TV drama. I'd been extensively naked during the lap-dance-club movie, and had actually worked as a pole dancer in a lovely nightclub for six weeks, before discovering that my lungs couldn't take the onslaught of cigarette smoke. Yes, I thought; whatever 'art nude' was, I was qualified to do it. I just hoped that my back, which had never really recovered from my gymnastics injury, would hold up. And I hoped that I hadn't chosen a murderer to do my headshots.

The very next weekend, I borrowed Lawrence's car and drove myself there. I was very excited, afraid of being killed, and hopeful that these would be my best headshots ever. With an actual makeup artist, how could they not be? I didn't know *anyone* who'd had a makeup artist for their headshots – I was either about to level up, or be murdered. It seemed worth the risk.

David did not murder me. His wife made me a cup of tea, and he showed me around his studio, which he'd built at the bottom of his garden. He was friendly, knowledgeable and competent. Once my makeup had been done, he took the headshots in just a few minutes. Then, he moved things around in the studio, and put together a set that he'd designed to look like a Victorian boudoir. I wasn't entirely sure what a 'boudoir' was, but it looked extremely glamorous, I thought. He had fake windows that he shone coloured lights through so that the whole set had a warm, golden appearance. Luckily, I'd brought a long white Victorian petticoat with me, and a sheer champagne-coloured lace top that had a slightly Victorian look to it. And since we were eventually going to be shooting 'art nude', I thought that wearing a sheer top and no bra would show willing.

Friends, it is a testament to David Linaker's professionalism, creativity and flexibility that we never got around to shooting *any* art nude on this occasion. The combination of his set and my costume looked great together, and once he started photographing me, I discovered a strange, delightful and compelling thing.

I adored acting. I had ever since Immi and I filled our days with it and we didn't even know it *was* acting. And until my first afternoon with David, it had never occurred to me that good modelling is acting too. On his set, in my costume, I stopped feeling like Joceline, a young, poor actor from 2003. I felt like a wealthy, saucy Victorian lady, enjoying a warm, sun-bathed afternoon at home with her lover. I rearranged my blouse, freeing one breast. I pulled up my petticoat, exposing my thighs. I lost all track of time, as David adjusted lights, I adapted my poses, and the story of my character wove itself in my mind.

Eventually, David realised we'd been working for four hours, and decided that it was too late in the day to build the other set and shoot the promised art nude. He said he'd email me a selection of shots the following week. He also told me that he thought I should think about putting some of them on a photographer and models' networking website where you could display a portfolio. He said that he thought I should be able to get some paid work. And he booked me to shoot a bridal jewellery commercial for a high-street jeweller with him the following month.

He did not, on that day or on any of our numerous

later shoots, even slightly try to murder me. But he gave me all the tools, and the confidence, to embark upon a course which led not just to a couple of paid shoots a month to help pay my bills, which was what I'd hoped for, but to an entirely new and wonderful career.

Driving back to London, I knew none of this. But I was elated to have unexpectedly found something that I seemed to be good at. I was tremendously excited at the possibility of being able to earn some extra money doing it. And I was hugely grateful to have stumbled across a photographer who not only seemed to be an entirely trustworthy and decent human being, but who was really good at his job.

The next week, as promised, David's pictures arrived in my inbox. I'd hated my first set of headshots back when I was a drama student, but I barely recognised myself in these. The combination of David's exquisite lighting and post-production, and the disinhibiting effect of my being able to pretend to be a character rather than having to just be myself, were stunning. To me, at least. I couldn't wait to show them to everyone. And, since I still didn't have security clearance at work, and therefore had at least three hours a day in which I had to be at my desk but didn't have any tasks to do, I spent the time putting together my embryonic portfolio on the website David had recommended, made up of his shots and a few paragraphs I wrote to explain that I was a professional model who was happy to shoot art nude. I still had no idea what this was, but with new confidence, I was sure that I'd be able to do a good job of it. And I couldn't wait to put the jewellery commercial shots into my portfolio.

The website I'd chosen, which was the largest model networking site of its day, was international. I had no idea how many British photographers would actually see my pictures, and even less idea as to whether any of them would be prepared to actually pay me. David had suggested that I charge £40 per hour, or £250 per day. That sounded crazily high to me; it meant that a single day of working as a model would earn me more than a week at my office job. But I trusted his opinion, and I figured that even if I got a couple of hours' work each month, it'd make a noticeable difference to my finances. And if it felt anything like the shoot with David had, it'd be fun too. And it'd make me feel better about myself. Which was important; living with Lawrence had somewhat drained me of confidence.

I activated my portfolio on a Monday morning, at my office in the art college, and couldn't believe what I saw when I checked my email at lunchtime. I'd been offered five jobs, though even to my newbie's eyes, some of them were clearly best avoided. A photographer who wanted to get naked and pose with me while he took pictures with a timer. A photographer who lived in France and was inviting me for a very non-specific visit to his house.

But there was also an amateur photographer who lived in London and wanted to shoot some fashion images from his home, and a painter who was interested in doing a body-paint film shoot. And, good heavens, an art nude photographer, who wanted to book me for *two whole days*! Since he described himself as a person who actually shot this mysterious art nude genre, I scrolled through his pictures. They were absolutely lovely. He shot most of his work in the Scottish Highlands, where he lived; mostly landscapes, many of which had nude figures incorporated into the landscape around them. Twined around trees, climbing up rocks, wading out of lochs. If that was art nude, I definitely wanted to do it.

I wrote back to the three photographers who sounded legitimate. And suddenly I had four days of paid work. The shoot with the painter was only for two hours, but it'd still pay me more than a day at my office job.

I realised that I'd need to take a week off work. That seemed a risk, but I thought that I could afford to assume that I'd be able to get another temporary job after my week of trying out being a model. Since I'd have been paid decently, even if I couldn't find anything immediately, and if no more modelling jobs came in at all, I'd still be okay.

I handed in my notice, booked my first ever flight, to Inverness, and got prepared for a holiday from my normal life. I never went back to an office. Nude modelling was about to *become* my normal life. And my gratitude to David in Maidenhead, to Ron in Scotland and to all the photographers who took a risk and booked an unknown model back in 2003 will be everlasting.

Chapter Twelve

A Professional Model

Off I went to my first shoot with the amateur photographer in London who wanted to take fashion pictures. I had very few clothes. Lawrence and I shared a child-sized wardrobe and I'd had no money to buy much in the way of luxury items. I did have a couple of lingerie sets, though, and my Victorian petticoat and lace blouse. So that's what I took with me as I headed to the photographer's house in north London, for my first day of being a professional model.

It was an excellent experience. Not because it was good, but because I learned a lot. Firstly, I discovered that the photographer in question had given me a fake name. His appearance, when I arrived at his house, was quite at odds with his online persona. He was, he explained, using his *dead friend's* name for his online photographic activities. This seemed very odd, but he did at least give me his real name once I arrived. At one point during the day's shoot, as I was posing on the bed, he suddenly produced a dildo and asked if I might like to use it. I declined. He then attempted to strategically leave it in shot, on the bedside table. I discovered that being assertive was an important part of being a model. I didn't *want* to pose in lingerie with a random dildo sharing the shot with me, and I said so. The day progressed with no further drama, until it was time to finish. Whereupon the dead-friend-name-stealing dildo-wielder insisted that I slow dance with him around his sitting room before he'd pay me. With escape around the corner, I did what he asked, collected my £250, and left his house, never to return. Would the rest of my photographers, I wondered, all be this boundary-dodging?

My next shoot was with a professional photographer from Spain, who'd come to London to complete multiple studio shoots with a series of models. We only shot for two hours, but he was encouraging and helpful, and gave me a set of lingerie. This astonished me and made me feel as though I'd fully entered the modelling world. And after the shoot, which was in Camden Town, I went shopping and bought myself a black satin skirt to go with a sheer black vest top that I already owned. I had two new modelling outfits, and felt highly professional.

The next day, armed with my entire wardrobe of modelling clothes and all five items of makeup in my collection, I took a train to Gatwick Airport for my flight to Inverness. I felt important, taking a flight to *another country* for a modelling job. I felt as though everyone would be looking at me: 'Who is that girl on her own? Surely she's a professional model!' I had breakfast at McDonald's – the expensive version that comes on a polystyrene tray, not just an egg muffin like the normal, non-model person I'd been up until the week before. And, because my delight was too powerful to deal with alone, I called my mother. I also thought it was wise to let someone know where I was going, since I still believed it was all too possible that the ex-police officer who I was going to work with in the Highlands might actually be a murderer.

I explained where I was going, and that I would be shooting art nude, specifically *nude in landscape*. I was grateful that my parents were so liberal about nudity; it was nice to be able to be honest, and to tell her that I'd be in Scotland, naked in the outdoors. And my mother, with the charming optimism that she often exhibits, said: 'Oh! I expect they'll have some sort of giant fan heater to keep you warm enough.'

Oh, Mummy. What a beautiful idea. They did not. No one, in my entire career, has ever had a fan heater big enough to keep me warm, and most especially not when I'm outside. But my job would be 100 per cent nicer if they did.

So, still being stared at by all the people in the airport, who couldn't believe that a young woman such as myself could possibly be travelling alone at the age of only twenty-five (honestly, I was delusional), I found my departure gate, boarded my easyJet flight to Scotland, and landed to find Inverness in deep fog. My photographer, Ron, was waiting for me. He was charming; steady, humorous and considerate. We had a two-hour drive back to his house, and he'd packed shortbread and a thermos flask of tea for the journey. He drove me down roads that became emptier and windier as we travelled west, past pine forests, over shallow, stone-lined rivers. It was beautiful. But it was December, and it looked cold. The idea of stepping out into that landscape with no clothes on seemed quite inconceivable.

But it turned into a lovely two days. It *was* cold, but Ron worked very fast. I was never naked outdoors for more than five minutes at a time. And just as I'd discovered in David Linaker's studio, modelling felt like acting. Dressed in a floor-length satin shift dress, I posed among the ruins of a stone farmhouse. I felt tragic, grandiose and, I thought unoriginally, very much like Lady Macbeth. And later, back in Ron's house with his big picture window overlooking a loch, he took some lovely portraits of me, wrapped in nothing but a tartan mohair rug. It was all satisfyingly Scottish. But it had started to rain, so Ron suggested setting up a backdrop in his living room and shooting some (finally, real) art nude. Whereupon I made a new discovery. Modelling up to this point had felt like acting, except where it had felt like having a fight with a fake-named man over a dildo. But art nude felt like ballet. Which meant that it felt like coming home to my own body, having been locked out of it for seven years since I'd had to abandon dance when I was eighteen.

I'd known I missed ballet and gymnastics; I couldn't bear to watch ballet on stage or on TV, for the wretched ache of remembering how it had felt to dance. Sometimes I dreamed of still being able to do it, to feel the joy and the freedom of being able to leap, and spin, to throw myself backwards and upside down, and to know that I'd land safely back on my feet. Although the poses I was doing for Ron weren't specifically either ballet *or* gymnastics, they were influenced by both. I was still strong and flexible, and I still had good balance. We did some pictures that I felt immensely proud of, when I sat next to Ron later, watching him edit them.

I'd wanted to model to get some headshots and to earn a little extra money. I hadn't expected it to feel like acting, and I definitely hadn't expected the catharsis of being able to feel a little like a dancer again. And to look like one. I realised that modelling could be my chance to fuse my acting career with my ten years of dance training, which I'd thought had been for nothing in the end. It felt like redemption. I hadn't known till then how much it had hurt to abandon my love of making shapes with my body, because I'd not allowed myself to think about it as years had gone by and my life as a dancer faded into distant memory. But my heart was full of happiness as I took my flight back to London, for a second week of modelling jobs I'd booked. I felt like the luckiest girl in the world. And modelling was about to heal another old wound too.

Chapter Thirteen

The Kinky World Reveals Itself

My body-paint shoot with the artist was at the same studio in Camden that my shoot with the Spanish photographer had been. It was run by two men of around retirement age and had a register of models available to book through the studio. This was, pre-internet, the way that models with no agency booked shoots, and the more old-school studios still offered the option. Since I was back for a second shoot in as many weeks, I asked if I could be on their model register.

'Of course you can!' said the younger (and friendlier) of the two owners. The other one looked at my chest. I have A-cup breasts. I always have, and I always will, barring disaster. But to this traditional glamour-studio owner, they were a deal-breaker.

'I'm afraid not. I don't think you have the right look.'

Although used to rejection as an actor, this should have hurt more than it did, given that it was a direct criticism of my physique. But, bolstered by the fact that I now had an entire month of paid work lined up, enough to take me to the end of the year, I took his chest-shaming in my stride.

And I don't want to sound unduly petty, but over the next three years, until the studio eventually closed, I was there almost every week.

'I'm back!' I'd sing cheerfully, as I passed the owners' office on my way to the dressing room. 'I've got another couple of photographers interested – they'd like to book next Tuesday, if there's any studio space free? It's the only availability I have all month!'

Childishly, I enjoyed flaunting my small-breasted nude model success, and I liked bringing the studio money by way of bookings. I hoped it'd make them think differently about what shape a professional model needed to be. Of course, it was entirely their choice to decide who made it onto their register, but it was nice to show them that there were actually plenty of photographers for whom my physique was no problem.

I was never on their register, and it didn't matter – the internet modelling world was booming and I had all the bookings I wanted. Now, if anyone suggests that I might want breast implants (and of course, people sometimes still do, because people can be idiots), I think of my twenty-year career as a nude model, my beautiful and diverse-looking model friends, the five properties that I own as a result of my modelling work, and of the successful creative collaborations in many genres that I've been part of. And I smile. Because good teeth are more important than big breasts, in my view. So that's what I got fixed.

Sorry, how boastful; I think I wrote it because I hope the studio owner who turned me down is reading this.

On this second visit to Camden, I was spending the afternoon with a painter who'd had the idea to do some designs on my body with UV paint, and then to film me, wearing the completed design, dancing under UV light so that all that would be visible would be his artwork. That sounded great to me, and Malcolm, the painter, a round, jovial man in his fifties, made me feel immediately comfortable. He chatted companionably as he began painting colour onto my body. We discovered that we lived within walking distance of each other's flats; although his, as I later discovered, had the luxury of multiple rooms. He took some lovely images and experimental video footage. It was tremendous to be dancing again, even though it was only the improvised movement that my injured back could cope with. And before I could quite believe it, our two hours were over. I was sorry; it had been fun and I liked Malcolm.

Malcolm then did a surprising and very welcome thing. He was heading to an exhibition that evening, near to Waterloo. He asked if I'd like to go along; he had friends who were exhibiting their work there, and I might enjoy it. I'd never been to an art exhibition, other than the Tate Gallery with my parents. It sounded like exactly the sort of thing a professional, city-dwelling model would do – I agreed immediately. It was only 6 p.m., and the gallery wouldn't be opening until 8, so Malcolm suggested going to get dinner somewhere nearby. My share of the meal would probably cancel out a lot of what I'd earned that day, but since moving to London I'd rarely gone out for dinner, and it seemed like the most glamorous possible way to wrap up an afternoon of modelling.

We went for pizza, where we continued to talk happily throughout the meal. And at the end, he surprised and delighted me by insisting on paying the bill. This is not, by the way, and in case you were wondering, a preamble for my announcing that he suddenly turned into a murderer, sex pest or similar. He just paid for my meal. Almost no one outside my family had ever done that for me before. And it struck me that I'd just spent some entirely pleasant social time with a man who was the age of my parents. This seemed incredibly unlikely and remarkable to me. These days, because of my job, I'm used to having close friends in their fifties, sixties, seventies and even eighties. But at the time it was new, and felt extraordinary. So off we went, my generous employer and I, to the exhibition, which was being held in a hip, undercroft area beneath Waterloo station. Malcolm guided me through the door into the gallery. And quite unexpectedly, my world changed, irrevocably and forever.

The first thing I saw was a bronze statue of a woman. She was nude, kneeling, and her hands were tied behind her. Seeing it felt like an electric shock. I was stunned. And I immediately felt horribly visible, as though everyone in the crowded gallery would be able to see the effect it had had on me. And as the first of the shock wore off, I realised that it wasn't the only statue. There was a series of them, and every single one included some kind of bondage. One figure was bent at the waist, secured in a set of stocks. One was on all fours, with a collar around her neck and cuffs on her wrists and ankles. What on earth, I wondered, frozen, was I looking at? It was like a mirror, reflecting the inside of my mind back at me. All my fantasies were laid out before me in this gallery. It was overwhelming.

Malcolm had noticed nothing of this, having spotted

a friend of his. He introduced me to Ray, another artist who'd also organised the event. He was polite and friendly, but I was wildly distracted. Who'd made these sculptures? Were there any more in here? I excused myself and walked further into the gallery. And there, on a wall, was a collection of framed sepia-toned photographs, hanging all together and clearly the work of the same artist. And just like the sculptures, they all depicted women. One picture was a back view of a woman bent over what looked like a church pew. In the foreground was a whip, lying menacingly on a table. Dear God. Another depicted a woman caught in the act of lowering her Victorian-style bloomers. In another, a woman knelt in profile, glancing up anxiously towards the camera. It was like seeing my dreams brought to life in front of me, in artistic form. I felt hot, and giddy, and utterly transfixed. If there was art like this, I *wasn't alone*, I realised. It's hard to explain how much that meant to me. Someone had *made* these images, and these figurines. And whoever they were, they must, at least on some level, be like me.

I've heard some Christians talk about their recollection of meeting God, of having a conversion experience. I never related to it, though I didn't doubt their sincerity. But, in recalling what it was like for me that night in the gallery under Waterloo station – the sense of peace; the hope of not being alone and strange after all, in the way that I'd feared all these years – I realise that what they describe doesn't sound dissimilar. Once, as a confused sixteen-year-old, I'd had a sexual experience when I thought I was looking for a spiritual one. And looking at this work that was designed to be sexual, I had what felt like a spiritual awakening. I was part of something. And whatever that was, it was here in this room with me.

The people who'd made it were in the room too, though I didn't know it. Ray, the organiser, suddenly appeared next to me. I hoped he hadn't read my facial expression. I don't know what it would have told him.

'Do you like this work?' he asked, indicating the sepia prints. 'The photographer is sitting at a table over there; he'd like to meet you.'

He was *here*? And I could *meet* him? We'd only been in the gallery twenty minutes. I was going from having no idea that art like this existed to meeting the artist who'd created the most electrifying work that I'd seen in my entire life, all in a dizzyingly short period of time. Giddily, I followed Ray over to where a tall man in his sixties, wearing purple-tinted glasses and black nail polish, was sitting. He stood up to greet me. And just like that, I met China Hamilton, one of the best-established and most loved creators of BDSM-themed erotic artwork in the UK.

'What did you think of my work?' he enquired courteously once I was sitting opposite him at his table, and Ray had absented himself again.

'I liked it very much!' I exclaimed, redundantly. I think that my feelings about his work were written all over my face. I'd never felt so young and ill-equipped to deal with a situation in my life. I didn't know how to talk about photography. I *certainly* didn't know how to talk about the wonderful, arresting darkness of the world he'd created in his sepia-toned prints. I literally did not have the vocabulary. I had never heard the term 'BDSM'. I'd never had my own private computer, so I'd never tried to search out anything relating to my interests. I'd been sure that I was alone. There hadn't seemed any point.

'You're very beautiful. Would you like to model for me?' asked China, blessedly far more comfortable in this arena than I, and not, as far as I could tell, in the grip of an overwhelming cocktail of unexpected emotions.

Of course, I said yes. So we chose a date in a couple of weeks' time, and he invited me to stay at his house in Suffolk overnight, since he preferred to shoot after dark. *Like a vampire*, I thought later that evening, looking over his work at the gallery again, but this time, imagining *myself* in the pictures in place of the models I was looking at. My conversation with China had only been brief, but he'd made mention of a 'BDSM scene' in London; from the sound of things, there was a whole network of people who knew each other, were into similar things to China, and who organised social events.

It seemed quite unbelievable, but as Malcolm and I shared a taxi back to our respective flats later that night, he corroborated the story. In fact, there was an erotic life-drawing class that ran every week, within walking distance of my home, and they did bondage-themed classes. I could work with them if I liked. And, as I confided with excitement that I was going to work with China Hamilton, Malcolm asked if I'd like to come over to his flat the following week for dinner, and to do a short shoot to try out some bondage so that I wouldn't be a complete beginner when I got to Suffolk. Thank goodness I said yes. Because my first experience of being tied up was not at all how I'd expected.

Dinner at Malcolm's house was delightful. He was

single, unfeasibly wealthy to my twenty-five-year-old, struggling-actor's eyes, and marvellously bohemian. We ate dinner sitting on the floor in front of his fire; the meal consisted of wine, grapes, crackers, and a huge slab of Wensleydale with cranberries, which I'd never had before, and which seemed like the most sophisticated type of cheese there could possibly be. Malcolm had piles of books all over the place, many pieces of art, and cameras stashed in all sorts of unlikely corners. This new glimpse of how some Londoners lived entranced me. In two weeks of modelling, I'd met at least twenty new people, almost all of whom I liked, and many of whom seemed to live pleasure-filled existences, full of art, wine, meals out, sex, parties and hedonism. I was quite enchanted, and wondered, if I stuck around, whether *my* life could be a little like this too? Up to this point, my experience of living in London had involved spending almost half my income on rent and council tax, riding the tube to work and to auditions, reading books from charity shops and cooking mainly vegetarian meals because I couldn't afford to buy meat. I'd been dimly aware that the proliferation of restaurants, theatres, art galleries and nightclubs around me must have meant that *some* people could afford to go to them, but my friends were also mostly struggling actors, and we were living a parallel but quite separate existence from whoever these other Londoners were.

But now I knew some of these Londoners. And one of them was about to tie me up and take photographs of me. Malcolm didn't know an awful lot about bondage either, but was happy to give it a go, since he, I think, felt a little responsible for the fact that I was about to go and work with one of England's most famous sadists. He had decided to tie me to a chair, which seemed perfectly reasonable to me. He didn't have any ropes but had bought a lot of rolls of bandages for another art project, so decided to use them instead. Tying me to the chair with multiple strips of bandage took about twenty minutes, during which we carried on talking as normal. And once I was firmly attached to the chair, Malcolm surprised me by adding a blindfold.

As an experienced bondage model these days, I know that he should have checked with me first – some people who are perfectly fine with bondage don't cope well with blindfolds, just as some people don't like being gagged. And possibly, I wouldn't have been so scared if he'd told me that's what he was going to do. However, I can't blame him. He wasn't experienced with bondage either, and he definitely didn't mean to scare me; he just absentmindedly forgot that I wouldn't be expecting it.

And although the idea of being blindfolded appealed to me very much in the abstract, the unexpected reality was terrifying. Abruptly, I felt quite sure that my cheery, collegiate new friend was about to murder me, and that the entire shoot had just been a ploy to lure me into a false sense of security. Without being able to see where Malcolm was anymore, I completely panicked. Fortunately, not being gagged, I could explain.

'I'm really scared; I don't like it! Please will you let me out?'

Malcolm agreed, but then discovered that knots in bandages tighten in a way that makes them difficult to unpick with your fingers, especially when you're in a hurry.

'Hang on,' he said cheerfully, 'I'll just go and grab a knife.'

A *knife*?

I heard his footsteps as he left the room en route to the kitchen. Surely he wasn't going to actually stab me? But I wasn't thinking clearly at all; it seemed perfectly likely that he was going to do *exactly* that. He hadn't thought to take the blindfold off, so I sat in darkness for what felt like an unreasonably long time, before his footsteps returned. I hadn't realised that I was crying until he removed the blindfold and I found my face was wet. And as soon as I could see again, despite the fact that Malcolm was standing in front of me with a steak knife, my sanity and sense of proportion returned. He wasn't going to kill me. We'd just embarked upon a bondage scene without talking it through properly, that was all. And since, now, I felt okay again, my desire to model returned. I'd been crying real tears, there was mascara running down my face, and I was sure it'd look wonderfully dramatic. I was still a little shaky, but did at least have the good sense to realise that my Jehovah's Witness-literature-fed, irrational belief that everyone wanted to murder me was highly distorted. So Malcolm did indeed take some pictures, and they *did* look dramatic, and we ended the evening as friends. We went on to work together for many years, and I never again felt at risk of being stabbed. But I did realise that I needed to work on trusting people a little more easily. Especially since my work as a model was clearly going to involve being alone with many different men, often in their houses. Which was exactly what I'd be doing with China Hamilton the following week.

In the intervening period between not being stabbed by Malcolm, and travelling to Suffolk to work with China, I'd done some research on him. He was genuinely well known in the photography and printing world, which made a murdering incident feel, irrationally, less likely to me. His work had been published in numerous countries, and, upon visiting the Waterstones bookshop on Oxford Street, I actually found his most recent book in the art section. I was impressed, not only by the fact that his work was in a *real* bookshop, but that the theme of his work was just as I'd seen at the gallery. Submissive women. Corporal punishment. Bondage. Sexual slavery. I didn't know how he was planning to shoot me, but it seemed reasonable to expect that it'd be something like his existing work. I couldn't wait.

I washed my hair, applied my makeup as carefully as I could, and put on my new black wool dress, which, I thought, made me look like a proper, serious model. How did he know I'd be good for the sort of work he wanted to do? I wondered to myself as the train from Liverpool Street station raced east towards Suffolk. Could he look at people and just *tell*? If so, perhaps he'd be able to explain to me where I fitted into this new world I'd just glimpsed. I sincerely hoped so.

He was waiting for me at the station, and guided me to his car. The drive to his house took almost an hour. And goodness, I learned a lot in that hour. China described himself, thrillingly, as a 'sexual sadist'. He said it a lot, with no sense of shame or reticence. It seemed breathtakingly bold to me, to be able to describe yourself like that to a stranger. He was married, but also had a slave, he told me. I tried to keep my face looking normal, as my whole body seemed to vibrate with wonder that this stuff was *real*, happening right now, in England, and that I had, perhaps, found someone who could guide me into it. He asked me what I fantasised about. And, as I looked out of the window at the lovely, tranquil villages and fields of crops rushing past, I found that it wasn't impossible to describe after all. I liked the idea of being tied up, I explained. And the idea of being hurt appealed to me too. China asked many interested questions, interjecting with anecdotes about other people he'd known with similar fantasies, and encouraging me to continue. He talked about sexual encounters without any sense of embarrassment, and in comparison to his stories, my own tastes felt, for the first time in my life, like something not so strange after all. Pedestrian, almost. But we were nearly at his house when he said the most remarkable thing of all, a thing that I played over and over again in my mind during the months that followed, for the comfort and peace that it brought me, as well as the sexual charge. 'You are a rare and special creature,' he began (he always spoke like that; I got used to it eventually), 'and what you are is a true submissive masochist.'

Was I? Was my sexual identity an actual, quantifiable thing with a name? It sounded right. According to China, there were plenty of masochists who weren't submissive, including some who were actually dominant but just happened to enjoy pain. But I wasn't one of those, he explained, because I'd described how much I'd enjoyed playing a slave in *The Tempest*, and how I loved the idea of having someone else control me, whether they hurt me or not. There were plenty of submissives who didn't like pain, China said. But since I was both, we'd work with both those aspects of my identity. What our shoot was actually going to involve remained curiously non-specific, but I found that I didn't care. I felt as though I could trust him.

And this, dear friends, was my first experience of what I now call, to myself, the International Kinky Family. Wherever I am in the world, when I meet people who've come to terms with their kinky sexual identity, are able to be honest about themselves, and are friendly towards others in the same community, they feel like family to me, even if I've never met them before. It doesn't matter if I find them physically attractive or not, or whether they're submissive like me, dominant, or a switch (someone who likes being either dominant or submissive, depending on who they're with). There's a connection, and it's one that I cherish. Of course, there must be some bad people in this world who'd present like this on first acquaintance, but my experience of people like China, who are capable of explaining their sexuality fearlessly to strangers, representing themselves honestly through their art, and welcoming newcomers into their sphere, is that most of them are people I would be proud to have as members of my family. So that's how I think of them.

At length, we reached China's house. It was beautiful, full of art and antiques, and smelled of woodsmoke. It was only early afternoon, and China wasn't planning to shoot until night-time. But he filled the time with education. He gave me signed copies of all his books. He showed me more prints, asking my opinion and gauging my reactions to each. Just two weeks before, I'd felt unbearably exposed just to be looking at China's work in a public place. But here, with the eyes of the artist himself on me, and with his explanations of his thought process behind each shot in my ears, it didn't feel embarrassing at all to explain why I liked some of the pictures especially. Next, he showed me the work of some of his own artistic influences, and told me about the people who'd shaped his life, both professionally and personally. He seemed infinitely experienced and wise. A couple of times, I caught myself with a feeling of regret. This world of sub-missives and masochists, dominants and sadists was real. These people were all around me. But I had a boyfriend already, and if BDSM wasn't his thing, that wasn't his fault. I may have discovered this extraordinary commu-nity too late to enjoy a BDSM romance, but I could at least experience it as part of my career. I'd be grateful for that alone.

It wasn't dark yet; I checked several times. I wanted to know what we'd be shooting, but the daylight was stubbornly persistent. What was China going to do with me next?

He was, I discovered, going to take me out for dinner. Being a model really was the most astoundingly pleas-ant job so far, I thought. We drove to a lovely, quiet restaurant with lots of space between the tables, for which I was grateful – China truly appeared to have no shame when it came to conversational subject matter. 'Of course, *I've* been practising anal sex for years,' he announced, casually.

He told me about sex acts I'd never heard of. He described the dynamics involved in a long-term master/ slave relationship. He shared details of kinky friends and their proclivities. I didn't have much to add to the conversation, but I was fascinated. It was like being at the theatre. China's monologue continued; I sucked in details to savour later. I ate polenta, which I'd never tried before. We drank Pinot Grigio, which I'd never heard of. I loved every second of the meal. And then we drove back to his house. Finally it was dark, and we were going to take pictures.

China and I went on to work together for many years. During that time he introduced me to lots of new experiences, and we shot a wide variety of beautiful, intense work. But some of my favourite pictures are from that first shoot. He, knowing that I was a complete beginner, and also, I think, having confidence that I'd be back for more, sensibly began very carefully. He didn't tie me up, or hurt me at all to begin with. He just directed me, precisely and unapologetically, into various poses. He didn't say please. He had very specific ideas about how everything should look. I tried my best to do everything he wanted. I stood facing the fireplace, with my legs apart, looking over my right shoulder. 'Don't try to look sexy. Just listen to me,' he directed. And I did.

He gave me an antique pair of silk panties, and photographed me standing, looking down and lowering them. He didn't need to tell me to look ashamed. I was perfectly comfortable with nudity, but being instructed exactly *how* to remove my clothes made it feel an entirely new and unfamiliar experience. I felt as though I'd never been naked in front of anyone before in my life. And a sense of beautiful, dreamy unreality settled over me. In his timeless house, lit by firelight, with a silver-tipped cane resting on the fireplace, and his erotic photographs all over the walls, it didn't matter that he wasn't actually *doing* anything to me. It was enough to be in a world where all the things I'd dreamed of felt suddenly possible. I'd found a place where people *did* get caned, naked, before fireplaces. And that felt magical to me.

He did, eventually, tie my hands behind my back. He wasn't a serious bondage rigger; as he explained, he preferred to tell his submissives not to move, rather than making it physically impossible for them to do so. What an entrancing idea, I thought. So the rope around my wrists was merely symbolic, just for the pictures. That's not, of course, how it felt. It made me feel fantastically vulnerable, and I longed for more. And once he'd taken that sequence of shots, he untied my wrists, before wrapping the rope around my waist, and then looping it between my legs and pulling it tight.

I'd not known about crotch ropes. The feeling was shockingly exciting. The rope was rough, and it was tight. It hurt. It felt incredibly invasive. I could, of course, have untied it again myself in a matter of seconds now that my hands weren't tied. But I didn't want to. It felt like the most perfectly complete experience. I know it's absurd, but I'd been starved of any of these possibilities, through the simple fact that I'd not known they existed. And now that I knew about BDSM, I was hungry to experience it all. Every single element of it felt precious, overwhelmingly erotic, and confusingly intense.

China continued to quietly take pictures, as I drifted into what I'd now recognise as subspace, the wonderful peaceful feeling of the rest of my brain shutting down, allowing me to focus on nothing but my immediate experience, physical and psychological.

Afterwards, he poured more wine. 'I thought you were having some kind of seizure,' he commented, looking amused.

God. It had certainly felt quite hard to breathe. I hoped I didn't look ridiculous in the pictures. But the next day, when China sat with me, editing at his PC, I was delighted. I looked like the women in his other pictures. I'd joined the world I'd glimpsed for the first time at the gallery under Waterloo station. China gave me a stack of prints from the shoot to take back to London with me, along with the books of his work. I slept on the train home, and once I was back in my flat, I fired up our shared PC. I needed to find more fetish photographers. I was already committed to going back to work with China, but I'd let seven years of my adult life go by without finding out anything about BDSM. And I was determined to make up for lost time.

Chapter Fourteen

Diving into BDSM

I was immensely lucky to have started modelling in 2003. Once I started looking, I found a plethora of commercial bondage websites, some of which were in the UK and hiring models. They were mostly in the format of members-only online magazines, with picture sets posted on a regular basis. Some of them were even shooting videos, although many people didn't have a fast enough connection to actually watch them. Back then, pre-financial crash and pre-industrial-level piracy, some of these sites were making serious amounts of money, and were hiring models regularly. The work varied widely in quality, but I wasn't inclined to be snobbish. I contacted them all.

My first knock-back came from an unexpected angle: a webmaster informed me that, sadly, he thought I was too tall to be a believable damsel-in-distress. I was taken aback. I couldn't do anything about my height, and I knew, instinctively and definitively, that I didn't want to play dominant roles. I *felt* like a damsel-in-distress, and China had been able to look at me in a crowded room and sense that I was submissive. Surely my height wouldn't stop everyone from working with me? The idea frightened me; if my only chance to experience my heart's desire was through work, I needed people to hire me to play the submissive that I was. I'd rather not do it at all than have to play the domme.

Fortunately other producers were more accommodating. By the spring of 2004 I'd been a model for six months, and although most of my work was mainstream nude and fashion, I had at least one bondage-themed shoot a month booked into my diary. I'd also gone back and worked with China on multiple occasions, and had the beginnings of what I considered to be a very kinky portfolio indeed. So when a new model-turned-photographer friend of mine recommended Restrained Elegance, a glamour bondage website with a webmaster/photographer based west of London, I immediately wrote to him. I sent example shots from a couple of mainstream shoots along with a few of China's darkest, scariest-looking images of me. I chose them because I thought I looked especially fierce, dangerous and challenging. Surely, I thought, this would make Hywel Phillips, the webmaster of Restrained Elegance, want to tie me up and photograph me.

He replied within twenty-four hours. 'I'm afraid I don't think you have the right look for my site,' he said. 'Maybe some time in the future? And best of luck. Cheers, Hywel.'

But I was an actual submissive! And I was a real, proper model – how could he turn me down so fast? I'd just got an agent for fashion work and was doing runway shows all over London. And I was physically flexible. Surely that was a good thing for a bondage model? What was wrong with him? I hadn't even told him how tall I was, so it couldn't be that.

I now realise that the shots I'd chosen to send him were entirely inappropriate for his style of work at the time. He wasn't shooting pictures of women who looked like furious, captured warriors (I'd sent him a shot of me waving a sword. Because obviously, fighting was sex.). He didn't want scowling, combat-trousered Valkyries. He wanted soft, feminine-looking glamour princesses. This was perfectly evident from his work, and I'd ignored it because I didn't have any shots like that. Much as I was delighted to *be* submissive, I wasn't very comfortable *looking* submissive. It felt embarrassing, and exposing, and other than when I was with China, who made me feel as though submission was the only reasonable response to his personality, I found it difficult to represent myself that way.

But this was not to be borne. Restrained Elegance was highly regarded among models, and I did not want to be turned down by Dr Hywel Phillips. Probably, some of his models weren't even submissive. I definitely had something to bring to the table; I just needed to convince him of it. So I wrote back.

'I'm still fairly new to modelling, but I absolutely love your work, and bondage modelling is my favourite genre. I appreciate that booking a model who looks different from your existing pool is a risk commercially; I'd be happy to reduce my rate for the day to reduce the financial risk to you?'

My day rate was crazily high in my mind, anyway. Money was literally piling up in the filing cabinet in our flat (I didn't have time to go to the bank very often). I couldn't begin to spend all the money I was earning, I didn't have expensive tastes, my hobby was my job, and Lawrence wouldn't go on holiday with me. Earning half my normal rate would still be a great result, if it'd get me onto Restrained Elegance, I thought. And once I was there, I'd show him, without any doubt, that I was the best bondage model he'd ever worked with. I wasn't sure how, but I would not be spurned.

Hywel wrote back, accepting my offer, and booking me in for the following month. So when the time came, I packed a case with my new modelling clothes: a beautiful blue-and-white babydoll I'd bought while working in Dubai; a cute grey-and-pink cardigan with matching frilly pink skirt; a short red skin-tight flamenco dress; and a long black glittery evening gown. I bought some more products for my makeup kit (I was up from five items to nine now, though it'd be five more bloody years before I discovered eyebrow pencil). And I stopped on the way to the shoot to buy a box of cream-filled meringues. Arriving at the shoot with cakes would be sure to make a good impression, I thought.

I rang the doorbell, and Dr Phillips answered it. He looked up at me with an expression of stunned horror. Great – I guessed he'd not expected me to be taller than him. And I was wearing platform heels, just to make the whole effect even worse. Oh well. I began my effort to show him that I was the best bondage model he'd ever met. I did this by talking very fast, and very loud. I showed him everything in my modelling bag, including several pairs of thick woolly socks, which I believed at the time to be the very epitome of edgy, fashionable good taste. Hywel has a barefoot fetish, a fact that couldn't have escaped my notice from looking at his site, if I hadn't been quite so fixated on all the bondage and gags. I told him that I could do the splits. I showed him that my elbows could touch easily behind my back – I'd just recently learned that this was considered valuable by bondage riggers. Hywel continued to look at me with wide, owlishly startled eyes through his glasses, slightly stunned, and not altogether approving. I thought that I should probably try harder. Consequently, I raised my voice a little more. Maybe he couldn't hear me properly.

Summoning speech, Hywel asked me what dress size I was. 'Size ten,' I bellowed, cheerily, 'just like all the other models I know! It's weird, isn't it, how many of us are the same dress size?'

'Not really,' replied Hywel, not especially helpfully. 'Most of mine are size eight, and some of them are size six.'

Huh. Well, they were probably all about five feet tall too, and they very likely hadn't walked at London Fashion Week like I had. And none of *them* were working for China Hamilton. I started to wonder if perhaps I wasn't going to like Hywel very much. Not that it mattered. The point was that *he* had to like *me*. And the best way to achieve that, I thought, was to say 'yes' to everything he wanted to do, and model as hard as I possibly could.

Which is what I did. Looking back, I do look furious in every single picture. I'm not sure if I was still resentful about the dress-size conversation, or whether I was just concentrating so hard that I forgot to do anything except frown. But I think that it was mostly the effort of not showing how very much I was enjoying being tied up.

As I mentioned, China didn't do a great deal of rope work. So I'd not been properly immobilised with well-applied bondage before, and I'd not worn gags. The combination of both at once was really lovely. We shot mostly damsel-in-distress storylines, and it was entrancing to be able to struggle against the rope, but not to be able to actually escape. The last set, with me dressed in my babydoll from Dubai, was my favourite. Hywel tied me with a spreader bar between my ankles, forcing my feet apart by about a metre. Then, tying my hands behind me, he pulled them up towards the ceiling, which bent me forward into a strappado position. It was thrilling, even before he added the crotch rope and a big blue ballgag that he strapped tightly into my mouth. I loved posing like that; it was fabulously secure, made use of my flexibility, and I started to feel as though I was maybe beginning to show him that I had some potential as a regular model. The ballgag was making me drool in the bent-over position, and I discovered that I liked that too. It felt sort of. . . humiliating. I *did* like it. And the crotch rope, pulled up to the ceiling, felt great too. I experimented by bending my knees a little, which tightened it further. That was even better. I discovered that by moving around even more, I could make it seriously uncomfortable.

'You must have a very insensitive crotch,' Hywel commented at length. 'Most models find that kind of thing quite painful.'

Wow. Hywel clearly wasn't great at reading people. Did he really think that the reason I was doing such a thorough job of posing with the crotch rope was because I wasn't *sensitive*? Maybe he'd not actually met many submissive masochists. Maybe, as I'd suspected, he mostly worked with vanilla models. In that case, I thought I knew how to go about showing him that I deserved to be on his site. I'd show him just how *insensitive* I was. Insensitive to crotch ropes, big gags, nipple clamps, spanking, tight bondage. Whatever he wanted to shoot with me, I'd show him how a *real* bondage model could do it. I'd make him like me. I'd get an A grade in bondage modelling from him. And maybe, I'd start to like him back somewhere along the way.

That happened sooner than I expected. When the shoot was over, Hywel apologised to me.

'A lot of models write to me, and they *all* say that they love my work. They all say that they love shooting bondage. And they mostly don't really mean it. You're a good model for this genre, and I'd like to book you again. I'll pay you my standard rate. And I'll send you some shots for your portfolio.'

He did, and they were beautiful. On the strength of being on his site, more bondage shoots flooded in. I went to Switzerland and posed hogtied on a pirate ship, just as though my pre-school Captain Hook fantasy had been prophetic. I went to Italy and was tied up outdoors in a field. I got regular bookings with other bondage sites across the UK. I got a bit of fan mail, and I became a regular model for Hywel. I eventually learned that however often I packed socks in my modelling bag, he'd never shoot me in them. He eventually stopped looking at me with stunned horror when I arrived at his door. And we shot some work, eventually, that didn't feature me doing my special fierce bondage face. It took a while, to be honest. He was very patient.

I was a bondage model, and I was content. Not totally, because doing bondage at shoots could not
compare with a real BDSM relationship, and further
exposure to the kinky community kept reminding me of
this reality. But my job was a delight, every single day.
And in 2006, I realised I'd earned enough money for a
deposit on a flat. Lawrence might still be unkind about
my appearance and my work, but I was out-earning him,
and I was going to secure our future by moving us into
a home with four whole rooms. Also, a landing, and a
large, fitted wardrobe. Once I'd provided him with a
permanent home of our own, I thought that he'd probably have more respect for me. And then, maybe we
could discuss BDSM.

Chapter Fifteen

Biblically Unsuitable

Living with a giant, narcissistic, bodybuilding actor, though stressful, was less trying than it might have been, owing to our rarely both being home at the same time. As I developed a longer client list and started venturing abroad and touring for extended periods, Lawrence got a job touring with a group of male strippers. This surprised me considerably. Though an excellent actor, he was an abominable dancer. When I eventually saw the show, it made more sense: the dances were like the very simplest of 1980s aerobics routines, with every basic move being done four times (left, right, left, right) in order to fill up as much of the music as possible while taxing the memories of the performers as little as was feasible. I knew Lawrence had the confidence to cope with the job; he already had a high opinion of his beauty. He watched himself in the mirror while we had sex, and I often caught him running his hands lovingly down his own torso as he did so. Neither of us had any hangups about getting naked either, so this job didn't seem like a terrible decision, just a slightly surprising one. I was proud of him for passing the audition – since they'd reportedly hated his dancing, they must have thought he really was gorgeous, and that meant the awful egg white and salmon diet was maybe worth it. Possibly even the miserable, never-being-able-to-eat-out-in-a-restaurant thing was worth it too. Except that it wasn't.

I'd pole-danced in a club for a few weeks in preparation for my lap-dancing movie debut, and had imagined that Lawrence's show would be like a male, theatrical version of that; no physical contact with the audience allowed, and no explicit nudity. Owing to my own travel schedule, it was several months before I eventually visited the theatre he was performing at and watched the show. Before doing so, I dropped in on Lawrence in the dressing room where the cast was preparing. As I came in, one of them was leaning over a counter, idly looking at a porn magazine while stroking his semi-erect cock. This, bafflingly, appeared to be completely standard behaviour among the cast. Each performer, not wanting to appear on stage with his penis looking suboptimal, was working at getting himself as hard as possible before tying an elastic band around the base of his cock, trapping blood in the penis and therefore artificially enabling an erection to be sustained through the entire show. I'd never expected them to need erect penises, and wondered whether they wouldn't look rather silly, with their cocks waggling around throughout the (punch left, punch right, lunge left, lunge right) performance.

Once I was in the audience and actually watching the show, though, all was revealed. Once the 'dancing' bit of each number was over, the cast would face away from the audience to remove their velcroed-together pants. Then with a flag, towel or whatever fabric prop

they were using on stage for that number, they'd obscure
their dicks by draping the fabric over the top. Or in one
particularly outré piece, each dancer hid behind a large
sheet on a clothesline, and rocked his hips so that his
knob made the sheet dance around. Then they'd invite
a girl from the audience up on stage and, though the
rest of the audience wouldn't be allowed to see behind
the sheet, the chosen one would be invited to assume
various sexual positions while whichever performer
was on stage simulated sex with the invitee.

I know that as a fetish model I was in no great position to get all puritanical and shocked, but actually I
was, a bit. Lawrence hadn't mentioned any audience
participation, and I'd had not the least idea that they
had to have erections. I wondered if the girls who were
pulled up on stage were really okay with the sort of sexual contact that was expected of them with no prior
warning. Nevertheless, I didn't feel it was up to me to
dictate what jobs Lawrence should or shouldn't take,
and I understood the financial worries of an actor all
too well. At least, I comforted myself, he was working
for a reputable company and playing proper theatres.
But soon afterwards a cast member started getting them
some gigs moonlighting at private parties and he came
home with scratches on his back from excited women
clawing at him. I felt sorry for him. He didn't seem to
enjoy it, and it didn't feel right that anyone should treat
an entertainer like that, but I understood that he needed
the money so felt he couldn't turn the work down.

But things were feeling a little strange at home, and I
began to wonder whether he was being entirely honest
about what his work involved. The first time I sensed all

wasn't well was when we went into Ealing together to shop one morning. We had separate errands to do, so we planned to meet up again later. Off I went to M&S to look at modelling underwear. On my way out, I passed the bureau de change. There, surprisingly, was Lawrence, handing over a large quantity of US dollars. He had never been to America. I was puzzled, and went over to join him. 'What are you doing?' I asked, confused rather than suspicious. He looked horrified, then irritated. One of the moonlighting party jobs had been for an American, he said, who'd paid in dollars. That sounded unlikely – I'd certainly never have allowed a client to pay me in anything other than the local currency. But I knew he'd not secretly flown to America, so I let it go. Kind of, anyway. But I did feel uneasy, and wondered if some of his jobs were perhaps illegal in some way.

Coming home late one night, looking particularly drawn and unhappy, Lawrence confessed that one of the gigs he'd now done multiple times was for a single client, a man in Oxford who wanted him to perform a private striptease routine. Since Lawrence's dancing was poor, I couldn't imagine that much actual dancing was involved, which left me wondering what on earth my boyfriend was having to do to entertain the customer, not backed up by the other cast members, and with his artificially erect cock wrapped in elastic bands. I felt wretched for him when he came home late, increasingly frequently, discouraged by the seediness of some of his encounters, and with a headache from taking Viagra in order to get any sort of erection in the first place. Not to mention friction burns on his penis from the elastic bands. It just seemed miserable when I compared it to

the way I was being treated on my nude-modelling jobs.
If he'd seemed happy doing it, it would have felt fairer,
but several times, after coming home late at night and
climbing into bed with me, I heard him mutter into my
shoulder, 'I don't deserve you.' This wasn't like Lawrence, and it worried me. I was making plenty of money
and he was getting well-paid acting jobs. I wished he'd
stop doing the striptease jobs if they were making him
feel that bad. I didn't want him to feel as though he
didn't deserve me. I just wanted us to love each other,
respectfully and equally. And I wanted him to be happy.

Meanwhile, work for me was getting more and more
enjoyable. I travelled to Australia with the kindly photographer who'd fed me shortbread in Scotland during
my first week as a model. I featured in a painting
exhibited at the Royal Academy Summer Exhibition. I
appeared in the print commercial for the Erotica Exhibition in London, which meant I could walk past posters
of myself on the Underground. A wealthy Irish amateur
photographer flew me and two model friends all the way
to Botswana, to shoot on safari for two weeks, in a resort
more luxurious than I could have imagined, given that it
was described as 'camping'. My 'tent' had a hardwood
floor, its own bathroom, a huge bed, and a member of
staff who woke me every morning with tea. To be fair,
the tent also came with a number of giant spiders, who
sat high above me, too far up to reach, and as far as I
could tell, motionless for the entirety of my stay. This
made the visit somewhat less relaxing, but still, I couldn't
really believe that anyone would pay me to fly halfway
around the world, stay in luxury, and shoot for a couple
of hours a day. In common with my other photographers,

my employer never made any hint that he was looking for more than posing from me, and my time was my own between shoots and meals. As a result, I mainly watched elephants at their watering hole.

I couldn't help comparing my luck with Lawrence's increasingly unhappy-sounding work situation. It seemed especially wrong because he'd had a fair amount of success as an actor in the previous eighteen months, being cast in a couple of Hollywood movies with small speaking parts, which would certainly help him get cast in higher-profile projects in the future. I wished that his stripping work could make him feel as happy and fulfilled as my modelling work made me feel.

Meanwhile, through doing a series of naturist travel documentaries, I'd befriended another female model, Sam. Sharing bedrooms for weeks at a time, while not wearing any clothes at all, and depending on each other for support when the occasional elderly naturist became a little over-attentive, will do that for a relationship. We co-presented over and over again, travelling all over Europe and talking non-stop while driving back and forth across France through the night, en route to catch ferry crossings. Back in the UK, we shared contacts with each other, and helped each other get bookings. As a result, we often modelled together and started to feel like real friends. She, like me, had a long-term boyfriend and a close family. And unlike me, she was gorgeously curvaceous, with long dark hair that fell well below her waist. We ended up in the *Sun* newspaper one day, laughing nakedly in the snow on Bournemouth seafront, and I felt that her breasts were much more appropriate to the publication than mine. But despite these envy-inducing qualities, she was such a decent human being that we eventually became best friends.

But before that happened, Sam found herself in a horrible position. The first I knew of it was the week after Lawrence and I had finally moved house. I'd bought us a one-bedroom flat in a part of Ealing that wasn't a roundabout, and the week before I'd come straight back from a giddy bondage-modelling trip on the other side of the world to pack up our belongings, and take the giant exciting step into home-ownership. It was a thing that I'd not have been able to consider when I was an actress, and I was happy to share it with Lawrence.

Since we didn't have an internet connection yet, I'd gone into Ealing Broadway to an internet café to do my work emails; Lawrence had left home early that morning for a job in Norwich. I logged on to my Hotmail account, and there, among the booking enquiries, was an email from Sam. It was a nice surprise; I decided to read it first.

It was only one line.

Hi Joss, do you know a woman called Lucy Payne?

I didn't, but I assumed whoever it was must be a model, maybe one Sam was planning to work with. We often helped each other out like this; it assisted us in avoiding having to work with anyone unreasonably difficult.

I replied right away.

No, sorry, why?

And then I got on with the rest of my messages. Back then, I could afford to leave my emails for a few days without checking them, but nevertheless, they'd mounted up. Almost an hour later I was ready to leave. I refreshed the browser one more time. Sam had replied.

I hope I'm wrong, and I'm sorry to have to tell you this, but Lucy Payne is telling people that Lawrence is her boyfriend. I worked with a photographer earlier this week who'd done some shots for her, and she said she could be booked with Lawrence too. He thought it was a bit strange because she's a lot older than Lawrence; he noticed the age difference when she showed him Lawrence's website, and because he'd thought it was odd, he remembered their names, and showed the website to me too.

People talk about getting bad news and feeling cold. I want to reach for a better word to explain it, but a freezing horror had enveloped me at my computer terminal; I didn't just *feel* cold – I felt suddenly *made* of cold. This was followed instantly by a feeling that the oxygen had rushed out of the air, leaving nothing to nourish my shrinking lungs. I felt my life as I'd known it evaporating like a puddle on hot tarmac.

I knew it was true.

Slowly, carefully, I stood up, being gentle with myself. I paid at the counter, approximating a smile for the café owner as I said goodbye. I walked cautiously, suddenly feeling it was important to look dignified, to *be* dignified.

On the busy street I stopped. The swimming, cold,

airless feeling was still with me, and I knew I had to find out the whole truth right away. Pain was on its way and I had to get the worst over with before the shocked anaesthetising numbness deserted me and I was overwhelmed.

I found a side street, and stood on a corner by a church in the June sunshine. My hands found my phone and I called him.

'Why,' I asked when he answered the phone, 'does Lucy Payne say she's your girlfriend?'

There was a horrible pause.

Did I say I'd known it was true? Perhaps I hadn't really known, not until that silence.

'Oh God.' There was another pause. 'I'm sorry. She's my client.'

I heard the words, but didn't understand the meaning. 'Your client? For what? Why does she say she's your girlfriend?'

'She's not my girlfriend. She's my. . . She's my – client.'

And suddenly, I did understand. Beautiful, powerful Lawrence, with his striptease jobs bringing him into contact with excited, horny women. With his private dancing gigs for audiences of one. With his growing, carefully nurtured actor's CV, and his girlfriend who loved him. Lawrence.

'You're an escort.' The words sounded alien, a combination of sounds I'd never put together before. And how I wished they hadn't just come out of my mouth. Tears started to pour down my face, feeling scalding, and somehow dry in their hotness.

'Just with her, just her. Her husband's impotent; I met her at a shoot. . .'

His voice went on, but I don't remember the rest. In any case, his words were lies. I didn't know that yet, but I'm glad for my past, twenty-nine-year-old self that I didn't have to find out everything all at once, in the gentle June sunshine on that street corner in west London, on my own. What I do remember is that eventually, I got angry. Perhaps it was the thought of the dinner dates he'd doubtless had with her, happy to eat out when he was being paid to do so, that finally flipped me into brief fury. He said he'd come home. I told him I didn't want him to. I ended the call. And I sat down on the kerb in front of the church and cried and cried.

Time skipped forward; I don't know how long I sat there. And I certainly hadn't realised how much noise I was making, until an old Russian lady came out from the church to comfort me. 'He was my *only* boyfriend!' I sobbed. 'I thought we were getting married and he's cheated on me!'

'In the end,' she said, gently, 'you'll be glad. I am old, and I know.' I doubted that, right then and there. But I did think that I should try to stop crying; I'd had no idea it had been audible through the church's thick stone walls.

She went back inside. I wish I could thank her now, for being brave, and kind, in approaching a stranger in distress. In London, that's hard to do. But despite my best intentions, I subsided back onto the kerb. I must have started crying again, because the next thing I remember, two hipster guys of around my age were standing in the road in front of me.

'Are you okay?' the bolder one enquired, looking kindly.

'He was my ONLY boyfriend!' I repeated, nonsensically and somewhat hysterically. And added, 'I lost my VIRGINITY to him!' Because, you know, TMI never goes out of style. To their credit, they didn't look overly perturbed to have been confronted out of the blue by my tear-stained religious fundamentalism.

'Do you want to come to the pub with us?' he asked.

I'd like to find them and thank them too. Can you imagine the misery they'd have been letting themselves in for if I'd said yes? I can, all too clearly. Because I know exactly how un-fun I managed to be for the rest of that year. But even in my shock, I had the good sense to turn them down. It'd have been a terrible idea. And I was beginning to realise that I needed to start doing things that didn't involve sitting on kerbs and crying.

I got up. My joints felt loose, I wasn't sure my legs would support me, and I didn't know if I could muster the effort to get myself back home. Then I remembered I had a family. I called Immi. Somehow, I told her. I don't remember what I said, but I remember her response.

'He *fucking* did not! He *FUCKING* DIDN'T!' She wasn't disbelieving me. She was responding with the anger that told me that I was allowed to be angry too. Just like always in my life, my big sister knew how to make things better. Her out-of-character swearing helped me know that it was okay to break up with him.

'I'm coming to visit. I'm coming now.' And Immi, who had two children under ten, and who lived five counties away, started the journey that would end that night with her sharing a mattress in my new, not yet furnished flat, as I stared at the ceiling and wondered how on earth I could go to work and smile into a camera ever again. And how, if I didn't, I'd ever be able to pay my week-old mortgage on my own.

But first, as Immi started her journey, I made the benumbed trip back to my flat. Suddenly I couldn't bear to be in the clothes I'd put on that morning when I'd been someone's girlfriend. I pulled off the bohemian skirt with its cheerful silk ribbons, and the striped wrap-over dancer's top. I screwed them up into the back of my wardrobe, and never wore them again. I redressed (what does a just-cheated-on urban twenty-nine-year-old wear? I can't remember), and got back onto a train to central London. At Paddington station, I went straight to a private walk-in doctor's clinic; they offered HIV testing while you waited.

The doctor was only a little older than me, a South African lady. I explained the situation, briefly dry-eyed with the fear that was now settling over me. She took blood samples, and I sat in the waiting room, wondering how I'd tell my family if the test was positive.

It wasn't. The doctor called me back in, and mouthed 'You're okay' as I made my way across the waiting room to her. She told me I'd need another test in three months. And then she looked me in the eye and said, 'Don't take him back. Once a cheater, always a cheater.' I'm still grateful for the insight and kindness of the women I encountered on the day I broke up with Lawrence (though not to discount the kind hipster guys).

Chapter Sixteen

The English Disease

'Are you asleep?' asked Immi, out of the darkness, at three the following morning. I wasn't. I was doing maths in my head, wondering if I could keep the flat. I'd only been paying £300 per month in the orange-lit box on the roundabout. The mortgage here was £700, and it was still so new that it felt an awesome responsibility. Clearly, I couldn't afford to cancel work. In any case, I had a shoot later that very morning. As a model, I'd learned early that I wouldn't be believed if I cancelled a shoot with a new contact at short notice, and I was as paranoid about this then as now, so I certainly had to go.

Immi kindly said she'd entertain herself and then stay one more night with me so that I wouldn't have to come home immediately to an empty flat. I packed a bag of underwear, and took the train into Berkshire.

I'd never worked with the photographer before, and the planned shoot was unusually hard BDSM for me at that point in my career. This was a mixed blessing. On one hand, I'd hardly slept, hadn't managed to eat anything, and was controlling my emotions only with a brittle veneer of cheerfulness. I wasn't in a good state to process four hours of intense physical pain. On the other hand, it did at least distract me from the miserable grief and worry chasing each other around my brain. And the genre of the shoot allowed for my probably pained expressions to pass off as good acting.

My photographer, thankfully, was not talkative. He was a hobbyist, shooting mainly long rolling takes of video, which kept small talk to a convenient minimum. He seemed pleasant but relatively emotionally removed, so my psychodrama could play uninterrupted in my head. He tied me up, cut off my clothes, and applied various clamps to my nipples, which hurt plenty but not enough to entirely distract me from my internal pain/anger/panic cocktail. Being gagged helped, as I didn't have to improvise dialogue. I doubt very much that I could have done a good job of it, unless he'd wanted a monologue about mortgage affordability and broken hearts.

It wasn't until the photographer finally cut the cable ties restraining me at the end of the shoot, and unstrapped the big ballgag I'd been wearing, that I realised it had only just been in time. I ran for the ladies' room, and vomited extravagantly. Then, because I needed a lift to the station, and because I didn't want the photographer to think that he'd caused my dramatic reaction, I gathered myself to leave the ladies' room and tell him a brief, unemotional version of the truth. What I did instead was to leave the ladies' room, burst into tears and throw myself into his unprepared arms. Which, I think you'll agree, will have left almost the same positive professional impression.

He was very kind once he understood what was

going on. During the afternoon I'd begun to fixate on
the worrying reality of needing to arrange further STI
tests, and when I mentioned that, he was generous
enough to tell me about his own experience of friends
going through the same worries when he was at university. It made me feel a little less sordid to be reminded
that I wasn't the first person ever to find herself in this
situation.

But over the next couple of painful, scary days, my
worries about STIs started to loom larger in my mind.
At my insistence Lawrence had stayed away, but we'd
spoken on the phone. I asked him if he'd had other clients. He denied it. But I'd started to wonder – what if *all*
the private 'striptease' jobs he'd had were actually his
excuse to go and have sex with strangers for money?
Perhaps in response to all the worry, I started to get the
symptoms of what felt very much like flu, but a quick
paranoid Google search told me that many STIs, including HIV, can show themselves initially with flu
symptoms. This was the worst possible time to have to
leave the UK for a ten-day naturist documentary pre-
senting job. All I wanted to do was stay home, try to
repair my heart, and get tested for every sexually transmitted disease I could think of. But I comforted myself
that at least Sam would be there too.

Sam had worried that I'd resent her for bearing the
news that had sent my life into a state of emergency. The
opposite was true; I felt closer to her, knowing that she'd
been prepared to risk our friendship to protect me. And
if my creeping, miserable suspicions were right, time had
been of the essence. If he *had* been sleeping around, I
guessed that he might not have used condoms, since he

struggled to get an erection when using one. So the longer it went on, the longer I could potentially have been in danger of catching something from him. Looking back with a more rational head, I see that STIs aren't the end of the world. Most of them are curable, and even the ones that aren't can be treated successfully and aren't an automatic death sentence. But I was a child of the 1980s, when the infamous AIDS advert was everywhere. And the Jehovah's Witnesses had loved to talk about it. The twenty-nine-year-old me was scared of the social stigma as much as the possibility of dying young. Also, I was beginning to vaguely comprehend the fact that I had the chance to start again at relationships, to maybe, sometime far in the future, find happiness with someone new. And the idea of Lawrence's infidelity being carried with me in my body, potentially forever, kept me awake at night.

We arrived in France. My flu symptoms had developed into a raging sore throat, and white spots were appearing on my tonsils. Charlie, the filmmaker who produced the naturist films Sam and I starred in, kindly took me straight to a doctor in the rural part of southern France in which we were staying, where I was issued with antibiotics. Later that day, we had to start doing pieces to camera, describing the huge, rambling campsite we were staying at, and it helped to be busy, especially with such supportive friends by my side. But talking was becoming agonising, and after three days, the antibiotics still hadn't made a difference to how I felt. I began to fucking hate Google. And my body. And, for the first time, I began to hate Lawrence. Afraid, and in pain, it finally felt reasonable to me to hate the cause of these feelings, however taboo that emotion might be, according to the Bible.

Lawrence had promised to get tested for every STI possible in my absence. It was a promise he kept. When we'd been in France five days, his results were due, and he'd said that he'd telephone me immediately. I carried my phone with me all morning. I described the campsite's charming river. I showed the camera around the shower block. I enthused about the swimming pool. I wondered if my boyfriend had infected me.

Just before lunch the phone rang. Charlie, Sam and I all jumped. We'd been on edge, and I imagine both Charlie and Sam were wondering how they were going to go about comforting me if Lawrence *had* picked up something incurable.

It was Lawrence, of course. He didn't have HIV. His hepatitis results were negative. He was clear of chlamydia. But . . .

'I'm sorry. I have gonorrhoea. It's treatable – they said not to worry. If you've caught it, it'd have been recently, because I've not got any symptoms yet. They said you'd just need an antibiotic, and to get tested when you get home. I'm so sorry. I love you.'

My 'flu' was gonorrhoea. I felt so dirty; I'd thought we were monogamous. I'd thought I'd be as safe from STIs as my parents, my sister. I felt cheap, and I felt outraged.

'You don't love me! You fucking cheated on me!'

My sudden, furious outburst echoed through the tranquil campsite. I slammed the phone down. I mean, in my head that's what I did. You can't actually slam a mobile phone down. All you can do is press the End

Call button really hard, which is what I did. Sam and Charlie burst into applause. 'I've been *waiting* for you to get angry!' congratulated Sam.

'He's given me gonorrhoea!' I repeated loudly and unnecessarily, stunned. Somehow, whoever he'd fucked had managed to reach out, through him, and infect my body when I was completely unaware that I could be at risk. It felt like such a violation.

Charlie, an ex-paratrooper with an extremely chivalrous concern for the wellbeing of his models, dealt with my hysterical outburst by immediately offering to take me back to the country GP. I couldn't wait to get the evidence of Lawrence's unfaithfulness out of my body; we went there straight away. Charlie had seen plenty of sexually transmitted disease during his army days back in the 1960s, and comforted me with details of how gruesome treatments used to be back then. This may not sound as though it would have been comforting, but it made taking a course of antibiotics seem a very small thing in comparison.

I saw the same doctor and told him the story that was now beginning to feel familiar enough to really be mine. My boyfriend had cheated on me. He'd just been diagnosed with gonorrhoea. Could I please have an antibiotic targeted to treat it?

The doctor looked amazed. 'Gonorrhoea? That disease is *unheard of* in France.'

This seemed unlikely. The English called syphilis 'the French Disease' back in the fifteenth century. Maybe blaming STIs on near neighbours is a universal constant.

'We call it the *English Disease*,' the doctor elaborated disapprovingly.

He picked up a big medical book and started searching through it to find the right medication. And it occurred to me, in the silence as I waited, to mendaciously claim that Lawrence was French. I didn't, of course. But I do sometimes think it would have been fun, on a day that had been greatly lacking in entertainment value up to that point.

With new antibiotics, Charlie, the English Disease and I returned to the holiday resort to resume our film making. My English Disease and I did a piece to camera about the on-site restaurant. As my English Disease started to decline in strength, we visited the beach together, where the heroic French antibiotics in my system ensured that I got a monstrous case of all-over sunburn. The disapproving French doctor had tried to warn me about this side effect but I'd thought he was trying to make a stupid joke about blushing. The week ended, and with my sunburn peeling, I packed, abandoned my deceased English Disease in France, and drove north with Charlie and Sam, to return home to a flat that was now all mine. I felt empty and lonely when the door shut. I'd never wanted to live alone, but now I'd have to, because the flat only had one bedroom, so I couldn't move someone in unless they were going to be my new partner.

Which, naturally, would never happen. Clearly, I had phenomenally stupid taste in men. Just like I'd thought back when I was sixteen years old, disgusted with myself for being kinky, I realised that if allowed to, I'd continue to seek out men who'd hurt me, who'd be bad for me, and who wouldn't respect me. If I hadn't been looking for a dominant partner, I'd never have been so stupid as to fall for Lawrence. Rather than risk another self-destructive, masochistic choice, it would be safer to live alone, and enjoy having a career, good friends, and a family I loved. That would be enough. And in case it wasn't, I would also have a white carpet, and a white sofa. And a pink bedroom, and silly gauzy curtains that let the light through. I would have scented candles, and furry rugs, and no giant economy boxes of battery-farmed eggs in the fridge. It would probably be okay.

I did have the faint realisation that I could, armed as I now was with knowledge of a kink scene across the globe, maybe one day find a partner who was kinky too. Not just big and selfish, like Lawrence had been, and which I'd fooled myself was the same as dominant. I could find a real dominant man, if there were any nice, unattached ones. But I felt a *very* old, bruised, jaded twenty-nine years old. I'd wanted to have just one sexual partner. Even in such circumstances, I felt as though I'd be cheating on Lawrence if I started again. He'd been an entirely unsuitable partner for me, and to be fair to him, he'd known it and had tried to warn me. So perhaps I'd forfeited my one chance at a relationship. I concluded it'd be best not to think about it. Maybe I'd have another chance when I was forty, or something.

So I went back to work. My dad came to stay. I saw a lot of Sam. I organised a tour of the Netherlands. I packed up Lawrence's stuff for him to collect, and found two Rolex watches hiding in among his sweaters. The filing cabinet contained flirty Christmas cards he'd kept from some of his clients. It didn't hurt as much as I'd have expected, to know I'd been sharing him with such a lot of unfamiliar women. But three months later, on a location trip in northern France for Restrained Elegance with Hywel Phillips and a couple of other models, one of the girls asked me if I had a boyfriend. I stumbled through a brief explanation of my recent breakup. 'But,' she asked, 'don't you miss him?' It hadn't occurred to me that I had that right. I'd ended it, after all.

'Yes,' I said, hearing the truth in the statement, and realising the scale of how much I did, and probably always *would*. 'I miss him every day.' And suddenly, I was crying, and felt as though I'd never stop; as though a part of me was doomed to be eternally sitting in an internet café on Ealing Broadway, discovering that Lawrence wasn't mine.

I jumped up. I cry easily but I try not to let my employers see me do it. I'm especially wary of showing sensitivity in front of BDSM photographers; it must feel awful, tying someone up if they seem emotionally fragile. Leaving the building as quickly as possible seemed a good choice.

I sat on the terrace as the sun sank to the golden hay bales on the horizon. At length, I heard footsteps behind me. None of the models knew each other well, and I dreaded having to field the sympathy of another woman who probably had a much more fluid approach to relationships than me. But it wasn't one of the models.

It was Hywel. He sat down on the ground next to me, at a respectful distance. I was glad. Though he was an undemonstrative person, and not a man who I imagined would be particularly comfortable with splashy outpourings of emotion, I did at least know him better than I did the models. We'd worked together at least seven or eight times in the three years I'd been modelling, and I liked his combination of boundless kinky creativity and endless nerdy fixations with technical quality. Especially, bafflingly, lenses. He was an ex-university physics lecturer, and seemed kind and honest and thoughtful. If I had to share my feelings (and I was doing a fantastically damp job of continuing to cry), I was glad it could be with him rather than the varied most-popular-girl-in-the-school individuals indoors.

We talked for a long time, until the sun had disappeared altogether from the sky. He reached out, tentatively, and briefly encircled my shoulders with his arm. It was a curiously moving gesture, coming from someone as physically guarded as he was. I sensed that he felt extra-curricular physical contact with his models to be something only entered into in extremis. I appreciated the effort it took him to break out of his own personal space in order to comfort me.

AND OH MY GOD, YOU GUYS.

My husband-to-be had just touched me for the first time.

I was quite right about his reluctance to put his arm around me too. We got married five years later, in 2012, and he still winces if I hug him for more than five seconds at a time. Also, he still loves lenses with an abiding, expensive passion. We have separate bank accounts.

Chapter Seventeen

Spanking Finds Me

While my personal life had taken on the feeling of a particularly nasty reality-TV show, my professional life had become a haven of productivity and calm. Having been modelling for three years, I'd developed a client base, and found myself working with people I already knew at least as often as I was booked by new photographers. This was a peaceful state of affairs, and meant that I also started getting booked up further in advance. It gave me a feeling of security to know I'd be able to pay my mortgage each month.

However, stability wasn't exciting, and I was craving more drama from my work, more sensations and more challenges. The bondage photographers I worked with behaved, by and large, in a predictable fashion. Once I was tied up, they'd photograph me, film me and untie me again. This in itself was fun and satisfied my long-held fantasies about being kidnapped and captured, but it hadn't addressed my desire to actually be punished.

Then one day, an email appeared in my inbox, from DSH Productions. I clicked on the portfolio link and my life became abruptly more interesting. DSH was a video-production company. Dallas, the owner, shot *nothing* but spanking videos. D stood for Dallas. S and H stood for Spanks and Hard. And certainly, from the look of his sample images, he did exactly that. A plethora of beautiful girls with bright red bottoms pouted at the camera on his landing page. And a twenty-second preview clip showed Dallas himself, using a thick leather strap harder than I could have imagined on a slender young lady who was lying face down on a padded bench. I felt a deep longing to be that woman.

Simultaneously, I knew that I couldn't take up his offer of work. Though my non-fetish photographers generally seemed relatively accepting of my bondage work, I was convinced that the mainstream shoots I relied upon would dry up if I followed my heart and shot spanking videos too. Looking back, I don't know what had given me that opinion, though it's true that plenty of the vanilla photographers I worked with insisted that their work was non-sexual and was nothing to do with the porn world. Some of those photographers *were* quite judgemental towards models who shot work of a more obviously sexual nature. But I wonder if residual guilt about being kinky at all played a part in my fear of judgement.

So, I wrote back to Dallas. I thanked him for the offer, and confessed that his work looked wonderful to me and that I'd love to try it. But I admitted that I didn't dare risk my mainstream work by accepting a shoot with him. I sent the email, and felt melancholy. The world on his website was where I wanted to be, but I didn't dare travel there.

Dallas, however, was very smart. He replied immediately, told me that if I ever changed my mind I should get in touch, and did a thing that guaranteed that I would. He gave me free access to the members' area of his website. I logged in immediately, alone in my flat, and started watching the first video.

I had a non-impressive internet connection. Every seven or eight seconds, the video would freeze while it buffered for several more. Then it would start again. For any other video, I'd have lost patience immediately. But I sat and watched the entire thing. Then I watched the next, and the next, and the next.

The style of video that Dallas shot was documentary-like. A model would arrive at his house; Dallas, in the role of a professional disciplinarian, would ask her why she'd been sent to him. She'd confess to driving without her seatbelt, smoking, failing to hand in her homework, or some similar minor infraction. Dallas would then scold her for a while about her irresponsibility, making her call him 'sir' as they discussed her behaviour. Then, he would make her stand in the corner for an extended period of time, with her hands on her head. The video would fade out, and when it faded back in again, corner time was over and it was time for Dallas to actually spank her. He would pull her over his knee and imme-diately begin spanking her, hard. Her bottom would turn pink and then red in a matter of seconds. Her pant-ies would be pulled down and the spanking would continue. Then, eventually she'd be allowed to stand up, before assuming a different position to receive strokes from some other implement. Whatever he chose, it always appeared to be significantly more severe than the hand spanking. Which is saying a lot. Eventually, with the model very often in tears, the spanking would be over and she'd be left to stand in the corner again, facing the wall. The camera would zoom in on her incredibly bruised and reddened bottom, and the video would end.

You could say it was a little formulaic, but to me personally, it was electric. Suddenly, it was all I wanted. The entire thing. The scolding, the formality, the corner time, the over-the-knee position, the giving in to authority and being punished until your guilt is paid off. . . I had to experience it. Suddenly, all my fantasies were about spanking, and in order to orgasm all I really needed to do was think about being pulled over his knee.

But Dallas, a fantastic-looking man from Hawaii, lived thousands of miles away, and I was booked up with six months of work that would make long-distance travel impossible. So I started some of the most entertaining research that I've ever undertaken. I needed to find a spanking company closer to home that could provide something approaching a similar experience. I was still worried about the implications for the rest of my career, but I found myself unable to stop the helter-skelter journey towards my spanking debut.

I found two companies of interest. The first, Firm Hand Spanking, managed to keep nudity conservative, and I appreciated their focus on spanking rather than maximum sexual exposure, so I contacted them to begin with.

Firm Hand Spanking wrote back, requesting a phone call. It turned out that they required this because so many of the people who approach them are men pretending to be women, indulging in a fantasy about being spanked as a girl. The producer phoned me when I was on a National Express bus, travelling from London to Yorkshire; needless to say, it was extremely awkward. Having established that I was a genuine woman, he enquired as to whether I'd been spanked before, before asking me if I'd experienced spanking with any implements. 'Yes,' I said, cagily, hoping that I'd not said anything incriminating that my fellow passengers could interpret as spanking-related. 'What sort?' was his perfectly logical next question. 'Paddle?' I mumbled into the phone. 'Wooden or leather?' he asked. I started to wish that I could get off the bus on the M1 and give myself properly to this conversation, which at any other time would have been a pleasure. Sadly, it turned out the producer wasn't going to be in the UK for several months, so I ended the conversation feeling no closer to my new burning ambition to get properly, thoroughly spanked in a movie.

Back to my research, and I found an entrancing-looking site. Girls' Boarding School seemed to be a large company with multiple websites and a huge cast of stunning models receiving hard spankings from the 'headmaster' of the school. Very appealingly, they paid models by the scene rather than by the day, which reassured me about a fear that'd been troubling me. One of the things that I'd heard many people say about fetishes was that some fantasies were best left that way. I was worried that my fantasy would be that kind. It was hard to guess how much spanking would hurt, based on nothing but watching videos of other people. I thought that one scene might be all I was capable of. It didn't occur to me to experiment with spanking off-screen instead – I assumed that anyone who wanted to spank me in a non-commercial environment might also expect sex, and the idea frightened me. Since investigating bondage for the first time on-screen at photoshoots had worked out well, doing the same with spanking felt less emotionally challenging than any alternative. But I didn't want anyone to be angry with me if I couldn't do a full day's shoot, and if they only paid me for what I managed to do, I thought I'd feel less pressurised. I emailed Girls' Boarding School, and they wrote straight back, inviting me for the following month.

The only problem, which I hadn't anticipated, was that they weren't in the UK. They were based in Majorca, and were willing to fly me there, and put me up overnight before sending me back to the UK the next day. This worried me. Travelling is one of my very favourite parts of my job, but I was scared about how irritated they might be if I couldn't get through more than one scene once they'd gone to the expense of paying for my flights. I said yes nevertheless – my fantasy was within my grasp, after all. But in the weeks that followed, my sexual excitement gave way to the much less pleasurable professional anxiety about providing a good service for these people who were trusting me to do the job.

I boarded my easyJet flight to Majorca, dressed in my favourite skirt, and made up to look as shiny, young and beautiful as I could possibly manage – I didn't want to be a disappointment. Half an hour into the flight, a headache started, pounding above my left eye. As the journey progressed, it got worse, until even shutting my eyes brought no relief. I knew it was because I was tense and scared, but I couldn't bring myself to relax. As the plane started to descend, I began to feel sick too.

Headmaster Tom, with a deep voice and German accent which I found instantly appealing, and his petite, pretty partner, Marie, were waiting for me in the arrivals lounge. They were pleasant but businesslike – we were going straight to the house, which doubled as their studio, and we were going to start immediately. I asked if there would be any other models at the shoot that day, and they replied that there wouldn't. This was a relief. Nowadays I love meeting other models at shoots, but since I was trying something new, I was worried about my performance being less good than that of a more experienced spanking model. And if I'm honest, I suppose I wanted all the 'headmaster's' attention to be on me. How embarrassing.

Girls' Boarding School ran a website purporting to be an English boarding school for girls, but the only property they had available was an airy, open-plan Majorcan mansion. They only had one student at a time, and they only had one teacher. They had no school equipment, and no one on set was under the age of thirty. Consequently, that day, the performances from me, the spankee, and Tom, the spanker headmaster, were all they had with which to create the vision of a boarding school for girls. Still dressed in the outfit I'd travelled in, we prepared to shoot the first scene. My character, Lucy, was sneaking back into school after an unauthorised night-time outing. It was 3 p.m. and broad daylight, but we persevered. Creeping through the sun-lit kitchen, she was to be discovered by the headmaster, who was to pull her over his knee immediately and give her a hand spanking, followed by an over-the-knee slip-pering with a flip-flop, which the producers had selected because it was light and wouldn't mark me too early in the shoot. I was grateful that the first video would be a sort of warm-up.

The preamble part of the story was over in seconds. I got the impression that Headmaster Tom was tired of scolding girls, because he pulled me over his knee right away. And then, finally, the first proper spanking of my life started. The first smack turned my right butt cheek into a flare of heat. The second smack landed on my left, equalising the sensation, setting my bottom alight. Then the third smack came down, onto skin that was already burning.

I didn't like it. Some fantasies *weren't* meant to be realised. I wasn't going to get through the scene, let alone the whole shoot. I started to squirm, trying to move my bottom out of harm's way as my body attempted to defend itself. Headmaster Tom's hand seemed able to anticipate everything I did; however much I wriggled, I couldn't escape. But after a minute or so, I began to discover the magic that being a real spank-ing fan can deliver to you. Much as it was hurting, I started to feel not hot, but warm; heated through and elated. It was okay. My fantasies *were* meant to be real-ised after all. By the time we finished the scene, I was beginning, through the persistent headache, to feel euphoric and floaty. And young, and beautiful. And proud of myself. I felt aroused, I think, too. But this must have been rather a distant secondary feeling – the sheer psychological wonder of realising I *did* belong in this world, that this really was a thing that I could do, gave me a feeling of tranquillity and joy. The feelings, in fact, that I'd always been encouraged to believe were available at church. Maybe I'd finally found some kind of religion after all.

The shoot progressed. In scene two, the implement Tom chose was a leather paddle. Today, I would recognise it as a fairly mild implement that wouldn't bruise me too much. But it was unfamiliar to me, and I was scared because it was big. Each slap with it would cover my entire bottom, meaning that there'd be no recovery time for any section of my exposed skin before the next stroke landed. For this scene, I was bent over a sofa, with my hands on the floor. I loved the position; it made me feel trapped because it'd be harder to move out of the pose than it was when I was over Tom's knee. It felt a little like bondage; like a perfect combination of my fantasies. It's still one of my absolute favourite things.

Each stroke did indeed hurt. My bottom was already sore from the first scene, but the heavenly endorphins circulating helpfully around my body had deserted me in the break we'd had between the scenes as I changed clothes and the crew reset the lights and cameras. I discovered a truth that would become familiar to me in time: spanking shoots get incrementally more painful as the day progresses. After a few strokes, Tom called for a cut. 'You mustn't scream so loudly,' he admonished. 'It doesn't sound realistic.' I hadn't been acting; I'd discovered another truth. For me, the fact that I *love* being spanked doesn't stop my body from recognising that I'm in severe pain. I've heard it said that masochists like pain because they process it in a different way from other people, and therefore experience it as pleasure, not pain at all. I experience it as both simultaneously and I wouldn't change it for anything.

I did, however, try to scream more quietly. I may have been partially successful. But scene three was to be the cane. I'd watched a few canings online and I was by no means confident that I'd be able to deal with it; the marks it leaves are so incredibly vivid and painful-looking that I was genuinely frightened about experiencing it. I was simultaneously full of fascinated anticipation. In this scene, I'd done something that made Headmaster Tom absolutely furious. He made me stand in the hallway, with heavy books held in my outstretched arms, while he waited to be calm enough to punish me properly. The addition of this was perfectly judged; it gave me time to sink further into believing that I really was in trouble, and deserved to be punished. It sucked me deeper into the scene.

After a few minutes, by which time I was shaking both with the effort of holding the books at arm's length and with fear, the headmaster returned to take me into the dining room, where he bent me over a table. Finally, after wondering about it ever since I was seven years old and had read a Roald Dahl book in a bookshop, I was going to feel the cane. Sadly, my memory deserts me at this point. I believe that I must have simply sunk so deeply into my character, then the endorphin high and the subspace, that I had no mental resources left to file the experience away properly. Since I couldn't remember it, I just purchased the video download online. I can see from the increasing blankness in my eyes that somehow, I'd checked out and was elsewhere. I can also see that wherever it was I went to, it was somewhere I liked.

It had been everything I'd hoped for. The shoot was over, and I felt euphoric, relaxed and calm. The tension headache that had developed on the plane had finally abated, and I lay inert on a downstairs sofa while Tom and Marie took care of unloading the footage onto hard drives for editing later. Kindly, they offered to take me out for dinner before dropping me off at my hotel for the night. I vaguely, happily agreed, and must have been the most peculiar dinner guest; still surfing on endorphins and adrenaline, I gabbled enthusiastically about the shoot, how I wanted to do more spanking, how I loved everything, how beautiful Majorca was, how good the food tasted, how big my glass of beer was... I felt, in the moment, excessively affectionate towards them both. Now, as an experienced model, I recognise this feeling of overwhelming connection with whoever just spanked me, and I'm able to ignore it and behave like a normal human being. It's like a kinky, short-term version of Stockholm Syndrome. But with no previous experience, I felt as though I was in love with Tom and Marie, and wanted to stay with them and keep doing spanking scenes forever.

This, I imagine, was not what they wanted, and it is my hope that they didn't realise the strength of my feelings. On the other hand, we left the restaurant without having dessert. Very wise of them. But once I was in my hotel room, I stripped off and looked at my bottom in the bathroom mirror.

It had turned black. From the very top of my butt cheeks right down to the crease where bottom meets thighs, my bottom was one solid bruise. The bruise was a neat oblong, as though I'd sat in a tray of ink. The flesh beneath felt hard and swollen, painful and alien to touch. I'd been aware that sitting down at dinner had been a little uncomfortable, but hadn't expected such a dramatic visual result. With no experience of this, I felt sure that I would be damaged for life, but couldn't bring myself to regret it. It felt entirely worthwhile, to have experienced that extraordinary feeling. I fell into bed, and there discovered another gift that spanking delivers to me: I slept more deeply than I ever remember doing before. I slept the way you would if you'd spent the day climbing a snowy mountain. Or the way you'd sleep in a cool hotel bed after a twenty-four-hour flight that you've spent awake. I slept in the sweetness of a post-spanking cocoon. I wish I could bottle this feeling. However many times I do spanking shoots, the result is always the same.

Chapter Eighteen

Becoming Amelia Jane

Back in the UK, comforted with the knowledge that I *could* take a commercial-length spanking, I threw myself into finding more spanking work. It became immediately apparent that Ariel Anderssen, my submissive character, needed to adapt to the new genre. I'd chosen Ariel as my stage name when I started bondage modelling, in recognition of how much I'd loved playing Ariel in *The Tempest*, and it had felt perfect for all the BDSM work I'd done up to that point. But submissives don't necessarily make good spanking 'Bottoms' (the industry word for someone who *gets* spanked, as opposed to 'Tops', who do the spanking). Being quiet, obedient, willing and enthusiastic about being spanked doesn't make for a very dramatic dynamic, and I wanted to be a very dynamic Bottom indeed. Part of the fun of being a spanking Bottom is that you can be utterly vile, incredibly argumentative, monstrously confrontational, and unwilling to back down. Of course, since the Top holds all the cards, you'll never actually win in the end, but trying to outwit the Top and argue your way out of being punished is such a joy. When I do it well enough,

I can make myself believe that of *course* this time I'll get away with it, which makes every spanking feel a bit like a new experience.

Ariel Anderssen, my kinky, submissive self, was not the right kind of character with which to launch a spanking career. So I decided on a different girl, who'd have a different name. As a young child, I'd loved the Enid Blyton series about a large, badly behaved doll called Amelia Jane. The teddy bear, the patriarch of the toy cupboard, sometimes had to be quite severe with her, and I always longed for her to be punished. I also related to the fact that she was the largest toy in the cupboard, didn't really fit in, and was wild, bendy and outrageous. I decided that I must be Amelia Jane in all my subsequent spanking roles.

Which left me with the question of a surname. Blyton's Amelia Jane doesn't have one, but if I was going to play a real-life girl, I'd need a realistic-sounding one, preferably one that matched my English accent. I hardly had to think about it at all. As a Jehovah's Witness, I'd grown thoroughly sick of hearing about Joseph Franklin Rutherford, the second president of the Jehovah's Witnesses, and the originator of many of the religion's joyless rules for life. He was responsible for the lack of birthday and Christmas celebrations which had isolated Immi and me at school. 'Well, of *course* no birthdays,' I imagined him lecturing. 'Didn't you know that King Herod beheaded John the Baptist on his birthday? Birthdays are TOO DANGEROUS to celebrate. Christmas? No, of *course* we can't celebrate Christmas. Jesus wasn't born in the winter, so Christmas is pagan and must be ignored at all costs. Wall's ice cream? On

NO ACCOUNT must you eat it. It has blood plasma in it (it doesn't), which is the same as eating blood, and in the Old Testament, dead animals' blood had to be sacrificed to God. Don't deny God his blood sacrifice!'

It was easy to imagine. I knew his voice: we had a recording of a number of Joseph Franklin Rutherford's lectures, which we'd listen to on our record player. I can assure you that he most definitely wasn't interesting. Even sped up to the wrong speed, he was extremely dull. Don't ask me how I know; you know the answer already. As an adult, I realised that since he'd made up a lot of the rules himself, he may well have not really believed any of it. Maybe he just wanted power over people. I thought I'd maybe found a fitting eulogy for the man responsible for the worst bits of my childhood. The endless meetings, the scary door-to-door work, the embarrassment of having to stand outside during school assemblies, the lack of birthday parties or invitations to other children's parties. My new spanking character would share his surname. Doubtless he'd have been against spanking models; it's hard to imagine that a man who disapproved of further education, popular music or eating black pudding would have had a liberal approach to erotic-film making. We shall never know for sure, friends, and it may sound spiteful of me but every time someone barks 'Rutherford!' at me in a spanking movie, I feel a mean sense of triumph. Honestly, if you feel like revenging yourself upon someone (they can be dead – mine is and it doesn't take away any of the pleasure), I urge you to appear in a porn film using their name. It'll do you the world of good.

So, with my new identity in place, I got on a long-haul

flight to shoot with Dallas. Despite being clearer about what to expect following my Girls' Boarding School experience, I was still nervous, because even to a novice like me, it was clear that his work was in another league in terms of severity.

Dallas is a perfect on-screen dominant. If I was writing erotic BDSM fiction, my hero would look like him. Tanned, athletic, handsome and the owner of dazzling white teeth, he looks the way I thought everyone in Hollywood would look. I, naturally, regressed immediately upon meeting him to the uncool teenage girl who was in love with her teachers and flirted via straight As. I'd obsessed endlessly over what to wear and somehow had ended up wearing one of my least favourite dresses. I felt awkward, far too big, amateurish and star-struck.

And as though designed specifically to ramp up the stress of the day, the hotel suite was full of people. Cool, fetish-club people. And there were several spanking models, two of whom were going to shoot with Dallas before I did. I was going to get a chance to watch. These days, I know never to do this. When given the choice to be punished first, or to wait and watch someone else, I always go for the first option. For me, it always looks *so* much worse than it feels. Of course, I'd watched lots of Dallas's movies already, but being in the actual room was more difficult, not least because it meant that, in all likelihood, I'd have an audience when I got spanked afterwards.

The model before me was a spanking legend. Named Kailee, she has the most astounding pain tolerance that I've ever seen, and seems to absorb hand spanking,

strapping and paddling with hardly any kind of reaction. The entire scene was difficult to watch, but the
final strapping pushed me into a sense of premature
despair. Kailee lay face down, secured to a bench. Dallas
picked up a massively long, thick leather strap that
didn't look as though it should ever be used upon a
human being, let alone a petite young woman. Kailee
looked exceptionally calm. Her dark eyes were oddly
blank, her bottom almost unmarked from the spanking
that had gone before. And then Dallas swung the strap
back and began.

I wanted to look away. It was fascinating, but ghastly.
Given the lack of reaction from Kailee, you'd be forgiven for not being able to judge just how painful the
strapping was, but the welts rising on her skin told their
own eloquent story. Slowly, silent tears began to course
down her face. She wasn't the only one in the room crying; another of the models started to weep in sympathy.
I couldn't do that; I felt too envious. Then, shockingly, I
realised that Kailee was bleeding. Not from a single
cut – her entire bottom seemed to have started oozing
blood, as though the skin was simply disintegrating
under the onslaught of leather. Dallas, sensibly, decided
that the scene was at an end. And Kailee stood up, looking perfectly serene, smiled and said, 'I'm flying now!'
She slouched over to a sofa and collapsed into it. I suspected, based on my Girls' Boarding School shoot, that
I wouldn't be able to find that headspace the way Kailee
had. I was pretty sure that I was going to have a much
harder time absorbing my spanking.

Of course, I guessed that Dallas was perfectly capable of judging his models' reactions and tailoring the

spanking accordingly. But once we were sitting side by side on the suite's sofa and the cameras were rolling, this didn't seem massively comforting. I was really scared, and painfully self-conscious. The fact that I was a fan of his work made it all far worse. I didn't feel as though we were equal. He was famous; I'd done one spanking movie. He had decades of experience; I wasn't sure that I could even *do* his style of shoot. And his beautiful, very experienced spanking-model girlfriend was behind the camera. I wondered if she'd think I was terrible if I couldn't do it.

Watching the movie back now, I'm appalled by how awkward I was. Dallas is excellent throughout; his calm, authoritative, good-humoured self. But having anticipated and expected every single element of the shoot, I found myself paralysed by all of it, especially regarding talking. It was as bad as it had been with Mr Lewis, my long-ago basketball teacher. To begin with, much as I wanted to, I couldn't call Dallas 'sir'. In fact, I could barely speak audibly at all. The scene was meant to have a real-life element to it, but I couldn't bear to portray the kinky, eager newbie spankee that I actually was. I resorted to very quiet truculence and an almost total lack of eye contact. Dallas was remarkably patient, given that he had to give me each instruction at least twice. Partly because I was taking refuge in playing an utterly nightmarish character, partly because I was so overwhelmed that I simply found myself failing to do what he said, over and over again. And really, there was very little to do. I had to lie over his lap, keep my head up so that the camera could read my facial expressions, and answer his questions politely. I couldn't keep my head up. Once the spanking started, incredibly hard, to my newbie's senses, the pain made me want to bury my head in the sofa cushions as though I could distance myself that way from how overwhelmingly it hurt.

'I didn't know it would be so hard,' I bleated, after a couple of minutes. Which wasn't true. I'd known. I'd just thought that I'd be tougher. Dallas actually laughed.

'This *isn't* hard. Do you want to see hard?' I didn't. This was unbelievable. What I wanted was to do exactly what he said, stop trying to play an argumentative character whose desires were entirely opposed to my own, and make him pleased with me. *That's* what I wanted.

But I was paralysed by self-consciousness. Dallas asked me a direct question.

'Yeah,' I muttered, into the sofa cushion. Knowing what he actually wanted me to say but not able to volunteer it.

'Yeah?' queried Dallas, looking entirely relaxed and unconcerned, and resuming the increasingly hard spanking. It was too hard. I couldn't even begin to stay still, and in comparison to the pain, calling Dallas 'sir' suddenly seemed like a more or less achievable task.

'Yes, sir. I don't like calling you that.' I loved calling him that. I was tremendously confused. How could anything be so excruciatingly awful and altogether wonderful at the same time? The spanking was unbearable. And the spanking made me feel as though my entire life had just been a holding pattern for this joyful feeling. As though I was doing the thing I'd been made for.

None of this will be evident if you watch the video. It's all buried under layers of denial I'd been so successful at forming that even my work as a fetish model hadn't managed to brush them away yet. I could do the work, but I couldn't show what it meant to me. I continued, whiny, disagreeable and resistant. While secretly, my heart soared with gratitude to Dallas, who'd had the confidence to write to a vanilla-looking model and the integrity to be honest about his own interests, to offer me a shoot, give me access to his membership site, and to work with me, calibrating my tolerance and coaching me through a whole new level of sensation. I couldn't say thank you, much as I wanted to. But I could at least call him 'sir'. Just about. Though not at the same time as actually looking at him.

Now, as a more experienced model, submissive and play partner (someone who engages in BDSM on a repeated basis with another person who may or may not also be their sexual partner), it's still hard sometimes to express how good doing BDSM with the right people makes me feel. But I know that if I don't tell them, I'm still to some extent hiding beneath the ghostly layers of denial that my conservative background and early self kink-shaming set me up with, and I don't think that's acceptable. So now, when I work with Dallas, and with the other Tops and dominants that I enjoy shooting with, I always try to let them know what a good job they've done, and how precious and important the experiences that they give me are. I realise now that good BDSM involves sharing your feelings – just like good sex of any kind is about sharing, being honest, and paying attention to your partner. I didn't have the emotional intelligence to do any of that at my first shoot with Dallas, and didn't fully explain how our first meeting had felt to me until years afterwards, when I sent him this chapter.

We were nowhere near done. He chose four implements, and he used them all. A leather paddle, a strap, some sort of God-awful rubber thing, and a long wooden ruler. By the end of the scene, I'd cried extensively, rubbed almost all the makeup off my face, and was so shaky that when he told me to go and stand in the corner next to the sofa, I wove alarmingly from side to side as I approached it. I was having trouble maintaining the disagreeable character I'd bizarrely chosen for myself. I felt happy, and peaceful, and sleepy, and very affectionate towards Dallas, and towards everyone else in the room. Also the hotel. Also the entire city.

Dallas conducted a brief interview with me, after the main scene was done. He asked if I actually liked spanking. And, to my shame upon watching it back, I lied. Not deliberately, but because I was still in a tangle of denial that even doing my second, stupendous spanking shoot hadn't fixed.

'Well, it's the *only* thing that makes me feel better if I've done something wrong,' I simpered. Which was nonsense. It sounds plausible, but it was rubbish. This is what I should have said, if I'd been up to my current levels of emotional honesty.

'Well, Dallas. I think I like it more than anything in the whole world, actually. Especially with you. I have a crush on you. Most of my orgasms over the last six months have been as a result of looking at your work. So, yeah. I'm pretty sure that I like spanking. It turns me on, and it also makes me feel happy and at peace in a way I can't even fathom right now. It probably does

*make me feel better if I've done something wrong, but
that's mainly because being turned on mostly does make
people feel good, doesn't it?'*

But, I wasn't ready for any of that.

And sadly, my part in the shoot was over. I'd planned
to head to the airport. Having discovered the multipli-
city of cheap hotels that weren't online, I'd intended to
take a room in one before flying home the next day. But
Dallas and Sierra invited me to stay the night in their
suite. Which probably sounds as though it was some
kind of preliminary to wild, Hollywood-style threesome sex.

What actually happened was this. We tidied the
suite. Dallas shot another spanking movie, with yet
another model. I helped with camera work, and was
intensely grateful to be able to be quietly useful, as
opposed to the diva I'd been on-screen. Then everyone
else left the suite, and the three of us were alone. Dallas, like the gentleman that he is, said that Sierra and I
should share the massive double bed, and he would
sleep on the couch in the adjoining sitting room, where
he'd been spanking models all day. But first, he called
room service and ordered cookies and milk for us all.

It had been, for me, the most magical day. I knew I
was only at the beginning of my journey into being a
real-life spanking model, but it had felt at once like
coming home, and like finding myself in an unfamiliar
alternative universe where being kinky was normal,
accepted and welcome.

Sitting on the plane back home was, predictably, an
uncomfortable experience, but Dallas had invited me
back to shoot with him again, and I felt as though we

were beginning to be friends. I'd found a world where I fitted, and it was full of lovely people. Nothing was ever going to go wrong, ever again. My life was going to involve spanking, and bondage, and friendship, and adventure. The end.

It's not the end. Something ghastly happened next.

Chapter Nineteen

The Underside

Everyone in the spanking world, so far, had been extraordinarily nice to me. Even the other spanking models, who I'd been scared to meet, having had the idea that we might all be in some sort of never-ending competition for a limited number of shoots, were warm and welcoming. Adele Haze, a well-established spanking model and blogger, wrote a post about me to let people know that I was on the scene. It was surprising and kind.

And I had no shortage of kinky people to meet and to play with. Another established spanking model invited me to come and stay with her and her husband, and we spent a joyful afternoon doing a fully costumed school-detention role play in their dining room. I felt awfully bohemian and liberated to be having so much fun with people I wasn't romantically associated with, and it felt simple too. Emotionally bruised from my breakup with Lawrence, I didn't want romance, but I loved being a useful extra play partner for my new friends. There was no pressure on me to be anything but a kinky role player, and I loved it.

I was excited to meet even more spanking-industry professionals in the UK. However, I was so new that I was completely unprepared to deal with what was by far the worst experience I've had with a professional spanking producer. Inevitably some readers will think that what happened is more representative of my industry than it is, but I assure you that it isn't. I don't know anyone who's had a remotely similar experience. It was bad luck, and highly atypical of a BDSM shoot.

I'd been booked for a multi-model video shoot on the South Coast. When I arrived at the location for it, a nightclub that the company had rented for the day, I was immediately impressed by how many people there were. This must be a really professional company, I thought, noticing all the crew members. Since I was early, I started introducing myself, and discovered the first warning sign: they *weren't* all crew members. Several of them had been charged a fee to come and watch the day of filming. As a general rule, I don't care who's on set, as long as they're adults who are aware of what's being filmed. But the fact that they seemed highly uncomfortable talking to me and didn't want to make eye contact or give me their names made me wonder. The fee I was being paid was unusually low for a spanking production. In fact, it was lower than my normal day rate for a non-spanking, non-bruising shoot. So I wondered why we weren't being paid more, given that we were not only making a movie, but putting on a stage show for a bunch of men who didn't want to shake hands with me.

Then the other two models showed up. It was a large venue, and I didn't know their names. So I asked, 'Are you here for the spanking shoot too?' Both looked puzzled, and said that they weren't. However, it turned out that they *had* been booked for the spanking shoot. They just hadn't been aware that they were going to be being spanked.

This was a massive, frantically waving red flag, and we all should have recognised it. However, I was determined to like this new world of spanking production, and thought that somehow it'd all work out. Maybe the other models were only going to do simulated spanking, I reasoned. They were chatty and friendly and I thought it'd eventually get explained to us properly.

The story was about three fashion models at a casting, where a couple of fashion designers would spank them into doing their very best posing, runway walking, etc. A fairly light-hearted storyline, which seemed to match the low pay. No mention had been made about the potential for any bruising, and since the other two models clearly weren't up for anything painful, I anticipated playing an absurd diva character in a playful movie with relatively light action. That sounded fun.

It wasn't until shooting commenced that things became alarming. First, we were all spanked by one of the two Tops (a man and a woman) playing the fashion designers. That was fine with me, but the other two models, who had not expected to do real spanking at all, were both in tears within a couple of minutes. Crying, in itself, isn't necessarily a bad thing. I'd cried in my first shoot with Dallas, and I'd been having the time of my life. But normally, the director does at least stop filming to check that the model's okay to carry on, especially if she's new. I kept expecting the director to call a halt to proceedings, and now I wish that *I* had done so. Theoretically, either of the other two models could have called for a cut in the action, but in a room full of people, that can be remarkably hard to do. I suppose we all kept hoping it would get better.

It didn't. The action was harder than I was used to, with my very limited experience. But worse, the Tops had none of the caring, pastoral attitude of either Dallas or Tom, the Girls' Boarding School headmaster. With their experience, I now see that they should have called a halt when they could see the distress they were causing to the other two models. No matter what the director wanted, the person doing the actual spanking is always directly responsible for the person they're hurting.

The more spanking you do, the less you tend to mark, but I was still a relative beginner, and so I started to bruise as we progressed through a range of leather implements. The other two models, neither of whom had done *any* spanking before, were beginning to look seriously bruised. And, of course, spanking on top of bruises hurts more. Neither looked in a good emotional state, and one of them started to look shocked and withdrawn.

I should have stopped the shoot myself, but dealing with my own pain and discomfort with the audience had me preoccupied. I think all three of us just wanted to get to the end. We'd been filming for most of the day by then, and were expecting to wrap up the story. But first, the director said that we needed to shoot a caning scene. I'd expected this, despite it not having been mentioned, but the other two models hadn't had any idea of such a thing. The one who was looking especially shaken up flatly refused – good for her. So we were down to two. The two Tops stepped in either side of us to begin the caning, taking it in turns with each stroke so that each of us had a little recovery time. I don't know how many strokes had landed before the other model, in tears and horribly marked, said that she couldn't carry on. It was certainly more than six. And at this point, we should have just stood together and insisted on calling an end to the shoot, but, as a beginner, and deeply invested in making a good impression on the people in this exciting industry, it didn't occur to me to do so. They needed a caning scene, and since the other two models were incapable of giving it to them, I felt that I should do the rest of it. So instead of agreeing that I too was done, I offered to carry on so that they could get the footage they needed without the other model having to take more.

What the director then suggested was completely unacceptable. Since he was paying for two Tops, he decided that they should carry on the rest of the scene as though there were still two Bottoms, but that they should both cane me, since I was the only model still prepared to go ahead. Which meant double the number of strokes that I'd originally been meant to take. I should have refused, or insisted they do half the original number each. But I was upset, dealing with the still unfamiliar adrenaline rush of the caning up until that point, and still, somehow, trying to apply the Christian values I'd grown up with to the situations I found myself in. What would Jesus do? Well, he'd obviously take the caning, wouldn't he? To save the production, and to protect the other models from being forced to carry on. And I was confused – I'd *liked* caning, at the one shoot where I'd done it. It didn't feel the same here, but maybe if we carried on, all the nice feelings would emerge, as they had at my other shoot.

So the caning progressed. I don't know how long for, but it seemed interminable. During a short break to move cameras, one of the Tops murmured to me, 'When we start up again, we're going to go faster, not slow like we have been.' I didn't think they'd been going slow, and I should have said no. But I wanted them to like me. I was the only kinky model there and I wanted membership to this club, despite the fact that the kinky people at this particular shoot were behaving abysmally. I shouldn't have cared. They didn't deserve to be liked and I shouldn't have given a damn how they felt about me. I dimly, hopefully wondered if maybe faster caning would be less painful than what we'd been doing up to now.

Of course it wasn't. It was awful. Within a few more strokes, I was crying. But worse, I wasn't able to hold my position. If you can't stay still, good Tops always either wait until you're back in the right position before carrying on with the caning, or they restrain you in some way. Moving during a caning is dangerous – you can get hit across your kidneys, sustain damage to your coccyx or get cut. But with one Top's stroke landing only a second after the other's, they didn't have time to react if I moved. And I couldn't help doing so. I couldn't have then, and I couldn't now. It was too hard, far too fast, and out of control. I landed on my knees, over and over again. Dimly, I was aware of pain across my lower back, but I was far past any ability to call 'cut' on my own behalf.

Finally, when it was over, I felt sickened, with none of the euphoria I'd felt at my previous shoots. None of the sense of achievement. And none of the warm feelings of friendship towards the other participants. Except for the other two models, my fellow survivors of the day; I certainly felt connected to them.

We were told we could go. Changing back into my street clothes, I looked in the mirror. There was blood seeping onto my panties from the highest of the cane marks, which had landed across my lower back. Looking closer, I could see that I was cut in several places. Goddamn. Did this kind of thing scar? Kailee had bled at the shoot with Dallas, but they'd worked together before, her tolerance for pain was well known in the spanking industry, and she'd requested a hard scene. None of that applied to us. And, since they'd caned another model with the same implement, what about the risk of infection? They'd cut her too – all three of us were vastly bruised, but the two of us who'd been caned both had thin cuts, oozing blood. What an absolute mess. All three of us took the train back to London together. Luckily I'd scheduled a few days off. The other two were both booked for shoots the next day, having not been warned about marks. They didn't know what they were going to do about cancelling work, and we promised to stay in touch, to check that we all healed and to support each other as best we could. I was glad to have the connection with the other two, but going back to my flat, I felt tainted and ashamed. I'd not stood up for myself, or for the other two models, who'd needed protection from the careless Tops and the irresponsible producer. And for the first time, I had bruises on my body that I wanted to erase. They didn't feel like badges of honour, they felt like dirt, like a bad memory that might not fade.

So when, two days later, one of the other models went to the police and made an accusation of assault against the producer, I thought that she was perfectly right to do so. And although I didn't feel as though I'd personally been assaulted, I was happy to make a witness statement to the police to corroborate her story. I'd seen her distress and pain, and her confusion over the content of the shoot.

Two very young officers came round to my flat. I'd not had to explain my sexuality or my work to vanilla officials before, and I felt ashamed of my industry. I trusted that most of the people in it weren't like that, but I'd met the very worst example of predatory producers and careless Tops, all in one day. I was embarrassed to have to describe their behaviour to the police.

The next day, I still felt dirty. And what was more, afraid. I didn't know if I wanted to be kinky anymore. Maybe, just like I'd thought at sixteen, in the depths of my depression, I *was* a hazard, but to myself. How could I possibly explain what had happened to us at that abysmal shoot to anyone in my family or circle of friends without them thinking badly of me, my sexuality and my profession? One of the models had told her story online, on a modelling forum. I went to read it, to gauge the reactions of the vanilla photographers who frequented the site. I was scared that they'd condemn all of us for not walking out. Mainly, people were being

kind and supportive towards the models, but horrified
by the behaviour of the producer. But one reply stood
out to me, partly because I knew the man posting.

Hywel Phillips, the webmaster of Restrained Elegance and the photographer who'd speculated over the
insensitivity of my crotch during our first shoot together,
weighed in on the discussion. In his typical, thorough,
scholarly style, he expressed sympathy for us, and his
disappointment in the producer for not taking the
ongoing consent of the models seriously. But he also
explained, for the benefit of the vanilla photographers
in the discussion, that BDSM, when it's done with
integrity, bears no relation to the shoot we'd found ourselves part of. He talked about mutual respect, safe
words, discussing storylines and implement choices
beforehand, and taking responsibility for your models.

I decided that I'd write to him; I wanted to thank him
for the post, which had made me feel safer and more
hopeful about the community of kinky producers again.
And coming from him it was particularly reassuring.
Though most of what Hywel shot was very glamorous,
and relatively light-hearted, I knew that he liked hard
BDSM play too, because we'd shot a video series called
Long Term Bondage only a few weeks beforehand and it
had been very intense and challenging indeed. We'd done
slave training and hard bastinado (foot whipping) and
I'd slept in a small cage in the studio overnight. Hywel
wasn't going to judge me for being kinky, because he was
at least as kinky as I was. And remembering how much
I'd enjoyed our conversations in breaks during the *Long
Term Bondage* shoot, it reassured me that sadism and
dominance were not in themselves characteristics that

made a person dangerous or unpleasant. So maybe he could help.

He helped a great deal. He invited me over to his studio, where he was working in his office while another photographer shot with a model upstairs. We sat and talked, and I told him the whole story in detail. He listened calmly. He said he knew that it was difficult for submissives to insist on anything mid-scene, and that I shouldn't blame myself for not having been more assertive. But, firmly, he said that I should never let that happen again. I agreed. And then he did the kindest and most helpful thing he could possibly have done. Since it was the end of the day and the other photographer and model were about to leave, he offered to do a short bondage shoot with me that evening. Nothing harsh or sadistic, and nothing nude, since I was too bruised. But we could shoot bondage as a way of affirming to me that I was still kinky, and that I could still respond to BDSM the way that I had before the disastrous spanking shoot.

Hywel was, and is, so incredibly smart. He tied me in soft, beautiful nylon rope for a picture set that he later titled 'Love Bondage' when it appeared on his website. In the safety of his studio, with no paying customers watching from a corner, no traumatised models, and nothing but friendship and respect between us, I realised that, of course, I was going to be okay. My body would heal, and my trust in the industry I'd chosen would return. And in the meantime, if I wanted to push my limits, I'd do it with Hywel. He'd kept me safe through our twenty-four-hour bondage movie project; the keys to the cage were within my reach all night while he slept. And he had incorporated my ideas with his in the most respectful, collaborative manner possible. He was kind, and he had integrity. And, travelling home on the train that night, I had an idea for another movie to shoot with him. It *wasn't* gentle, but it could, I thought, have a level of emotional warmth to it. I was glad that we were friends.

Chapter Twenty

The Arrival of a Real Dominant Hero

One of my least favourite things about some submissives, and about myself when I notice I'm doing it, is the way in which it's easy to revel in the drama of needing to be rescued by a big, strong, dominant man. But that's what I'd needed. The comfort of vanilla friends hadn't been enough for me; I'd wanted my dominant, sadistic friend to rescue me, and make everything feel better after my stupid spanking shoot experience. He *did* make everything okay again, because he understood what had gone wrong better than my vanilla friends could. I felt comfortable with being kinky once more, and enjoyed the feeling that he'd looked after me. Did it feel a little romantic? I suppose that it did. I didn't think much about it at the time, but afterwards I felt a bit ashamed of having fallen into the role of damsel-in-distress so comfortably.

But circumstances were about to conspire to balance out the dynamic of our friendship, and though at the time it was horrible, it was for me an important change. It's easy to like everyone who employs you, looks after you, comforts you when things go wrong and helps you live out your fantasies in a safe environment. It's not till something goes wrong in their life that you really know your feelings for them.

Hywel was about to have his own episode of professional drama. For all the time I'd known him, he'd had a good working relationship with an established model who shot for him on a monthly basis. I knew and liked her, and he'd booked us together several times. But Hywel had been paying her a monthly fee, and she'd started cancelling shoots, citing health problems. By the time he took stock of the situation, she owed him around £2,000. The next time he tried to arrange a shoot with her, she told him that, with regret, she was ending her modelling career. He offered to set up a payment plan so that she could pay him back gradually for the money he'd advanced her, since he realised she might need a while to re-establish a career for herself. At this point, she startlingly announced that she didn't owe him any money.

After a few attempts to negotiate with her, Hywel eventually filed a claim with the Small Claims Court in the UK, which is used to arbitrate small civil cases. And the very next day, as he was at his studio preparing for a shoot, the police arrived to arrest him for sexual assault.

By this point in our friendship, we'd already been away on a week-long location trip, and I'd witnessed his physical guardedness many times; he was always clearly aware of maintaining professional boundaries. The accusation that his ex-model made was that he not only groped her, but uttered the following, fantastically unlikely couple of sentences: 'Phwoar, I want your tits. Phwoar, I want your pussy.'

At the point of writing this book, I have been married to Hywel for eleven years. I have never heard him even use the word 'tits', let alone 'phwoar'. He's not a big dirty talker. Furthermore, he is a thoroughly decent individual. If his models have any criticism of him, it's that he's incapable of saying the appreciative things that some photographers find so easy.

'That's beautiful! Gorgeous! Stay there! Yes! Beautiful!'

Hywel can't do this. Left to his own devices, he conducts his shoots in silence. The idea of his managing to rouse himself from his contented, lens-choosing, light-fiddling, non-verbal shooting state to announce *anything* about anyone's pussy was absurd to me.

Of course, the police didn't know this. They had to investigate the allegation. As it happened, the model in question appeared to have decided to leave the industry in a blaze of drama, and had made allegations about at least one other photographer too, which perhaps helped the police to see through her claims. The fact that she owed Hywel money may also have helped his case, as well as the fact that he was pursuing her to retrieve it through an official channel. But nevertheless, being accused of exactly the sort of thing that people outside our industry tend to assume is rife among photographers was a dreadful shock. So although Hywel was released again, quickly and without charges, he was considerably shaken up. Just as I, the month before, had seen a dark side to my industry that I'd not glimpsed previously, he was now fully aware of his vulnerability, as a male photographer shooting female submissive-themed work, in a studio on his own.

He emailed me. I was free that afternoon, so I got straight onto a train out of London to go and see him. He met me at the station and we went to a café, where I bought him cake; several cakes. We sat and talked for hours. I knew that allegations of sexual assault needed to be taken seriously, but I'd have bet my career on what the model had said about him not being true. He was always, *always* appropriate towards his models. Sometimes, to me, a little annoyingly so. Tying people up is a physically intimate thing to do, but I'd rarely met a bondage rigger who managed to make it so businesslike. His behaviour towards me, and to all of us, when we'd been away on the location trip to France had been exemplary. And he'd been an absolute model of kindness and decency when I'd been off balance after my recent spanking shoot debacle. Probably, he could have taken advantage of my guilt, and there'd never been a hint of any such thing.

On a personal level, I was distressed that Hywel, the very best of men, had spent most of a day in a police cell for something he hadn't done. On a more abstract level, though, it disturbed me in a more complicated way. It felt entirely wrong, somehow obscene to me, that he'd been arrested. Hywel was a dominant. I wanted him to always be in control. That was what I felt he deserved. I also felt, suddenly, very protective of him, and disgusted with the model for her fraudulent, self-serving claim.

Other than listening to Hywel, and buying him cakes, I wasn't sure what I could do to help, so I asked him. The Small Claims case was still coming up. Hywel had a considerable paper trail to demonstrate the fact that he'd paid her for work she'd then cancelled, and he had copies of all the emails in which she'd cited her ill-health as the reason for not taking further shoots. He had evidence that all had seemed cordial between them in their correspondence until he'd tried to arrange to get his money back from her. Hywel wondered if I'd be happy to write a brief statement to speak of the perfectly good working relationship that I'd witnessed between them on many occasions, as well as to describe my experience of being one of his regular models.

I was more than happy to. I wrote it as soon as I got home, and in doing so, wrote a sentence which, though perfectly true at the time, would have been comically impossible for me to write a month later.

Dr Phillips has never touched me in a sexual manner at any one of our numerous shoots. His behaviour towards me has always been entirely professional, and lacking in any sort of sexual undertone.

Well, it was true at the time, and Hywel won his case. The other photographer who was accused by her also continues to work professionally, with no other allegations of misconduct, to this day. It was a horrible episode, but it had made me feel that we were equals. I wasn't just his emotionally fragile, newly single model friend, or his inexperienced, spanking-shoot victim friend. We'd looked after each other, and that, I hoped, was how our friendship would continue.

I wondered if, in the same way that I'd needed to ease back into shooting after my bad experience, he'd need to work on feeling comfortable being alone with a tied-up model again. I was pretty sure I could help with that. I'd been thinking about another video series to shoot with him, and had come up with a movie we eventually called the *Bondage Driving Test*. It was the story of a woman who knew she was submissive, and who was looking for a dominant partner. To this end she'd come to a specialist dating agency, where the owner took her through an assessment to see which activities she most enjoyed and was best suited to. It was a simple (and, as always, unlikely) scenario, but because it was so wholeheartedly consensual, I thought it'd be emotionally comfortable for him while he had the memory of the assault allegation fresh in his mind.

It'd represent a change for me too. Up until that point in my career, I'd been uncomfortable playing kinky characters. They felt too close to the real me, and I hadn't been ready to share that with anyone who cared to watch my videos. It was so convenient and comfortable to hide behind a vanilla character who hadn't chosen what was happening to her. Being Cinderella was a nice, camouflaging refuge. Also, I was scared of feeling like a slut. I'd heard the way photographers sometimes talked about models who shot more unapologetically sexual content than I did; they could be disapproving and judgemental. And I still felt embarrassed about wanting to be tied up and hurt. I thought at the time that it'd have been so much easier if I were dominant. It would seem to fit my feminist worldview better. I might feel empowered to admit to wanting to torment and dominate men. Admitting to being submissive still troubled me; it felt like admitting to being weak. So making a video about a woman seeking out her fantasies, exactly as the real me *was* doing through fetish modelling, felt awfully exposing.

But if I was going to tell that story – and I wanted to – I felt Hywel would be the perfect person to do it with. I wrote him a script and sent it over. He replied immediately, saying he liked it and arranging a date.

I always looked forward to working with Hywel, but in the taxi to his studio that morning I was especially excited. I think, on one level, I felt as though I was saving him; like Jesus, again. But I was also beginning to realise how comfortable I felt with him. And I was wondering about suggesting, if the shoot went well, the idea of possibly playing together off-screen. Hywel didn't have a play partner, and since neither of us was looking for a romantic relationship, I thought that it might be a good idea. I'd begun to feel like an immensely experienced, casual BDSM player, having played with an entire five people with whom I wasn't in a romantic relationship. I was a single, kinky, independent lady, and it gave me confidence.

At the studio, Hywel greeted me, looking amused and a bit ashamed of himself.

'There's something about this storyline,' he said. 'It's really hot. It might be a bit uncomfortable to film.'

Well, I had written it to be hot. It certainly was for me. And if Hywel found it a turn-on, that was even better. I'd suggested it because I'd thought he'd like it, after all. And I knew that he was more than capable of staying professional while we were filming. I realised I rather hoped that he wouldn't want to be 100 per cent professional later, because of my plan to talk about playing together. I felt powerful, knowing that I'd written something that he could connect with. And I hoped to do a good enough job to make him want to do some non-filmed BDSM with me too.

The shoot was delightful. Although I'd written the storyline, I'd left the specifics of what BDSM action should go in each scene to Hywel, assuming that he'd prefer to have some control over it. Scene five was probably my favourite: the nipple-clamp endurance test. In scene four, Hywel had tied me so that I was kneeling on a bed, with my hands tied behind me and my elbows bound together. This part of our fictional assessment was to find out how long I could stay with my elbows tied like that. In reality, we both knew the answer to this; having shot lots of bondage together already, we were aware that I could stay in that position for around thirty minutes. So, since waiting for me to hit my limit would take a while, Hywel decided to combine it with a test of my pain tolerance.

Nipple clamps come in many different designs, ranging from barely painful at all right through to excruciatingly severe. A lot of the milder types are adjustable, so there's no need for them to cause more pain than the wearer chooses. The type that Hywel chose, however, were the most painful in his collection. They're called clover clamps, and are not an adjustable design. They're made of steel, with hard, textured rubber tips that bite into your skin. And most painfully of all, if the chain connecting the two clamps together is pulled, the clamps don't slip off; instead, they tighten.

Although my character hadn't worn nipple clamps before, I had. And while I knew that they were painful, clover clamps provided a kind of pain that I loved.

Furthermore, there was no way for Hywel to get them attached to my nipples without touching me. They're not especially easy to apply – they need to be attached a little behind the nipple in order to be really secure, and that involves stretching the nipple away from the wearer's body. I liked having his hands on me, but the clamps immediately started to burn and I hunched forward, instinctively trying to lessen the stretching feeling of my breasts being pulled down by the weight of the clamps and connecting chain.

'Stay in position,' ordered Hywel. 'Shoulders back!' and I discovered that I could. It hurt more, but my character wanted a good mark in her assessment, and I wanted Hywel to enjoy playing with me.

Which isn't to say that he didn't need to repeat himself several times. I adjusted perfectly well to staying in the position Hywel had chosen, but only until he picked up the connecting chain and pulled it towards him, tightening the clamps and sending flares of new, sharper, deeper pain through my nipples.

'Shoulders back!' he repeated, more sternly. I started to hyperventilate. And although I didn't know it at the time and only found out when I watched the video back, I also moved my knees as far apart as possible, entirely unnecessarily – and started writhing around with my hips. Because... well, what? Because Hywel was being hot and dominant and sadistic, and I was single. And for once, worries about being professional were a long way from my mind.

Eventually, after a lot more experimental tugging on the nipple clamps in different directions, Hywel was ready to remove them. Whereupon his professional

mask slipped a little too. Up until that point, he'd successfully played the role of a dispassionate examiner,
simply doing his admittedly kinky and peculiar job. But
as he prepared to take the clamps off (by far the most
painful part of the entire nipple-clamp-wearing oper-
ation) he said, with great relish: 'This is really going to
fucking hurt.'

It did really fucking hurt, he was quite right. And I
enjoyed having got under his skin a little. I thought that
perhaps he was enjoying himself as much as I was. I
hoped so.

'How are your arms?' he asked, as he had done at
intervals throughout the scene, back in his dispassionate examiner role. I realised that they were finally
beginning to go numb. So, moving in behind me, Hywel
began to untie my elbow rope. His body being so close
to mine as he did so felt delightful. I wanted to lean
back against him and feel the heat from his body against
my bare skin. I couldn't reach, but without even thinking about it, I felt my lips brushing against his forearm,
where it had been conveniently, tantalisingly, close to
my face. His skin was warm, and smelled clean and
delicious.

Touching him with my mouth felt unfeasibly intimate. We'd not discussed that; it hadn't occurred to me
beforehand that it might be something I'd want to do. I
hoped, vaguely, that I'd not crossed a line and made him
uncomfortable. We needed to talk about the possibility
of a play relationship in a break from shooting; it wasn't
fair to him for me to cross boundaries without discussion, any more than it would have been okay for him
to do it to me. And he'd been entirely appropriate

throughout. Had he, I wondered, even noticed the touch of my lips against his skin? I thought perhaps not; he was busy with the ropes. I wanted to kiss him again, but he was out of reach.

'Is there any spanking in this movie?' I asked Hywel when we reached lunchtime. I'd not specifically written it into the script, and I wasn't sure if Hywel actually liked it. We'd not shot much in the way of impact play, except for the bastinado in *Long Term Bondage*. But I knew we were moving on to suspension bondage that afternoon, so I was anxious that we might not get round to my new favourite activity.

Hywel *hadn't* planned any spanking. Shocked by the hideous marking he'd seen on my bottom after my previous spanking shoot, he'd been cautiously steering clear, to make sure that I healed thoroughly. But I was no longer marked, and spending the day with him without any spanking happening at all seemed like a waste.

'Maybe you should spank me now,' I said, shamelessly. 'Since it's lunchtime.'

'Without filming it?' Hywel looked quite put out.

'Yes. I mean, if you want to?'

This wasn't how I'd meant to ask about playing together. In my mind, I'd been planning to be an entirely different sort of character. A flirty, sophisticated, irresistible kind of person who'd manufacture some sort of reason for needing to be punished. But in the moment, it didn't feel right. I didn't want to be flirty and clever and manipulative. I wanted to be honest about what I was looking for, and to find out if that was something he'd like too. It was awkward, but it was truthful.

Hywel sat down on the corner sofa on the living-room set, upstairs in his studio.

'Then,' he began, looking quite as uncertain and hopeful as me, 'you'd better come over here and get over my knee, hadn't you?'

He had none of the assurance that I'd witnessed in Dallas, Headmaster Tom, or the people I'd played casually with over the preceding months. I wasn't sure that he'd actually ever done this before, and I knew that I couldn't expect him to suddenly become a massively confident spanking Top out of nowhere. Especially considering that he'd witnessed my traumatised response to my last spanking shoot.

As his right hand connected, very gently, with my bottom, I realised that he had no idea how much I loved this. I wanted a great deal more than light hand spanking, but how was he to know? I'd never been able to explain the heart of my sexuality to Lawrence, and my play partners since had all been experienced BDSM players who were used to figuring out their Bottom's tolerance as they went. If I wanted Hywel to properly understand, I was going to have to be braver and more explicit about what I wanted to experience. And while I appreciated that starting too gently was far more sensible and far more respectful than starting too hard, I realised that the middle of a shoot was probably not the best time for him to feel comfortable about potentially bruising me. But when, later, I invited him to come for dinner at my flat to talk further about playing together, I felt certain that, even if it didn't work between us, there was no way that he'd ever be anything but smart and considerate in his decisions regarding what we did together.

As I travelled home from the shoot that day, I felt warm and hopeful. Maybe we'd be successful play partners and maybe we wouldn't, but we'd be friends who shot hot movies together, and who respected each other's desires. There wasn't any room in my heart for romantic love anymore, and I'd never trust myself to fall in love again in any case, since I clearly had dangerously bad taste. But I wanted Hywel in my life, and to begin with, that meant him coming to my flat.

I started to wonder what I should cook when he came to visit. Something that made me look like a sophisticated single woman who owned a flat in London all on her own, obviously. And who, rather than having pedestrian desires for romantic, exclusive relationships, welcomed casual BDSM adventures. Probably while drinking expensive white wine out of a giant, fancy wineglass, and effortlessly entertaining a procession of men while wafting around in sheer, designer lingerie, barefoot on her white carpet. What kind of meal could possibly convey all of that? I wondered. Maybe something with asparagus. And I'd light all my scented candles. He'd be bound to like that.

Chapter Twenty-one

Dom/Sub

Hywel came for dinner, as promised. It turned out that he was allergic to scented candles; he took one distressed look at them and asked if we could blow them out. I was a little crestfallen. But my cooking was a success, and he was an appreciative guest. We'd found it easy to talk during our shoots together, and it felt no less comfortable to talk about the possibility of playing on a non-professional basis. We agreed easily on the limits of our proposed relationship – neither of us was looking for romance, so kissing on the mouth or actual sex were off the menu. But I liked the idea of having a proper, formal dom/sub relationship, rather than just doing individual play sessions when we felt like it. I hoped that he'd want to take control of some parts of my life even when I was away touring for work. I wasn't sure what, but I hoped he'd think of something that he'd enjoy controlling.

Since my flat was small and had no BDSM equipment in it – I'd only just finished assembling furniture – we decided to play at his studio instead. And so, the first time Hywel and I shared our real, off-screen selves with each other for a BDSM scene, it was in the familiar setting of the place where most of our relationship up to that point had played out.

Hywel made me wait in the model makeup room while he set things up. I was full of anticipation, but full, too, of worry. What if we didn't fit together well when there were no cameras to perform for? If I hadn't liked him so much, we could have just not seen each other again if it didn't work out. But he was an important friend to me. I didn't want to wreck that.

He led me out into the studio space, and I looked in delighted surprise at what he'd done. It still seems uniquely sincere and wonderful. Perhaps we all try to bring the best of ourselves to our sexual partner, whether or not our relationships involve actual sex. And what Hywel does impeccably is lighting. Although an experienced bondage photographer, he was new to practising BDSM, and he knew that. So he'd lit the set the way that only he could, to show me that he meant to do his best. The wrought-iron bed frame with its black cover stood in a pool of warm, muted light. BDSM implements stood on a table in deliberate semi-darkness. I couldn't see what he'd selected to play with – I didn't care. The skill and thought he'd put into the lighting told me that he was giving this his best shot, that he wasn't going to assume that he knew everything, and that he, too, wanted it to be good. It touched my heart. By lighting the room so beautifully, I knew I'd look okay too. And strange though it sounds to explain this, given that I'm a professional model who'd worked naked in front of him dozens of times before, I needed the confidence boost. My last relationship had not been kind to my

self-image; I worried about not being desirable. Hywel
had solved the problem. That night, I wasn't scared
about not being sexy enough.

Playing together was good, and it continued that
way. It became a regular pleasure, and he came around
to my flat more often. He introduced some rules. When
he came through the front door, I had to kneel until he
told me I could stand up. I liked to kiss his hand while I
was kneeling there. Actual kissing, on the mouth, would
have felt, ridiculously, like cheating on Lawrence, and I
couldn't fathom how I'd ever get past that. But I'd never
kissed anyone's hand before; it was a fresh experience
that held no memories, and I loved it – I felt like his pet.
And one night, as Hywel was preparing to leave for his
drive home, he announced that he wanted me to sleep
on the floor that night, rather than in my big, new,
metal-framed double bed.

I expect that sounds quite mad. I was an independent
woman, and exceptionally proud to be paying my own
mortgage on my own flat, after being so frightened that
I wouldn't be able to a few months before. My favourite
song was Destiny's Child's 'Independent Women'; I sang
it often. It was an important affirmation in my post-
Lawrence life. I'd bought my own house. I didn't have a
car, but I bought my own train tickets. I'd bought my
own watch. And the bed I slept in? I'd bought it. But
being ordered not to sleep in it felt like the very definition of erotic power exchange. I wasn't Hywel's
submissive because I was weak, or because I needed
someone to tell me what to do, or because I couldn't
exist on my own. I *had* power – professional and
economic – and I got to choose who, if anyone, would

dominate me. Giving aspects of that power to Hywel was a delight, but only because I had it in the first place.

So I pulled my duvet and pillow into the sitting room, and lay down on my white carpet, listening to Hywel's car pull away on the drive beneath my window. And I felt more content than I had for a very long time.

A few weeks later, I was walking back from the tube station to my flat, dragging my modelling bag behind me up the hill. A text came in on my phone. It was from Hywel.

No more orgasms till next time you see me

I stopped, rooted to the spot on the pavement, my arm, holding the phone, sticking rigidly out in front of me in shock. What?! I wasn't seeing him for *ten more days*. Did he have no idea how many orgasms I liked to have in an average week? I couldn't possibly do what he said. Especially, paradoxically, because the fact that he'd told me that was immensely hot in itself. Inconveniently, it made me want to have an orgasm then and there. Recovering slightly, I continued on my walk home with my mind whirring. Did that mean, I wondered, that next time he saw me, we were going to progress to actual orgasms? We'd not done that yet – at the beginning of our play relationship it had felt too much like sex for me. But things were going well, and the idea of *Hywel* making me come was far better than the idea of more orgasms on my own. I hoped that was what was in his mind.

And, though I tried half-heartedly to wait, I failed. I decided, fleetingly, that it wouldn't matter – I didn't have to tell him about having a forbidden orgasm. Except that, of course, I did have to. BDSM is nothing without honesty. And I was curious about how he'd react. He might have forgotten about it anyway, I thought. He might not care. But I wanted to know. I wanted more information about the sort of dominant I was playing with.

I was playing with an uncompromising one, it turned out. He *did* remember to ask, and I *did* tell him the truth. And, of course, he said that I'd have to be punished. He said this in the least sincerely regretful tone that I've ever heard. And I doubt that I was any more convincing in my ridiculous response: 'Oh no! But I'm very sorry now! What *are* you going to do to me? Will it be very, very dreadful?'

Because, though play had been fun, I wanted it to feel real. I wanted Hywel to have actual authority over me, albeit within limited parameters that we'd both agreed to. So this time, when he told me that I could have no more orgasms until after the punishment, I did what he said.

And, a week later, I found myself back in the model makeup room at the studio, waiting just as nervously, while Hywel prepared for whatever he'd decided to do to me. But this time, I wasn't scared about whether or not we were compatible. I knew that we were. I was just scared about how much it would hurt. And this time, when Hywel came to collect me, he didn't look nervous and hopeful, the way he had the time before. He looked determined and focused. He walked me downstairs in front of him, and I opened the door into the main studio. I froze, scared, in the doorway, and Hywel propelled me forward. In a circle of cold light, in the middle of the black shiny floor, lay a fur rug. Above it hung the electric winch that Hywel used for suspensions, and there were ankle cuffs dangling from it. I suddenly felt quite certain of what the punishment would be, and it wasn't one that I'd find easy to enjoy.

Back when we produced our *Long Term Bondage* series, we'd shot a foot-whipping scene. It was by far the most painful of the things that we shot, and Hywel had used a small black leather strap that looked innocuous but was, for some reason I've never understood, absolutely agonising. A curious and frightening feature of bastinado is that, unlike impact play on other parts of the body, the pain doesn't fade as quickly. So, each new stroke lands upon skin that's still busily sending out pain signals, and the pain builds extremely fast, from painful to unbearable in a matter of a few seconds. It's unique in this quality, and it is intense, even when a light implement is used. The black strap was not light. On the contrary, it was horribly severe. It wasn't something I could possibly keep still for only by using willpower, which was why the cuffs were there. At Hywel's instruction, I lay on my back while he buckled the cuffs around my ankles. Then he tied my wrists securely to my knees. That way, I couldn't reach up to protect the soles of my feet.

And of course, when Hywel picked up the implement, it was the black strap. No other choice would really have made sense, given our history with it. He knew it was the worst, and that's why he'd chosen it. And on some level, I'd have been disappointed if he hadn't. I wanted to see what he was like when I'd broken his rules, and I wanted it to be different from when we were playing normally. I guess I wanted to know that we could do BDSM in different gears. Although, in that moment, I wasn't sure I was ready for this particular one.

The first stroke was painful. By the third, I was already screaming. And it went on, and on. The pain built steeply, until the entire sole of each foot was burning unbearably. And even when Hywel paused, after every twelve strokes, the agony did not cease. And there were many, many strokes. At least a hundred.

My screams developed a gravelly, breathless tone. I struggled to get my feet out of the path of the strap, but Hywel had winched them up so that there was no slack in the rope – I couldn't evade the strap's descent. Unlike the way it is with spanking, I could see the strap as it fell – I was facing up. It made everything worse.

Sheer blinkered panic started to set in. It hurt too much. I couldn't take any more, not a single stroke... and then, the most remarkable thing happened. The pain had increased, and increased, and had become entirely unbearable. And then, suddenly, it was gone. Each stroke was still landing on its target with the same ferocity, but it was as though something had switched off in my brain. I could still feel the heat coming from the soles of my bruised feet, but it felt pleasant and warm. I'd crossed over into a type of subspace that I'd never experienced before, an altered mental state that was so complete and enveloping that it drowned out the physical sensations of the bastinado entirely. It felt like sleeping. It felt like flying. Hywel noticed, and stopped, thank goodness. Because my body had stopped sending warning signals, and it's not safe to be the recipient of sensations that you can't feel anymore.

Hywel must have unfastened my ankles and untied my wrists. I didn't notice. I was a long way from being in possession of any kind of observational ability. But when I felt fully aware again, I realised that Hywel had joined me on the fur rug. My head was in his lap. My feet had resumed their burning. They felt swollen to twice their size, though they weren't. They felt as though the soles should be bright red, too, which they were.

'It hurts,' I whimpered, my voice feeling scratchy and dry after all the screaming. 'It hurts, and I deserve it.'

Which, friends, is part of the joy of BDSM. You can be entirely sincere, while still knowing on some level that it's just a game. Sometimes you can play it as though it were serious, as we just had, but simultaneously, we both knew that I didn't *actually* deserve it. We'd done it because we were a sadist and a masochist, and because it made us feel more connected, and because bastinado was one of Hywel's favourite things. And because, in the aftermath, the orgasm that Hywel gave me as a result of being punished for having an orgasm was far more physically intense and emotionally satisfying than the forbidden one had been in the first place. So while I wasn't in a hurry to do something deliberately wrong again, I liked knowing that the possibility for more, similar melodrama was always within reach.

Back on tour the following week, and on my own in a hotel room near Glasgow, I thought about Hywel, and how he'd lit the scenes we'd done together at the studio so beautifully. He turned out to be an excellent, intuitive and careful Top, but he'd taken the extra effort to bring all his skills to the table for our first play session. (Actually, not all his skills – I have limited interest in

astrophysics. But he'd brought the skills that I'd appreciate. And I had, very much.)

I wondered if there was anything I could give him as
a surprise. I thought about how he liked bare feet. And
the idea of having a slave girl. And I thought about
what I was best at.

In my heart, I am a dancer. I have been ever since I
was seven years old, since the first time that I stepped
into a ballet studio. I loved every single lesson I ever
took. And the day that I sat in an orthopaedic surgeon's
office and he told me that I'd never dance again, part of
my heart broke. It never really mended. I'm not sure
that any dancer's heart truly ever does. So, although I
was grateful for the approximation of dance that I had
in my modelling work, and although I was happier and
more content than ever before in my adult life, I still felt
as though my best self was the dancer that I'd been. I
wondered if somehow I could give that self to Hywel.

I thought that perhaps I could. I decided to make him
a barefoot slave-girl dance. I thought that I could
choreograph something that wouldn't hurt my back. It
didn't have to be massively athletic, I just needed it to
showcase my feet, include lots of toe-pointing, and look
submissive. I chose a track from the *Kill Bill, Vol. 1*
soundtrack: 'The Grand Duel' by Luis Bacalov. It's
beautiful, serene and slow. I could choreograph something that my body could cope with rehearsing. Over
the next few weeks, I added to the dance, phrase by
phrase, and anticipated performing it for Hywel. It
involved a lot of kneeling, a great deal of balancing on
demi pointe, and a slow striptease. I loved it; it felt ritu-
alistic and formal, and it felt as though it suited our

relationship. And finally, when I was home from Scotland, I invited Hywel to my flat, and told him that I'd made up a dance for him. He sat on my sofa, and I retreated into my bedroom to get ready. Suddenly I was afflicted with stage fright. I wondered if he'd think it was hopelessly weird and self-aggrandising of me to take it upon myself to make up a performance and force him to watch me. I'd done it plenty of times to Immi, and she'd not enjoyed it at all. I hoped that I'd judged his tastes correctly.

The song began on my CD player, and I rose up onto my toes. Then I stepped out into the sitting room and, not daring to look Hywel in the eye, performed for him. At the end, there was silence. My final position didn't enable me to see his face.

When he spoke, his voice was soft.

'Come over here.'

I went over and knelt in front of him, still not daring to look up. I'd wanted to show him the best of myself. I wasn't the dancer I'd been at eighteen. My best wasn't as good as I'd have liked.

'No,' continued Hywel. 'Not there. Come and sit on the sofa, next to me.'

I'd always avoided that. It felt too romantic, not formal and distanced enough. I'd wanted emotional boundaries. But I wanted to do what he said, and I felt vulnerable. I'd not danced for anyone in a long time, and never like this. I climbed onto the sofa next to him, and he encircled me with his arms. My face was against his chest.

'It was beautiful,' he told me, the warmth in his voice impossible to miss. 'I would like you to do it again for me. But first, you have to start breathing normally again. You are my beautiful slave girl, and I'm very pleased with you.' His t-shirt was wet under my face. I'd cried on him; they were tears of relief. Somehow it had felt important to me to show him everything that I was made up of, and this was a piece I hadn't given him before, because it was too close to my heart. Of course, I wanted to dance for him again. I loved it when he was theatrically cross with me. But I discovered that day that I loved it most when I'd pleased him.

Part Three

A Massive Masochistic Moth

Chapter Twenty-two

Dominant Boyfriend

This is my story, so I don't want to tell other people's private stories more than I have to. But I must explain that Hywel was married when I first started working, and then playing, with him. Everything we did was with the knowledge and consent of his wife, and the fact that he was married made me feel safe in the knowledge that he wouldn't look for what I couldn't provide for him: love and romance. At the time that we started playing, I'd actually hoped that I'd be useful for helping them to stay together. Since they weren't doing BDSM within their relationship, I didn't feel as though I was treading on ground that belonged to someone else, and I hoped that Hywel would be happier if he could explore BDSM with me. So the first time he came around to my flat, I also extended the invitation to his wife. She was, and is, a wonderful person, and is also these days a valued friend who comes to stay with us regularly. I wasn't prepared to play with Hywel unless it was fine with everyone involved, and since I knew they'd struggled, despite their very best efforts, to keep their marriage in good health, I felt optimistic about helping with that. Being a kinky safety valve of sorts, perhaps. Or some kind of surrogate.

We'd been playing for several months when Hywel telephoned me. I was at home in my flat, and delighted to hear from him, but he sounded unhappy. He and his wife had finally decided to divorce. They were both very sad about it, but recognised that to protect their precious friendship, living together wouldn't work for them in the long term. I was sorry for them; I hated to think of either of them being unhappy or lonely. They'd been together ever since they were undergraduates. Deciding not to live together anymore seemed like a huge, momentous step.

Hywel went on to explain, as kindly as he could, that he didn't think we could play together anymore. He'd tried to create a sort of patchwork relationship for himself, he explained, with different people providing the things that, ideally, he'd like to have from one person. Since he wasn't going to be in his primary relationship anymore, he wanted to try to find love and romance in the future. He knew that wasn't something I could give him, he explained, so regretfully, he needed to stop playing with me and, eventually, begin the whole process of trying to find a partner again.

He said that of course we'd still be friends. And naturally, we'd carry on shooting together. I couldn't argue with the sense of what he was saying. He was a clever, kind and decent man, and a caring, skilled dominant. He *deserved* a wholehearted relationship, and if that was what he wanted, I didn't want to stand in his way. He was right.

And yet. . .

Only a couple of weeks before, we'd been shooting in a hotel suite in Kent. The suite itself looked like something out of my Barbie house: Swarovski crystals everywhere, a giant round bed and white-velvet furniture. It was absurd, but photogenic and entertaining. We'd shot some wonderful pictures, including a collection of shots with me in a five-point set of shackles, with oversized metal collar, wrist and ankle cuffs connected by chains that were too short to allow me to stand up. Hywel had photographed me in the shower, as my hair gradually became drenched and my makeup started to wash away. In the pictures, my irises look completely black; mid-shoot I'd dropped into subspace despite the fact that really, nothing was happening to me. But things had been going very well in our dom/sub relationship, and almost everything we did felt like an act of dominance and submission – even photoshoots. We'd had dinner in the hotel restaurant, and I'd slipped my shoes off and teased Hywel with my bare feet under the table. And staying in the suite that night, I'd expected to sleep on the floor, because that's what had fitted with our dynamic. But at bedtime, Hywel didn't order me onto the floor at all. He enfolded me in his arms and announced that he wanted me in the (ridiculous, Swarovski-encrusted) bed with him that night. And when I woke the next morning, it was because his hands were on me and he'd pulled me tight against him. It had felt beautiful.

And hadn't it, I wondered now, as I put the phone down and sat, stunned, on the arm of my sofa to think, felt romantic too? It had. And if sex had been an option, would I have liked it? I thought that I would. My feelings were complicated. When we were doing straight dom/sub play, I didn't feel as though I was doing anything wrong, but the idea of kissing, sex or actual love filled me with guilt. Lawrence had cheated on me on a quite literally industrial scale. It didn't make sense to feel any loyalty to him. But he'd been my first sexual partner, and I'd only ever expected to have one. Nevertheless, over the last few months, when I'd looked at Hywel, I'd sometimes imagined a life in which we were free to give each other more of ourselves. And now, the words of Take That's song 'Patience' came to my mind.

I wondered, what if it was just a question of time, and of patience? Because I wanted the best for Hywel, and if that meant him starting again and finding a partner who could give him everything, then that's what he should do. But I wondered – could that partner possibly be me after all?

The timing was poor. I was about to set off on a round-the-world tour with Ron, the art nude photographer from my first week as a model; I'd be away for almost two months. But I hoped that we could figure it out. So I emailed Hywel, confident that this time he wouldn't respond with 'I don't think you've got the right look for me' as he had to my first email to him, five years before.

Hywel agreed that we should try giving a real relationship a shot. We only had time to meet up once, for dinner, before I left for Singapore the next day. We held hands under the table in the restaurant. We didn't want to lose the theatrical formality of our dom/sub relationship, which had been such fun, and of course there'd been plenty of affection and intimacy within that friendship. But now we realised we had more facets to explore. Like holding hands, which felt good. And kissing. And actual sex. And my calling Hywel something other than 'sir'. I still liked calling him that, and I'd fantasised about a 24/7 dom/sub dynamic. But both Hywel and I agreed over dinner about the importance of real-life equality. We wanted to make things last between us if we could, and we both felt as though having equal decision-making power for the non-sexual bits of our relationship was the only way to have a connection that was long term, meaningful and healthy. Hywel only felt safe and comfortable expressing himself as a dominant sadist if he knew that, in reality, we'd share decisions and responsibilities. He didn't want to be the only adult in the relationship. And I'd never abandoned my sixth-form feminist stance. I *am* an independent woman. I'm not, in the words of the Bible, 'the weaker vessel'. And I don't need to be spanked because I lack self-discipline, or because I can't work on my own personal development without the assistance of a male authority figure. I like to be spanked, and tied up, and dominated because it turns me on, and it makes me happy. Hywel and I were in agreement: for us, BDSM was a sex game. Certainly it was one that we enjoyed abandoning ourselves to for extended periods, and sometimes we liked to play as though it was entirely serious, the way we had with the bastinado punishment. But, sexy though the word 'slave' was, for both of us, in real-life decisions we agreed that we would be equals.

Having discussed all that, but not having had time to put any of it into practice, it didn't feel great to be setting off for Singapore having only seen Hywel once as my possible boyfriend. But at least we'd had a chance to talk about it face to face. And as I travelled from country to country and my round-the-world tour progressed, I became more and more excited about coming home to Hywel, and giving a real sex life another chance.

I got close to not having that chance. In Singapore, I had a photoshoot with a local photographer, who took me to a rare derelict building: an old hospital. Singapore is very built-up and there's not much unused land, so it was a treat to be shooting somewhere deserted. I was worried, though, because my understanding of the law in Singapore was that it was illegal to be nude where anyone could potentially see you. There was no one at the derelict hospital except for us, but I was anxious enough to ask the photographer about it. He explained that the concern over that particular law was mistaken. Actually it *was* legal to be nude outdoors, so I had nothing to worry about. Reassured, I spent the next couple of hours shooting classical ballet-themed artistic nude shots in the abandoned building. It was warm, and the location was atmospheric, and I had a super time.

I was getting dressed in an alcove at the end of the shoot, when I heard an unfamiliar voice. A police officer had turned up, attracted by the photographer's car parked outside the hospital. It appeared that we were trespassing.

I wasn't delighted. Laws of trespass vary from country to country, and I'd assumed that the local photographer would have had permission to be there if it wasn't publicly accessible land. But there was nothing to be done; I stepped out of the alcove to greet the police officer myself.

'What have you been photographing?' asked the officer. Reluctantly, the photographer handed over his camera, and the police officer started scrolling through the images – whereupon his demeanour changed entirely.

'These are pornographic,' he stated, baldly. He picked up his radio and spoke into it. I couldn't translate, but it didn't feel good. He told us that he'd called for backup. And he seized our passports.

I'd never had my passport taken away from me when abroad before. It is an awful, vulnerable feeling. The officer walked with us down to the car park, whereupon a police van and two more police cars pulled up. There were only two of us: the photographer and me. I couldn't imagine why they needed so many officers. It was frightening, especially since now, everyone was conversing in Malay.

It seemed certain that we were about to be arrested. I was meant to be leaving the country the following day. I suddenly felt very far from home.

The most senior police officer took custody of our passports. He put me in the back of one of the police cars, and everyone took turns looking through the pictures on the back of the camera. They all appeared to have an opinion on them, but I didn't know what anyone was saying. And an awful thought, so dreadful that it was almost funny, occurred to me. Didn't Singapore allow judicial caning? I was sure that it did. Was *that* what was going to happen to me? It seemed preferable to a prison sentence, but I felt as though I had an eternity, sitting in the back of a police car, to consider what the British tabloids would make of *that* story.

STAR OF SPANKING MOVIES SENTENCED TO SINGAPORE CANING!

How genuinely humiliating that would be. I like humiliation play as a general rule, but only because it's not, actually, humiliating. It's just fun. The *actual* humiliation of being sent back to the UK, having been ejected from Singapore after being caned in a blaze of publicity, would have felt like the end of the world.

I continued to sit in the police car, as everyone outside continued to argue. And it suddenly occurred to me that I might not be able to go home to Hywel at all. What if I got a custodial sentence? Would he wait for me? Though I didn't know it at the time, I could have received a one-year sentence for obscenity. For being irresponsible, and not checking the facts for myself. I should never have trusted the photographer. He wanted to get his atmospheric nude shots, so it hadn't been in his interests to tell me the truth – that we were breaking the law.

Finally, the senior police officer came over to the car, and spoke to me through the rolled-down window.

'These pictures are obscene,' he stated, in English. He looked at me, assessing my reaction.

Obscene? By local standards, I couldn't argue. But still, it hurt to have my naked body described that way. I'd been doing ballet poses. I'd not done anything sexually explicit. I'd never thought of nudity that way. But I was in their country, and I'd broken their rules.

'I'm awfully sorry,' I began, sounding just as hopeless as Amelia Jane Rutherford does when she's finally been trapped into admitting that she's done something wrong and is hoping to avoid the worst punishment. 'I honestly didn't know.'

There was nothing else for me to say. It was the truth, but it didn't sound especially convincing.

The officer looked at me in silence. Then, he flipped something in my direction. Automatically, I caught it. It was my passport. They were letting us go.

Back in the photographer's car, he was full of good cheer and excitement. 'That's what happened last time they turned up at my shoot!' he exclaimed. 'Eventually they let us go!'

Last time? What an idiot. This had happened to him before, and he'd taken the same risk again, with a model from halfway around the world. The police had erased his pictures, but he had an extra memory card in his camera; he was delighted that he still had copies.

'Please, please don't upload them!' I implored him. 'At least don't publish them until I'm out of the country...'

I didn't trust him at all. He dropped me off at my hotel, and I started packing frantically. My flight to New Zealand was scheduled for noon the next day. The sooner I could get through airport security and out of Singapore, the better.

The next day, every single official in any kind of uniform made me jump guiltily. I kept remembering that they had my name, and they knew where I'd been staying. At any point, they could change their minds and come back for me. We got to the airport, and I shuffled shamefacedly through security, terrified that my name would set off some kind of alert.

Finally, the plane took off, and I was out of Singapore.

Only then did I dare email Hywel to tell him what had almost happened to me. It was Hywel who went and researched what the repercussions could have been. I wouldn't have been caned – they don't do that to women. But a *year* in a Singapore prison. How ridiculously naive I'd been.

Hywel was waiting for me at the airport when I returned to the UK two months later. He drove us to my flat, and made me promise never to go back to Singapore, irrespective of the exciting photoshoots I might be offered there in the future. I was happy to promise him that, and I loved it that he cared enough to insist. I thought that if I'd been imprisoned, he'd probably have waited for me to be released, rather than just casually moving on to another submissive who wasn't incarcerated overseas. Our relationship was new, but I felt as though our lives were already intertwined in a way in which my life with Lawrence never had been. It felt very good, and very safe, to be back home with him. Since I was jetlagged and exhausted from not sleeping on the flight, I went straight to bed. Hywel, concerned that my excitement at seeing him again would stop me from sleeping, tied me *to* the bed. After two months of vanilla modelling, it felt wonderful, safe and peaceful to be back with Hywel, and back in his ropes. I drifted easily to sleep, knowing that he was in the next room, waiting for me.

And then, friends, later that day, after nine months of playing together and two months of being apart, we embarked upon a new stage of our relationship. Which is a euphemism for saying that we had a great deal of actual sex. Very excellent, dom/sub sex. Over the next few months, Hywel and I did very little *other* than have sex; in my flat, in hotel rooms and at his studio. We discovered that, sometimes, just having vanilla sex felt right to us; loving, and warm, and friendly. More often, we fucked as though we hated each other, and it felt like fighting, just like my long-ago combat choreography. He hurt me and bruised me, wrote his name on the back of my neck in ink, made me his, and made me love him more completely than I'd ever imagined. I hoped I could give him what he wanted, and I put my whole heart into trying. It'd been hard to trust him not to hurt me like Lawrence had, and not to let me down. But he only hurt me in the ways I'd hoped he would, and he has never, ever let me down.

The next time I got to speak to Sam in person, we were driving alone through northern France. I told her all about sex with Hywel. Sorry, Hywel. It's what some people do, and I am one of those people.

'It's *really* amazing,' I told Sam. 'Hywel actually, properly cares about whether I'm having a good time.'

Sam, who is a year younger than me, gave me an indulgent, old-person's look. 'Well, yes,' she said. 'That's what real men do.'

And I am happy to report that both Sam and I, who, when we first met, were in almost identically ridiculous relationships, are now married to real men. They want us to have a good time; it's very nice.

You could be forgiven for thinking that once we were free to do real BDSM and sex in our personal lives, our desire to create BDSM artwork for Restrained Elegance might have atrophied a little. After all, both of us had started shooting bondage work to fulfil our needs, and the sexual frustration and loneliness that had prompted me to write the *Bondage Driving Test* story about a girl searching for a master was gone. Blessedly, for Hywel and me, we weren't done with being creative. It was a happy surprise to discover that we wanted to share our passion for BDSM just as much now that we were feeling personally fulfilled. Maybe even more so; I was acutely aware that there were many people in the situation that I'd been in until recently, and if they weren't getting to do BDSM personally, I wanted them to be able to enjoy the next best thing – like I had with watching movies from Dallas's website. And maybe watching our movies would push some of them into taking first steps towards finding their own BDSM experiences. I hoped so.

Hywel had booked another location trip to the same house in northern France that he'd taken me to the year before: the one with the terrace where I'd cried about Lawrence and he'd hugged me. He booked Kate, one of his very first models from when he'd begun running the site, and with whom he had been friends ever since. And he booked Sam too.

Hywel and I had busied ourselves writing scripts for a couple of feature-length bondage films to make while we were there. Hywel's was a horror story along the lines of *The Evil Dead*, but with more bondage. It involved Sam and me doing a lot of running around in the dark, screaming, and eventually suffering demon possession. Hywel, dressed as a monk (I enjoyed calling him Hywel-in-the-Cowl, which rhymes if you're pronouncing his name right), tied me to a table and delivered a severe flogging, lit only by candlelight. And when Sam and I eventually escaped the haunted house that we'd found ourselves trapped in, Sam discovered, too late, that I was still possessed, so I attacked her with ropes. Hywel had begun to teach me how to do bondage rigging so that I could help more at shoots. Although I'll never enjoy it from a kinky perspective, given that I'm submissive, I did like being useful. I liked trying to make the bondage neat and secure. I liked, if you can imagine it, trying to get Hywel's approval.

When I was home again, with time to reflect on it, I realised that having a genuine BDSM romance had made me much more comfortable with producing work that showed my sexual identity for what it was. Without really noticing, my reticence to express my fantasies to my friends and colleagues had washed away. In France, we'd shot plenty of off-the-cuff ideas, and from the security of a relationship with Hywel, I didn't mind what I admitted to liking. Consequently, many of my ideas on the location shoot had been fairly offbeat, but I didn't feel ashamed of them, even when everyone else unanimously refused to shoot them with me. Hywel *did* allow me to shoot a ridiculous video series in which I was demoted from Restrained Elegance Slave Girl to Restrained Elegance Pet Girl. Hywel made me write an explanation to accompany the videos when they went live on the site, because he thought that they might be a bit traumatic for our core audience. I hoped that no one would be traumatised, so I was happy to explain to the website members that being a pet girl was one of my current fantasies, and that they'd never see me doing anything that *wasn't* one of my fantasies. I had many, and I wanted to share them all.

From the safety of being in a relationship with a full-time bondage photographer, I started to relax about talking honestly with non-kinky people too. I'd kept the two parts of my professional life – vanilla and kinky – separate up until that point, using different names for my mainstream and BDSM work. I'd told some of my closer photographer friends about both, but now I discovered that there was power in being honest with everyone. I also discovered that when I started being more forthcoming about my own sexual identity and kinky relationship, other people shared more with me. I learned that quite a number of my 'vanilla' photographers were no such thing. They'd just kept quiet about their interest in BDSM, not wanting to make me feel uncomfortable and not wanting to be judged. I understood that; I'd heard many judgemental statements made about kinky people. But I started to feel as though, together with Hywel, I could do my bit to change the way the BDSM community was perceived.

Hywel has great integrity. Back when he was still a university lecturer and started Restrained Elegance, he did so under his own, not especially common, name. It didn't occur to him to be anything less than completely honest. He showed his work to his colleagues at the university, and when he handed in his notice, he explained that it was to pursue his career as a bondage photographer. When we started dating, his parents asked him who his new girlfriend was, and he showed them bondage pictures he'd taken of me. I'm just going to assume I was clothed. He's simply not any good at lying, prevaricating, or obfuscating the truth, and after Lawrence, that was of great value to me. Being his girlfriend, I noticed that people coped better than I'd have imagined with hearing the unapologetic reality of Hywel's lifestyle and career.

It made me imagine a different world. It made me wonder, if there'd been more people like Hywel in my life when I was growing up, would I ever have felt so confused and guilty about being kinky that I'd have contemplated killing myself? I didn't think so. What if someone like Hywel had been one of my drama school teachers? Wouldn't I have felt more at peace with myself, when I saw how comfortable he was with his own sexuality? I would have. And, as I met more and more people in my personal life and at work who were quietly into their own versions of BDSM, I realised that there were a lot of us around. There would have been other kinky students at my large sixth-form college, and even at my small drama school. There would have been kinky people at the churches I attended, and in the casts of the theatre productions I was part of. But because most of us couldn't face being honest about it, we as a society allowed young people like I had been to grow up conflicted, guilty, ashamed and lonely. I decided to dedicate the rest of my career to encouraging more openness. Whatever I did would be only a small contribution, but I wanted to do my part. If my honesty about my sexual identity could make someone like the girl I'd been feel more normal, then I wanted to try it. Because it was only from the safety of my current state of mind that I could acknowledge how bad things had really been in my head, and for how long.

In 2005, when I'd been modelling for a couple of years, and soon after the 7 July London terrorist attack,

I'd been travelling home from a photoshoot on the Underground when I'd spotted an unattended shopping bag in my carriage. I'd asked the other people on the crowded train whether it belonged to any of them – no one claimed it. So when we pulled up to the next station, I'd asked people to get off the train so that we could raise the alarm from the platform where we'd be safer. No one did what I said; presumably they'd taken the warnings in the wake of the attack less seriously than I had. So not knowing what else to do, I'd picked up the bag, and taken it from the crowded train to the less crowded platform. I'd carried it to the far end where there were no people, then cleared part of the platform and waited for station staff to notice my frantic waving at their security cameras. It had turned out not to be a bomb after all, and I'd boarded the next train home, only realising a few minutes later that I was vibrating with a horrible adrenaline comedown. I'd started thinking about what would have happened if it *had* been a real bomb. Maybe I'd have saved the people on the train carriage, and possibly I'd have died in the process. And it would have been the only useful thing I'd ever have done for society, I'd thought, spitefully. I was just a bondage model, doing a job that I loved but that was entirely unnecessary. Making sexy pictures for people to enjoy wasn't important or useful. Maybe I wasn't an enemy to society like I'd thought as a teenager, but I certainly wasn't any use, either. I was just indulging myself, making more money than I really deserved, living out fantasies through photoshoots.

I wasn't suicidal anymore, not in the way I'd been when I first discovered my sexual identity. But, looking back at myself in my twenties, I see that this incident was nothing like a one-off; my behaviour was regularly consistent with having a death wish. Despite having no relevant skills, I couldn't avoid interfering in situations where I thought other people were in danger. It happened over and over again. One night I saw two men beating up another, while his girlfriend stood aside on the train platform, hysterically begging them to stop. Forgetting that I only know how to *pretend* to fight, I launched myself between them. Miraculously it worked: they *did* stop. Sometimes, I think that my well-projected, outraged voice is as effective as martial-arts training. But I cried afterwards, from fear and shock, sitting alone on the train back to my flat. The fight had been on the platform, with a train approaching. I could have been pushed onto the line, and I realised I'd probably risked my life stupidly. I do hate bullies, but my behaviour wasn't rational. I wasn't risking death for other people because I was brave; I was frightened. I may have wanted to save them, but what I was really doing was trying to redeem myself. And doing that through dying was what my Jehovah's Witness childhood had prepared me for. Behaving repeatedly like some kind of Jesus/Batman hybrid from within the body of an injury-prone ex-ballet dancer wasn't very far from being suicidal, after all.

But now, a couple of years later but with a perspective shift resulting from my relationship with a man who felt no shame about what he was, I saw this attitude for the self-hatred that it was. My life and my work *were* valuable. Just like China Hamilton's photography was valuable; seeing it at the gallery under Waterloo had told me that I wasn't alone, and had led eventually to my finding happiness with a partner I was compatible with. Dallas's work had been valuable to me in the same way, as had Hywel's. The effect their work had had on me was replicated thousands of times across the world, when people accessed their websites to find not just arousal but beauty, inspiration and a sense of belonging. And since I've been with Hywel, I've never again thought in that self-deprecating way. Those of us who are capable of being honest about our atypical sexualities make it easier for everybody else to find their courage too.

Chapter Twenty-three

A Sadist in the Family

For the first couple of months of our relationship, Hywel and I existed in a sort of vacuum, mostly spending time alone with each other, but socialising with other bondage models and photographers when there was an opportunity. In a long-term relationship, of course you have to engage with real life too. We started to introduce each other to the people in our lives.

Hywel's mother and father were utterly delightful to me from day one. They are, respectively, a mathematician and a lecturer in electrical engineering. I was concerned that they might find me an odd choice for their introverted, intellectual son, but if they did, they never showed it. Hywel's father, an immensely practical man who I once found fixing the hinge on our bathroom door in the middle of the night, simply because he couldn't bear not to, finds my desire to talk about feelings all the time quite baffling, but is very kind about it.

'More introspection? Oh good. We've not done any of that for at least five minutes. Have another piece of cake.'

And Hywel's mother, the kindest of ladies, who finds

my version of being a woman (colour-coordinating out-fits, changing hairstyles several times a day, wearing makeup to walk on the beach) puzzling in the extreme, has never been anything but respectful and supportive of my relationship with their son. I appreciate her very much.

I was delighted to be able to bring a physicist home to meet my parents, especially my dad. My parents love hill walking, as we do, and Hywel has shepherded us all up Welsh mountains, with my father talking happily about particles the entire way, while my mother and I talked about feelings. Feelings and tweed. I was glad. Since I can't muster a passable imitation of someone who's interested in physics, at least I've been able to give my dad the gift of a family member who doesn't have to fake it.

But my niece and nephew, Philippa and Ely, were actually the first members of my family to meet Hywel. They'd come to stay with me in my flat, and I, hideously aware of my responsibility to keep them safe at the ages of ten and eight respectively, had taken them to London Zoo, where I'd been the very epitome of an over-anxious aunt. I'd driven them to the zoo in my car, because I was scared of losing them on the tube (or having to fight someone in front of them, obviously), and once at the zoo I clutched at them constantly, lest they should get lost within its grounds. I kept them hydrated with the intensity of someone conducting a dangerous scientific experiment. And on the way home from the zoo, when I stopped at Marks & Spencer to buy extra things for dinner, I made them come into the shop with me in case someone stole the car with my precious family members in situ. Having kept them safe all day, I hoped that the evening, which was to involve having dinner at my flat with Hywel, would be a less risky proposition altogether. I wondered, would he be any good with children? Our relationship up to that point had been the very antithesis of child-friendly. I wasn't sure what Hywel was really like when he wasn't being my dominant. But he was lovely. A little shy in unstructured social situations, he'd written a role-playing game for us all to play, based on the Harry Potter books. It's what Hywel's been doing with his friends ever since he was school age, and I was touched that he'd made the effort to try to ensure that the evening was a success.

We had dinner, lounging on the sofa and floor since I had no dining table, and Philippa and Ely were astounded that Hywel managed to eat three servings of banoffee pie. They still remember it, many years later, as though it was a stunt that he put on to entertain them. And Philippa, who'd always been artistic, complimented Hywel on the photo he'd taken of me that hung on my landing wall. It was from one of our early shoots together; a picture set loosely based on Andromeda from Greek mythology, chained to a rock to be sacrificed to a sea monster. I was fully clothed in the image, and there was only minimal bondage; I'd thought it was child-friendly enough to keep on my wall. It meant a lot to me that Philippa could see some beauty in Hywel's image – obviously it would be many years before she'd be old enough to view most of his work, but it felt good to at least have furnished my whole family with a basic understanding of Hywel's job. I felt that, given time, Hywel would be a good uncle to them both.

Of course, if you didn't skip the Prologue of this book (I HOPE YOU DIDN'T), you'll remember that Philippa eventually came to do work experience with us during her gap year, when she was considering taking a degree in film. It meant a great deal to me that she asked us, and that she felt comfortable enough with the subject matter to spend a month helping us to produce it. I was, and am, immensely proud of her maturity. (Sorry. This is how people talk about their children; this is my nearest approximation. It's probably sickening. But they're both so beautiful. YOU HAVE NO IDEA.) Ely has turned into a keen role player. He and Hywel play some of the same games. Honestly, I don't understand them, but the main thing for me is that Hywel has plenty of ways of connecting with my family that don't involve BDSM. As you'd hope.

And I've not even told you about Hywel and Immi. Until I took Hywel up to Nottinghamshire to meet her and her husband Phil, it hadn't occurred to me that they are, in some ways, eerily similar. I had essentially swapped one relationship – the one in which I'd spent my childhood trailing after Immi, trying to get her to stop reading books and pay attention to me; playing games about imaginary people; making her watch me dance; and annoying her with my great fondness for constant physical contact and affection – with another relationship where all the same things applied. Hywel and Immi love books. They love several of the same authors. Sometimes, they buy each other books. And they both retreat into books when they become overwhelmed by me and my talking. They both, probably, love me rather less intensely than I love them, because my feelings are perennially oversized, and my needy version of affection is perhaps impossible to match. Their good relationship, and their similarity to each other, makes me happy every time I see them together.

'Immi, can we live together when we're grown-ups?' I once asked her, hopefully, just before she moved out of our shared bedroom. She was non-committal. I did the closest possible thing: I moved in with, and then married, Hywel. Immi, very sensibly, continued to live with her husband Philip, who was recently ordained, having decided that he'd prefer to be a minister than a housing manager. And the wholehearted, accepting way in which my family have welcomed Hywel, my atheist, pornography-producing, kinky husband into their Christian household was never clearer to me than in 2018, when I decided to interview my family about my job.

Immi, Phil, Philippa and Ely were staying with us at our house in Wales for New Year. I'd started a YouTube channel, and since I'm asked about it over and over again by photographers who can't believe that my family would be capable of accepting my career choice, I asked them all if they'd appear in a video with me and tell the world their thoughts about my job.

Immi, naturally, refused. She was reading a book. She held it up high like a barrier, and hunched behind it disagreeably, like a tortoise retreating into its shell. Hywel looked very much as though he'd like to do the same. I reminded him that we were married, and that he didn't have the choice. Phil, who is uninhibited, extrovert and warm-hearted, agreed immediately. As did Philippa and Ely, by this time twenty-two and twenty years old. I asked them several questions (What did they think I actually did? What sort of things did they think I said in my videos? Were they grateful that I didn't charge them my model rates to hang out with me?) and they gave thoughtful, illuminating and entertaining answers. There was one question that was especially dear to my heart.

Many years before, when I had a blog dedicated to my BDSM work, someone had left a comment that had angered me very much. In a long and judgemental ramble, he'd accused Hywel of being abusive towards me. The writer said that he'd been abused as a child by 'people like Hywel'. He finished by saying this:

> *Also, it makes him nothing more than a pimp. God help if you have children, I'd be terrified to leave a child of mine with him. If he preys on you, who can at least defend herself if things go to [sic] far, what about a child*

I'd been remarkably lucky in my career in that I'd had very few comments like this directed at me, but I know it's a common assumption that dominants and sadists are dangerous to vulnerable women and children. I'm tired of seeing that kind of depiction in books and movies, where an interest in BDSM is often used as a shortcut to show a character as damaged, disturbed and sometimes dangerous. I wanted to address it with my family, the people I most want to protect in this world, and who'd had the most contact with both Hywel and me over the ten years we'd been together.

'I married a sadist,' I began, looking at Phil, Philippa and Ely. Hywel sank a little further down on the sofa, looking longingly over to where Immi was sitting, safely out of shot behind her book.

'Has Hywel ever hurt you?'

All three of them looked at me with blank faces. Ely started laughing. Then Philippa spoke.

'I'm not sure that he's ever made *eye contact* with me, let alone come near enough to *hurt* me,' she declared. Hywel looked grateful.

'Only when he chose you over me,' replied Phil, 'which is something that breaks my heart every day.'

'I don't think he's ever made physical contact with me,' said Ely, seriously.

And there we were. As I'd known, they hadn't been harmed, but it was nice to hear them say it. What was more, to hear that my family accepted my husband, and me, with our odd lifestyle, our stone dungeon, our boxes of rope in the utility room next to the washing machine, the spanking furniture in our dining room, and the steel collar that I sometimes wear. Just as we accepted them, with their house next to the church where Phil worked, with Phil's job as a representative of the Church of England, and his puzzling Amazon Wishlist full of books about God; the crucifix on a chain around Immi's neck, and Immi and Phil's faith that colours their life decisions and attitudes to the world, just as being in the BDSM industry colours ours.

At the time of writing, I've been with Hywel for twelve years. I could fill the rest of this book with stories about why he makes me so happy. But I think I've indulged myself quite enough. (Thank you for listening.) And it wasn't the end of the story. Finally comfortable with myself and my career, I wanted to see what I could achieve. I wanted to see how hard I could flex my sub-missive muscles. I wanted to see how far I could stretch my masochism. Now that I didn't feel ashamed of my sexuality, I wanted to examine it. And for that, I needed to work with the best BDSM practitioners I could find. Come with me – I found some treasures, and I want to share them with you.

Chapter Twenty-four

Alistair and the Military Caning

Alistair first contacted me only two months after I broke up with Lawrence. He said he was a fan of my work and would like to do a spanking shoot with me. At the time, I was suspicious. I was only working with a handful of spanking producers, all of whom were professionals. I was worried about being manhandled by an unskilled, creepy fan who didn't know what he was doing and who'd give me an uncomfortable day of trying to insist upon professional boundaries while he pushed the limits of my comfort with intimacy. I was also worried about something that didn't apply when I worked for professionals who showed their faces on camera:

'Do you have a partner? And is she okay with you doing this?' I asked in my reply.

His response was reassuring. He did have a wife. She wasn't into corporal punishment but was respectful of his desire to pursue his own interest. This impressed me, and I guessed that they must have a healthy, trusting relationship, which made me feel kindly disposed towards him. Having been cheated on myself, the idea of unwittingly hurting another woman in the way that

I'd been hurt was unbearable to me, but his response felt sincere, so I accepted the booking, with the caveat that while I was happy to do spanking-themed pictures, I wasn't sure until I met him how much actual spanking I'd be comfortable with.

Alistair, in person, made me like him almost instantly. He's well-mannered, respectful, sensitive, empathetic and highly imaginative. As we sat drinking tea and getting acquainted at the studio, I discovered we had more kinks in common than I'd expected too. He, like me, enjoyed melodramatic storylines, with interrogations, heroic agents captured overseas, themes of torture, courage, sexual threat, and complicated characters. Part of his reason for contacting me was that he'd enjoyed some of my self-scripted movies, feeling similarly that spanking could be used to enhance all sorts of stories, from romances, to thrillers, to rom-coms, to psychodrama. None of this guaranteed that we'd be a good match to work together physically, but being on the same page psychologically seemed a good start.

A slight disadvantage during our first meeting turned out to be that we'd booked a studio which seemed to also function as a corridor. Quite a *busy* corridor. I, dressed in a short gingham dress, posed bent over on a sofa. The studio owner walked between me and Alistair to answer the doorbell. As I slowly pulled down my panties, the studio owner returned, casually carrying a parcel. I changed into a business suit and posed at a desk, feigning petulance. The studio owner's friend arrived, pushing a motorbike through the studio, between us both. I started to feel ridiculous. I changed into a school uniform, and suggested that Alistair should set the camera on a timer to try some action spanking shots. Both the studio owner and his friend immediately appeared with cups of tea, and wandered over to a corner to discuss their faulty gas space heater. I started to feel a little desperate. So, perhaps, did Alistair, who offered to take me to the café over the road for lunch so we could talk more privately.

Over lunch, I began to like him even more. I tend to connect more easily with dominants than with anyone else; they're my opposite and we need each other, so I usually feel an affinity with them. Switches are harder for me to understand. I'd rather not do BDSM at all than have to play the dominant role, and I find it difficult to comprehend how anyone can like both.

But Alistair's emotional intelligence, and the empathy he had as a participant on both sides of the dom/sub divide, interested me. And I wondered how it would affect his style of Topping. I was curious, and suggested that, if we could find a studio that wasn't also a high-traffic corridor, we should maybe try a video shoot. I still had no idea if he'd be in any way accurate, skilled, or even a good role player. But when people are nice, those things maybe matter less.

So a couple of months later, we met for a video shoot. Alistair, with the emotional literacy I'd noticed on our first shoot, had selected a light-hearted story that didn't require hugely severe action, and which could develop in a number of directions as we figured out the dynamic we were comfortable with. He was playing the owner of a corporation; I was his new senior manager, with whom he was displeased. It was a simple enough, familiar scenario. I wondered how well we'd fit together in improvisation.

It is a matter of great regret to me that Alistair doesn't want to publish any of his work until he's done with his mainstream career. I can't disagree with him; I know many people who've run into trouble at work as a result of their kinky creative endeavours, and I don't want any friend of mine to be added to that list. But it's such a waste. Because Alistair, I discovered, is absolutely first class at role play. He's not only convincing, but manages to be funny, scary, pompous, domineering, apologetic, or whatever the story requires. Also Cockney, or French, or German, or frightfully posh. Never, before or since, have I met another spanking role player who's prepared to throw themselves so far into a character that they'll actually do accents. It was a joy. I think we filmed forty-five minutes of dialogue before we even got to the spanking.

Improvisation was what I'd spent my childhood doing with Immi. It was what I'd spent my years at drama school enjoying. And to find an amateur photographer who could match me for argumentativeness, imagination, sheer disagreeableness and absurd behaviour, all while gradually manoeuvring my character into a situation where she'd eventually have to accept a spanking, was delightful. My respect for him as a co-performer grew as the day progressed; he was an excellent Top – accurate, careful, and good at calibrating severity. I soon realised I could trust him with any implement he wanted to use. He could gradually increase intensity, judging my reactions flawlessly as he did so. He never marked me more than we'd agreed, even when, later in our working relationship, we progressed to severe, extended canings, the hardest that I'd shot in my entire career.

Perhaps it is unusual, but for me, the way in which BDSM reveals a person's character makes it a wonderful way of accelerating friendship. As a sub, it's hard to hide your real self when you're in so much pain that you're crying and shaking, when you're no longer quite sure what's real and what's part of the role play, and when you begin to feel as though the Top has your actual life in their hands. Similarly, if you as a dominant, deep down, don't like or respect the person you're Topping, I don't believe that it's possible to hide it in an intense scene. If you're a selfish player who's disinterested in your co-player's experience, there's no way to hide it when you're playing hard and deeply submerged in a role play. I liked the person that Alistair revealed himself to be during our shoots very much. It's strange that making videos in which at least one participant was completely unreasonable, unkind and manipulative toward the other can forge the beginning of such a warm, equal and intimate friendship. But that is exactly what it did.

Alistair soon became one of my favourite people to work with, and to date we've been friends for fourteen years. We've talked about everything in our personal lives. We've been away together on multi-day location trips, and I invited him to my fortieth birthday party. It's the sort of friendship I never anticipated when I started working in this business, and if I was still a Christian, I'd say I felt blessed. As it is, I just feel grateful and lucky that I've had the good fortune to meet him.

We've shot a wide variety of scenes, all of which I have loved. He's been generous at allowing me to bring my fantasises to his shoots too, so our work is a true collaboration which represents both of our sexual identities. I hope that one day the spanking world will get to see some of it. It is some of the work that I'm proudest of. Consequently, I was at a loss as to which specific shoot to share with you, but then I remembered my absolute favourite.

Alistair and I were staying in a beautiful old tower, rather like a lighthouse. It was furnished in a timeless style, and so it fitted a wide variety of potential story-lines. The main reason we were there was to shoot a long, multi-scene movie about a Victorian psychologist (Alistair) who has been engaged to treat the wife (me) of an acquaintance who'd reported that she is frigid and unobliging as a companion. Now that I look at it, I see that it has some similarities with *The Taming of the Shrew*, and is, naturally, absurd. You can't fix people's wives by terrorising and caning them. And even if you could, you shouldn't. However, this was the story that we wanted to tell, so we were shooting it over multiple days.

Both he and I are quite emotionally sensitive, and Alistair, by the end of day two, was beginning to feel guilty about his character's indefensible behaviour. I, knowing how unhappy playing any kind of aggressor makes me feel, was entirely sympathetic. We had the whole evening, so it seemed a good idea to shoot an entirely different storyline, one where Alistair could be unequivocally in the right, and entirely justified in his actions. We both liked military storylines, and I'd had an idea that I thought he'd be perfect for.

Ever since playing Ariel in *The Tempest*, I'd enjoyed reading military memoirs. They were sometimes hot, but I also found them motivating. It's easy to get caught up in the challenges of your own career, and there's nothing like reading the experiences of someone who's definitely dealt with far more than you in the line of duty to contextualise your own hardships. Sometimes, if I'm struggling to get through a challenging shoot, I imagine what a Special Forces soldier would think of it, and what they'd make of my effort. It's a technique that's got me through a lot of freezing-cold art nude shoots, as well as some spanking shoots with less-than-ideal co-performers.

So my idea was for Alistair to play that sort of military hero. The type who'd been through real interrogation and torture. Since Alistair's a Switch, it was fun to give him roles where he can use his experience as a Bottom to add complexity to his Top characters. At the point at which our story started, his character would be semi-retired and employed as some kind of civilian discipline consultant for the armed forces, brought in when they wanted to deal with problems unofficially.

Of course, this wasn't realistic. But part of the pleasure of BDSM stories is that they don't have to be plausible enough for an unkindly inclined critic to accept. They just need to convince the participants in the moment, so that they can give an emotionally committed performance.

We decided my character was in trouble for publishing a highly controversial, anonymous blog, exposing bullying within her regiment. She'd been found out, and her blog had been deemed to breach the confidentiality clause in her contract, for which she could be discharged from the army altogether, and prosecuted. However, we agreed that my character should be sufficiently valuable to the army that they preferred to retain her.

Furthermore, her blog had drawn the high-ranking officers' attention to a real problem that they acknowledged
should have been addressed, so they were disposed
towards being lenient with her. Which meant that disciplinary action should be kept private and unofficial.

Alistair and I fleshed out this story while having tea
in front of the fire in our tower. We both liked it, since
it gave the rare opportunity for both of us to feel as
though we were in the right, but to also feel regret for
our actions. That seemed sufficiently mind-bending for
us – we liked complicated characters who could be
pulled in multiple directions emotionally as the scene
progressed. It meant that neither of us would be able to
predict where the scene would end up going, which is
one of the primary delights of good improvisation. And
to add to the drama, we decided that my character
would recognise his as one of her heroes. Perhaps she'd
even read some of his books.

Alistair set up the cameras and microphones; we
planned to shoot in one rolling take to allow for maximum emotional intensity. I got changed into a satin
pencil skirt, blouse and black stockings, which is what,
in spanking-porn world, off-duty soldiers wear when
they're sent to meet mysterious strangers for unspeci-
fied disciplinary procedures. Of course.

Segueing from being friends into our roles is always
potentially difficult, so we normally create the separ-
ation between the two by one of us leaving the room
and coming in again. This time, that clearly needed to
be me. So I went out, shut the door and knocked.

'Come in!' barked Alistair, sounding most unlike
himself.

I entered. He was standing, facing the fireplace. I couldn't see his expression. I approached, hesitantly. And when I was close enough to be standing on the same hearth rug, he turned around.

I gasped, recognising the military hero from the author's photo on my favourite inspirational book. And I couldn't help smiling in pure fangirl delight, before remembering that I was here because I was in dreadful, potentially career-ending trouble. And then I noticed the way that he was looking at me. My hero was staring at me with something close to disgust, as though I was a traitor.

Before I realised, my eyes had filled with tears. I blinked them away. If he already thought I was a traitor, I at least didn't want him to think I was a cowardly one. In under thirty seconds, Alistair had made me believe the entire story. I hoped I could make him believe it too.

Alistair's character explained that my one disciplinary option as an alternative to court martial was to submit to a judicial caning. My character was shocked, having had no idea such a thing was even a remote possibility. Alistair's character recommended that I accept the court martial. He explained that the caning would have to be severe enough to leave lasting marks, so as to appease the senior officers. And as a past recipient of such treatment himself, he thought it too unpleasant for me to choose. I, having expected to see the end of my military career, grasped at the faint hope that I might be able to get through the caning and rescue my future, while atoning for an act I had begun to regret.

As was our habit, the preamble to the caning itself was extended. It gave us both time to begin to sink deeper into our characters. I'm sure this type of play wouldn't be for everyone, but for both Alistair and me it was part of the pleasure. Not least, for me, because it gives me time to distance myself sufficiently from my real self so that I can experience things like canings as though I'm feeling them for the first time. Recapturing first-timer's magic is worth it, but making myself feel unprepared, ironically, takes a lot of preparation.

While being uncompromising, Alistair's character was as kind and respectful as the scenario allowed for. He turned his back as I raised my skirt in the way that he'd directed, and only turned round again when I'd lowered my panties and taken the position he'd also chosen for me, bending over with my palms resting on the fireplace and my feet apart. He even gave me words of advice. He told me that if it was unbearable, I could call a halt and revert to the court martial. He told me that he'd pace the strokes to give me time to recover a little between each. And he warned me again that the strokes were, of necessity, going to be very hard.

It was excellent acting. I picked up on his reluctance to do this to a woman. It made me determined to make it easy for him by being brave. And it made me scared; the reiteration of his promise that the caning would be severe ensured that my hands were shaking a little as I gripped the fireplace, determined not to let go, and not to scream.

The strokes *were* hard. Alistair is fantastically accurate; I suspect that playing racquet sports is excellent training for using spanking implements well. And his accuracy ensures that he can afford to play hard, safe in the knowledge that the cane won't hit the wrong place and cut me. This knowledge helps me to relax, stop worrying from a professional model's perspective, and to simply process the pain.

I don't know how long the caning was. I was already well into an altered mental state as a result of the role play, and the additional pain, when it came, took all my energy to process. There was no room left for analysis, but I do remember it ending. I was still standing, though now the shaking in my hands had spread to all of me. My eyes were dry, and I was breathing in shallow gasps. Alistair was behind me. Briefly, his hand squeezed my shoulder. 'That's enough. You did well. And that's what I'll say in my report.' As is often the case, the kindness affected me in a way that the severity of the caning had not. Feeling the full humiliation of having been punished by someone I looked up to, and now being in need of his comfort, made my eyes start watering again. I took my time to adjust my clothing before I turned around and tried to meet his eyes.

When he dismissed me, I felt like fainting with relief, then left the room and came back in, immediately not upset at all anymore, but elated, and full of things I wanted to discuss. Alistair was himself again, my talented, imaginative, empathetic friend, and one of the people I trusted the most with my body and my emotions. We hugged, drank more tea, and talked about our favourite bits of the scene. I told him about all the things he'd done that had been unexpected, and clever, and hot. He responded by being very kind about *my* performance. We behaved like ridiculous movie stars at a press conference, praising each other excessively, on a post-performance high that, blessedly, we didn't record. So no one need ever know, except that I just told you.

'You were so brave.'

'*You* were so brave! *So brave.*'

'Was that stroke too low?'

'It was perfection! Poetic!'

'Your diction, though. A triumph!'

'Your posture; a revelation!'

It may sound like an awfully odd way to spend time with a friend. We'd spent most of the day pretending to hate each other, and for a break during the evening, we'd pretended to be strangers. But it's such a treat, and I feel as though every hour I spend doing melodramatic role play with friends counts like twenty-four hours spent together doing anything else. It's a privilege to be trusted with another person's fantasies, and to feel safe to share your own.

I will never take these friendships for granted, especially when I think back to my ashamed sixteen-year-old self, who believed that she'd never be able to admit the subject of her fantasies to anyone. Now I can share everything with my friends, and the more I do it, the less shame I feel.

And, dear Mr Lewis, *that's* the kind of scenario I was saving calling someone 'sir' for. So perhaps you can see why I was unwilling. Love from, your best gymnast and worst basketball player.

Chapter Twenty-five

Drago and the Sex-Talk Masterclass

Working with Alistair became comfortable and easy. Having worked together for years, our shoots felt the way meeting a friend for a regular game of golf probably feels. You know each other, understand each other's game, and can switch between being friends and being competitors with no effort at all. (I don't know why I chose golf as an analogy; I've never played. Sorry, dear golfers, your hobby is probably very much like caning, but my opinion may not be trustworthy.) The fact that shoots with Alistair were both physically and emotionally demanding did nothing to change the fact that they also felt very little like work. They felt like friendship, and they felt safe. But the fetish world will not see what we shot together for many years, and my desire to help produce BDSM movies that people can enjoy right *now* compelled me to keep looking for collaborators.

BDSM, even something as formal as caning, can be done in many different ways, to the extent that it can feel like an entirely different activity depending upon the scene. But until I met Drago, I didn't really know that.

The first time I worked with him, I was doing a studio day. I'd been hired by the studio owner, who then sublet me to individual photographers for short shoots. Drago simply booked three hours at the beginning of my day. His email before the shoot briefed me that he was hoping to shoot some BDSM-themed images with an emphasis on implied corporal punishment. Feeling that even fake spanking was better than no spanking, I took the booking. In person, Drago was a cheerful, athletic-looking man, wearing unusually stylish clothing for a photographer, many of whom dress identically in uninspired black combat gear. He was, I guessed, somewhere in his mid-forties, and he seemed possessed of exceptional patience – forty-five minutes of the shoot had gone by before the makeup artist had finished unpacking her kit. This made me nervous. Many photographers don't feel as though their models are really working until they start posing, so I prefer makeup artists to be quick in order to allow me to feel that I'm giving the photographer value for money. Drago seemed unworried, and remained calm and friendly. After an hour and a half of hair and makeup styling, we eventually only had around forty-five minutes in which to actually shoot. It was a rushed affair, and it left me feeling regretful. He'd been a pleasure to talk to, but with the studio owner and vanilla makeup artist in attendance, I hadn't had much opportunity to find out anything about him, or about why he was shooting spanking-themed pictures. I thought that I'd like him, given the opportunity. He was courteous, intelligent and funny. I assumed he was dominant too, and having finally reached a point in my life where I didn't feel

any sense of shame about being kinky, I always regretted missed opportunities to get to know other kinky
people.

As it turned out, I did get to know him. He booked me
again, this time at a more private studio, and with no
makeup artist in attendance, since his editing was excellent and I'm competent to do my own makeup as long as
it's not meant to be wildly avant-garde. This time, Drago
was hoping to make my bottom look as though I'd just
been caned, and his plan was to use lipstick to make the
marks. I wasn't sure how effective this would be – real
cane marks are raised welts, not just red lines. I felt comfortable with Drago, and we didn't have anyone watching
us disapprovingly, so I suggested maybe doing the cane
strokes for real instead.

I hadn't really thought it out. Up to that point, I'd
only ever done caning either in private with play partners, or at video shoots, where acting was required.
Doing caning on its own, out of context and simply to
create the right visual effect, was surprisingly difficult.
Since I didn't need to project the idea of being in unbearable pain for a video shoot, and because I didn't want
to distract Drago, I decided the best course of action
was to not react at all, and let him concentrate on getting the right level of marking for the pictures. As
though I was a canvas, I thought. But my attempt to
distance myself from what he was doing seemed to
worry Drago. He does not, as a rule, travel around the
country caning totally silent models. This was usually
part of his sex life, as it was mine, and during canings,
presumably his sexual partner didn't try to ignore the
entire thing. I hope so, for his sake. Being ignored is

awful, especially when you're trying to be sexy; I have
expertise in this matter, friends.

After a few fairly light strokes of the cane, he asked,
tentatively, 'Are you okay?' and I realised that my silence
was probably rather eerie.

'Oh yes, I love it!' I enthused, sounding both hysterical and artificial, since the effort of not screaming had
been considerable, and I was feeling a bit wobbly. 'It's
just that normally, I'm either doing this for videos or for
sex. So I'm not sure how to react.'

In any case, the marks were super, definitely more
convincing than lipstick, and we were able to shoot our
stills, which turned out beautifully. However, the conversation had made Drago think about shooting videos
of his own, or perhaps we'd have ended up there anyway. Which brings me onto the story of our next shoot,
where everything became considerably more interesting, and unexpectedly educational.

It was December, and Drago had booked us rooms in
a lovely country-house hotel in Shropshire, with the
intention of doing a shoot split over two days. The first
part would be shot in artificial light at night, the second
part shot the next morning, utilising natural light. And
this time, as well as taking stills, Drago was planning to
make a video. The vast majority of my spanking work
has been in the form of improvised, dialogue-based,
punishment spankings. I generally play unwilling, vanilla characters who don't want to be spanked, are
incredulous and indignant about the whole thing, and
who tend to be quite hostile towards the person doing
the spanking. Drago wanted the opposite: a dreamy,
consensual-looking spanking movie, with minimal

dialogue, an emphasis on pleasure, and an implied sexual relationship between the two characters.

That probably doesn't sound particularly difficult. After all, I was a professional actress, had shot several sex scenes as part of mainstream productions, and was (obviously) a big fan of spanking. But the sense of potential emotional exposure was considerable, and outside Drago's hotel room door (ominously named 'The Boardroom') I had a moment of performance anxiety. I didn't know if I'd be too embarrassed to act the way I would in private. Pretending to hate being spanked had always been a useful emotional refuge, a barrier between my work and my private self. I was concerned that breaking that barrier down would feel unbearably intrusive.

But I'd agreed to the shoot, I liked Drago, and I knew it was the sort of film that I'd enjoy watching myself. I decided that by acting as though I was comfortable with doing something that felt so personal, I'd be able to *become* comfortable with it. It had worked for me at drama school when we'd done nudity classes, crying-technique classes, mimed being parts of heavy machinery, and pretended to mate like animals. Surely acting like I was enjoying a spanking wouldn't be harder than all of that. So I knocked on his door.

The room was gorgeous, panelled in dark wood with a four-poster bed and a separate sitting room with masculine leather furniture, like a library. Formal, old-fashioned, expensive-looking. Perfect for a spanking story. As, in all honesty, was Drago. Tonight, he was dressed formally, and looking exactly like the authoritative, sophisticated romantic lead that he was going to be playing. Drago's clothes really are the best.

Naturally, all this made me feel awkward and nervous, so I began to gabble about everything except spanking. 'Ooh, look at the walls! Did you have a good journey? I almost burned the carpet with my curling tongs! What time are you going to have breakfast? How's work? Which lingerie do you prefer? Ha ha, what a funny picture! Ooh, look at the walls!'

Drago, wisely, ignored all of this, and started to explain the story of the movie. I was going to enter the frame first, while removing my dressing gown and, dressed in nothing but lacy lingerie, stockings and suspenders, I'd kneel on a chair as though waiting. In front of me on the window sill lay an array of implements. As always, the cane caught my attention. It was the most severe of his collection, and I knew that however romantic and consensual the storyline, the pain it would cause would be real. Trying to get into the headspace of someone about to be spanked by their lover, rather than by a relative stranger, I was impatient to start, if only to prove to myself that we could do it without hideous awkwardness. Whoever I'm working with, I want them to have a good time, and this only applies more when I'm working in my favourite genre. Most of us don't get to do quite as much BDSM as we'd like to, so every opportunity is a privilege. I wanted to make a good film, but I also wanted Drago to feel comfortable, and to have fun.

Having set up his cameras on tripods and lit the scene to his satisfaction, Drago was ready to join me on-screen. 'I wonder,' he asked, cautiously, 'if you're okay with us role playing some dialogue?' That was what I'd expected – I knew we weren't making a silent movie, and our previous experience of shooting stills together had highlighted the fact that doing spanking in silence felt very artificial indeed. 'Of course!' I replied.

'Is there anything you'd prefer me not to say to you?' he asked. And in doing so, increased my respect for him. Most don't ask, and some Bottoms can react very badly to some words. I didn't think I was one of them, but hugely appreciated his thoughtfulness. I'd not thought about it for a long time, so I quickly leafed through my mental filing cabinet, trying to think of spanking scenes I'd not enjoyed.

'Just don't call me stupid,' I eventually replied, 'or ugly. Please don't say I'm ugly.'

Drago looked surprised – he wasn't planning that kind of scene at all. But I hoped that by telling him a couple of things I wouldn't be okay with, he'd feel more confident that anything else he said would be fine with me.

We were ready to start, and suddenly, I wondered why I'd agreed to do a movie with someone with no perform-ance experience that I knew of. Acting isn't for everyone, and Drago had, up to this point, seemed quite emotionally reserved, very correct and not especially keen on giving away information about himself. Rather like Colin Firth playing Mr Darcy in *Pride and Prejudice*. I couldn't imagine Colin Firth in a BDSM scene. I imagined Drago was going to confine himself to lines like 'I'm going to cane you now. Bend over and touch your toes.' And some-how, the sense of romance and the feeling of sexuality would have to come from my responses. I tried not to dwell on how odd it would be if he behaved like a stiff-upper-lipped headmaster while I moaned with pleasure and made sex noises. But there wasn't room for worrying about how the final edit would look; I just had to do my best to work with whatever performance Drago was capable of producing.

As a result, the on-screen Top version of Drago that I met that evening knocked my socks off. (Not actual socks. I'm using that as a euphemism for 'the version of Drago that I met that evening was fantastically hot and not at all like Colin Firth'.) Arriving in the frame behind me as I remained kneeling in the chair, one of his hands found its way into my hair, as his other hand caressed my bottom. 'Who,' he began quietly, in a seductive, caressing voice I'd never heard before, 'is your master?'

This was unexpected. But thankfully, it was a world with which I was familiar. 'You are, sir,' I replied, hesitantly. Was that what he wanted me to call him? I should have checked before we started recording. We were trying to start the story *in media res*. My character would know what to call him; these would be things they'd have said to each other many times before. They'd already be comfortable with each other. We needed to be too.

I arched my back, pushing my bottom against his hand, as though wanting more of his touch. I *did* want more. The magic of acting is not convincing an audience of the truth of your situation, it's convincing yourself. And Drago was doing a fine job of making that very easy to do.

'And who,' he continued, in that silky, seductive tone, 'is my slave?'

That word. I should be bored with it by now. It should have lost its erotic power over me through being used at shoots. But in this dimly lit, wood-panelled room, it made me gasp. Could I reply to that? For me, in BDSM, words can be even more powerful than actions. You can switch your mind off to escape from pain; you can't escape from language. But this was a consensual scenario; my character would reply to his. So: 'I am, sir,' I responded.

And so it continued, with the dreamy, liturgical style of call-and-response; his questions, my replies. All the while, his right hand was on my bottom, caressing me through the silk and lace of my underwear. And far from worrying about the spanking, I started to crave it, the way my character would. When it came – Drago pinning me in place with his left arm as his right hand connected over and over again with my bottom – it felt heavenly. It couldn't have been easier to shake off all my customary indignant and incredulous responses. All I had to do was experience the spanking like the submissive masochist that I was. It was easy to moan, to arch my back, to find my breath quickening and my body responding. My character and I were one, united in our desire to please Drago and *his* character, and to make them want to go further.

Which he did. Pulling me up from the chair where I'd been kneeling, he guided me over to the four-poster bed, where he positioned me on my knees, with my legs apart, bottom high in the air, my face pressed against the counterpane. It didn't feel like a spanking position. It felt like a sex position.

I trusted him. He wasn't going to do anything to me that we'd not discussed and agreed to. And his intentions were perfectly clear. He had the cane in his hand.

Many years before, when I was a worried teenager who thought she might be a masochist, I'd asked my sister what a masochist actually was. She replied that it was a person who experiences pain as pleasure. That may be true, but it isn't a reflection of how it feels to me. I experienced the first cane stroke as definite pain. But behind the pain raced pleasure, trying to catch up, to fill me with euphoria, even as the first line across my bottom burned and throbbed. In Drago's story, I was meant to enjoy it. I did.

Each stroke hurt. Each one took me higher. I probably screamed into the counterpane. I know that I reached back at one point, the instinct to protect myself being hard to fight. Drago grabbed my wrist, twisted it behind my back and held it there. And each time a stroke stung me into trying to rise up from the bed, he guided me back down into my original position. That night I learned that, on-screen, he would never allow any deviation from the position he'd chosen for me. It was strangely comforting to know that nothing I did would change the course of the caning. You can't submit if there's nothing tangible to submit *to*, but I submitted to the caning and to the exacting position, and each enhanced the other.

Eventually, the caning was over. It wasn't enough; it almost never is. I rely on the sanity of the people I work with – I can't see the marks on my own body, and my perception of pain is an unreliable indicator for physical damage. So he was right to stop, and given that in the story, the entire spanking scene was just a preamble to a whole night of excellent sex, I figured that my character would be satisfied with the amount of action she'd enjoyed. What we were not done with, however, was the Drago Bee Masterclass in specialist dirty talk.

'Say thank you for your punishment,' he breathed, in that gentle voice that allowed for no argument at all.

'Thank you for my punishment, sir,' I responded, speech, as always, feeling far more difficult than it had before the spanking. My voice seemed to be coming from far off, faint and quiet. 'Thank you for caning me, sir,' I continued at his direction. 'Thank you for dominating me, sir.' This was embarrassingly hot; on some level I feel that a professional spanking model should be over finding simply saying *words* associated with spanking overwhelmingly erotic, but apparently I was not. This was an entirely new experience, and later I wondered if I'd even have needed the spanking in order to find myself in this state of hazy, disoriented subspace. His use of language was the absolute best. Better even than his clothes.

'Say thank you for making me your bitch,' Drago concluded. I, naively, hadn't seen that particular sentence coming. I hesitated, unsure whether either I *or* my character could volunteer such unequivocal submission. Drago made it easier: 'Or I can resume the caning?' Undoubtedly, he could. And much as I wanted him to, I felt it wouldn't have fitted the story. Clearly, the characters were transitioning from foreplay towards actual sex, and my character was perhaps not quite so masochistic as I was. Possibly she found talking less difficult, also.

So. 'Thank you for making me your bitch, sir,' I said, with a reluctance that was confusingly both feigned and real. I didn't want to say that out loud. It was fabulous to say it out loud. My mind couldn't untangle my feelings. I felt as though I was drifting into a half-waking fog. The pain hadn't done that on its own. It was the scenario, the feeling of entirely voluntary submission. It felt extraordinary.

Drago stopped the cameras, and became Colin Firth again. 'Are you all right?' he enquired cautiously. 'That wasn't too much? Were you okay with saying all those things?'

At work, I try to deliver the maximum professionalism that I can, to make things as easy as possible for my employers. Professionals shouldn't need aftercare, I felt, and they shouldn't lapse into subspace. I struggled to remember my professional self.

'Of course! I loved it! You were great! You're *very* good at this!' I enthused, truthfully but far too loudly. I couldn't remember what the normal version of me sounded like. Jesus. I wasn't being the real me. I felt as though I'd left the real me in the scene, on the bed. *This* me was the acted version, cheerily offering to retake any shots that hadn't worked, chattering and repacking my suitcase, asking about how he planned to edit the piece. My job is to make shooting intimate-looking things a comfortable, drama-free experience for the producers who hire me. It requires my helping to establish boundaries between on-camera and off-camera behaviour. It had rarely felt so difficult. It was after 11 p.m.; I went to bed in my own room shortly afterwards, still trying to process the emotional intensity of what we'd just filmed, and not quite believing that my job involved getting to do it all again tomorrow. Which we did, and it was a delight.

One of the great privileges of doing my job is that not only do I get the chance to sample other people's versions of BDSM, but I get to join them in their world, and try to figure out what they need from me to help bring their vision to life. I love BDSM, but separately, I love *shooting* BDSM. It's like double submission: submitting within the scene, but also serving the project to the best of my ability. And I quite like submitting; you may have noticed.

I don't know how long I'd need to do this job for to stop feeling bewildered delight at the different ways in which good players do BDSM. Every time I work with someone who does it well, I come away thinking '*This* is the heart of my kink!' It isn't; I love it all. Often, I come home from shoots armed with new ideas that I want to try; my tastes keep expanding, the more skilled Tops and dominants that I meet. I've worked with Drago many times since, and each shoot has been a tremendous pleasure. I get performance anxiety every time, though in truth that might be part of the fun.

I love spanking, and, in the right hands, I like the cane. But as I became a more experienced model, my desire to stretch my mind and body more, to find out what I was capable of when teamed with the right people, only increased. The pleasure of over-the-knee hand spanking and simple bondage has never left me. But I always wonder – is there more? There's always more. And I found it, conveniently, in the very next chapter.

Chapter Twenty-six

Eric Cain, Rhymes with Pain

I'd been driving down the dirt road for about ten minutes when an armadillo ambled out of the shrubbery and in front of my rental car, its body gleaming in the headlights. I stopped and stared in wonder, having never seen such a creature in the wild before. The very last of the sun reflected red into the clouds on the horizon as I watched the armadillo gain the safety of the opposite verge, and then drove on.

I was far from home, but in familiar territory. Eventually, I saw the turning I needed, on the right, down an unmade drive with trees either side. It was entirely dark by now; the silhouette of a workshop loomed to one side of me as I drove on, towards the single-storey house that I knew was there, somewhere. I wasn't sure if I was on the right track. The grass either side of the car was high – was I just driving through the undergrowth, having missed the track entirely? But there was the house, glowing faintly white in the darkness. I turned off the engine and stepped out of the car, and as I bent to grab my bag from the passenger seat, I caught movement in my peripheral vision. I whirled around, and screamed.

My friend Eric was standing about two metres away from me, looking entirely perplexed. Understandably: he'd been expecting me. There was no reason for my having been shocked to see him. And I wasn't, just a little overwhelmed. About my height, but more power-fully built, with big hands and muscular arms, Eric looked a little threatening even when he was smiling, which he was. He was also carrying a glass mason jar full of clear liquid. We regarded each other, both equally puzzled.

Why is she screaming?

Is that chloroform?

'I'm making moon water,' announced Eric, by way of explanation. This should not have surprised me. He lives in an endearingly offbeat way, in the middle of nowhere with a determinedly affectionate rescued pit bull called Cooter, surrounded by vintage trucks that he's in the process of fixing, and trying to live in an eco-friendly, non-dairy-consuming, ethical and health-conscious fash-ion. He always makes me feel hopelessly conventional. I'd brought cows' milk with me. I wondered if he'd let me keep it in his fridge.

'I didn't see you,' I explained superfluously, in explan-ation of my bizarre screaming attack. Eric didn't deserve to be screamed at. He was my friend, had invited me to stay for five days, and had never given me a moment's reason to be scared of him.

Except, I suppose, that Eric singlehandedly produces the most intensely ambitious, sadistic BDSM movies that I've ever seen, let alone worked on. Of all the people I shoot with, he is the producer that the largest number of women want to talk to me about, and I've lost count of the number of photographers who've told me that they want their work to be like his.

I'd first worked with him in 2016. Because of the intensity of his shooting style (he films everything on his own, in one rolling take with nine cameras recording the non-stop action) he'd only booked me for a single hour, on two consecutive days. I'd hardly had time to speak to him, but what I *had* found out about him, I'd liked very much. He seemed calm, which I appreciated, and exhibited a complete lack of the boastfulness and insecurity I'd often encountered in dominants during my career. ('I've actually got a lot of money, did you know? And my dick is *really big*. And I can make you orgasm by just looking at you. Also, EVERYONE LIKES ME.') The two short shoots had been a pleasure, and I noticed that he'd paid attention to my responses during the first shoot, and adjusted what we shot in the second one to reflect my abilities and tolerance. This seemed both sophisticated and considerate of him, and I'd wanted to return. But there was something else too.

I'd had very few opportunities to shoot anything as comprehensively sadomasochistic as Eric's work during my career in Europe. Most of the companies who shot anything similar were also shooting hardcore porn, which I wasn't interested in doing. And although I'd done plenty of challenging shoots, few people were trying to shoot so many BDSM elements all at once. Spanking, of course. Nipple play, absolutely. Bondage and gags, naturally. But all together, at once, and taken to their extreme – not really. And what I *had* done of it had sometimes confused and troubled me a little.

Occasionally, I drove away from those shoots feeling unhappy, and I didn't know why.

The difference that I'd first noticed during my second hour-long shoot with Eric was the emotional tempera- ture of the entire experience. I didn't remember much about the detail of what we'd shot; it was challenging and painful and my memories of shoots of that type tend to be fractured. But I remembered this: the second that he'd got the footage he needed, he'd taken a knife from his belt and cut the ropes off me. I was free from the entire rig within thirty seconds. And then, immedi- ately, he'd put his arms around me. Not in a seductive way, but in a manner that felt comforting, kind and, most of all, friendly. I was shaking from the adrenaline/ endorphin cocktail that had flooded my system from the demanding shoot, and the feeling of emotional warmth from an almost total stranger was a welcome surprise. It made me feel as though we were collabora- tors, not adversaries. Which is how it should feel, because that is the truth of BDSM. I liked Eric's version of it, and I'd wanted to come back.

My chance to do so hadn't come until 2018. This time we'd been commissioned to shoot four movies for customers with specific storylines, and Eric had invited me to stay with him. It had been a lovely visit during which I'd spent a lot of time cuddling Cooter the dog, but I'd struggled to raise my game to meet the require- ments of his work. With the additional pressure of our customers' requests, we couldn't easily adjust the story- line to my on-the-day tolerance of each element, and I'd overestimated some of my abilities. Having thought my gag reflex was under control, I'd nevertheless choked on a giant cock gag, temporarily safe-worded over some severe nipple clamps, and lapsed into a semi-conscious state at the end of our final movie as a result of the intensity of the bondage. Now, later that same year, I was back, and I wanted to do a better, more professional job for one of the producers I liked and respected the most.

The customers who'd commissioned the earlier movies had done so again, which reassured me that we must have done at least some of what they'd hoped for in the previous attempt. Their trust in us to do a good job made me even more determined to do better this time around. And added to that, we had some new customers with stories they wanted us to make into movies. We had four days of shooting, and five films to make.

Because of working alone, setup time for Eric was considerable. Everything needed to be ready on set because all of the bondage positions were ambitious, and it'd be a struggle to sustain them for the length of the movies we were making. However hard I tried, I wouldn't be capable of staying tied up while we took breaks from shooting for Eric to set up equipment, read the script, or find items he'd not put aside for use. So for each hour-long movie, Eric was spending around five hours on the setup alone. I couldn't help with it, so during the daytimes of the first three days, I shot with other producers, returning to Eric's house in the evening to shoot each movie that he'd prepared for.

On the first evening, Eric tied me in a standing spread-eagle for a mammoth neck-roped, ballgagged, belt-whipping scene.

On the second evening, tied in an almost identical

position for an almost identical belt-whipping (but this time wearing sheer pantyhose and weighted nipple clamps), I played an undercover detective captured by the sex trafficker she was trying to track down. It had been intense, overwhelmingly painful, and had left my bottom so bruised that I'd had to sleep face down. This had in turn made my bruised nipples hurt so much that they woke me up in the middle of the night.

On the third evening, we shot a tight box tie/hogtie combination with foot torture and, again, nipple clamps. That night, as I lay in bed listening to a train pass by in the distance while creatures howled in the dark, I wondered how I was going to manage the fourth day. It was our last, we had two movies to make, and to add to the pressure, the customer for the first of the two movies was a personal friend. Busby Wilder, the friend in question, had visited Hywel and me at our house in Wales on multiple occasions, and I'd stayed with him in the USA numerous times too. He was a lovely man who'd started exploring BDSM relatively late in life, and had boundless energy and imagination. In him, I saw the life I might have had if I'd not had the internet to propel me into the bondage world during early adult-hood, and I felt grateful that I'd had a chance to take part in it during my twenties, rather than having to wait until I was in my sixties. I wanted Busby to have the best BDSM experiences possible, whether as a partici-pant or as a commissioning customer. He'd written a beautiful script idea, in which he wanted Eric and me to do a BDSM session with an emphasis on consent and willing submission. I loved him, and I wanted to do the best possible job, especially since it had been his story that we'd cut a little short earlier that year when my endurance had failed.

I wanted to do the best possible job for Eric too. While enjoying our non-shoot time together, he proved to be a kind, honest, highly entertaining and thoughtful individual. During a series of increasingly over-tired and hysterical late-night conversations over the week, we'd done an excessive amount of laughing about a wide and peculiar range of topics, including mortgages, erotic fiction, knitting patterns, my ridiculous stage-combat scripts, 1980s hair bands, lawn mowers and reincarnation. And during our shoots, he had relent-lessly, incrementally, carefully and safely, taken me to the absolute edges of my BDSM endurance for three days in a row, and had made movies with me that I'd be forever proud of. Now my body was bruised, my cour-age was failing, and, lying in the dark, I didn't know how I was going to get through two more movies, let alone do the good job that his skill deserved.

I don't mean to be unduly modest. I know that I'm an experienced, bendy, professional model and a trained actor. Generally, I feel that I can bring value to all my shoots; it's not like I go around tediously insisting that I'm not worthy all the time. But with the thoroughness of the bondage I was shooting with Eric came a profes-sional disadvantage that I didn't know how to manage. When I was tied up so tightly that I *couldn't* move, my ability to pose was taken from me. I couldn't do a good technical job of finding attractive positions when I was stuck in precisely one position, which I hadn't even chosen for myself. And all the verbal dexterity in the world was of no use when I was going to be gagged for the entire film. So I couldn't add value that way either. I wasn't even meant to be playing a character; Busby didn't *want* me to be a resourceful, courageous, resistant heroine. He wanted to see me submit. I was worried that I'd be boring. I was afraid that I wouldn't give Eric anything to work with. And I was desperately frightened that I wouldn't be able to endure the pain. Carefully, I gently pinched one of my nipples, imagining a clamp being applied. They were horribly bruised. And there was an extended belt-whipping scene in Busby's film too, the third of the week. Every customer would prefer their chosen model to start each scene with no bruises, but since every shoot with Eric always marked me, we'd scheduled our movies to end with the most severe in order to make me look as unscathed as possible for as long as we could. I reached back and touched my bottom. It throbbed. I couldn't imagine how I'd cope with a belt landing again and again on the same bruised flesh. I didn't want to safe-word. I didn't want to pass out. And I didn't want to disappoint Eric.

I lay there, worrying and trying to find a solution, as it got light. At 8 a.m., Eric got up and went over to the studio to prepare. I did my hair and makeup, and dressed in loose clothes that wouldn't mark my body. At 9 a.m., I was ready, but there was a lot of preparation to be done, and I couldn't help with it. So I worked out for a while, trying to stretch every conceivable muscle in the hope that by being physically prepared, I'd be able to endure the bondage positions better. Then it was 10.30 a.m. Eric returned to the house to pick up more kit, looked at me with kind incredulity as I lay on his floor pointlessly practising the splits, and left for the studio again. I realised that I was struggling to take in whole breaths. I lay on my back and tried unsuccessfully to concentrate on doing a drama-school breathing exercise.

It occurred to me that perhaps the best course of action was to take refuge in playing a character anyway. All my life I've enjoyed pretending to be someone else whenever I feel unequal to any situation. It's a natural and comfortable way to protect the sensitive, inner me from the more difficult aspects of the real world. If I could pretend to be someone braver than myself, and if I could imagine that Eric was someone I neither liked nor respected, it was possible that I could distance myself from the pain. I'd done it before at challenging shoots, and it had sometimes helped immensely.

But I realised I didn't want to cheat Busby, who'd wanted honesty. And I didn't want to cheat Eric, who would, I knew, be putting his considerable physical and mental resources into piloting us through the challenging, action-filled script. I wanted him to have my honesty. It was all that I felt I *could* give him, given that I wouldn't be able to move, speak, or take responsibility for any of the technical aspects of the shoot. If he could operate nine cameras, tie me up in multiple positions securely and safely, hurt me to the limit of my endurance and keep me there for an hour without letting me fail, then I could do the one thing that was being asked of me. Like an adult. Like, specifically, a kinky professional model who was getting to spend the day doing one of her favourite things, even if right now it felt like a very bad idea.

So, I decided, I would stay present. I wouldn't shut

my eyes and mentally retreat, and I would react honestly to everything. I wouldn't safe-word. When it was over, I promised myself, it wouldn't be because I'd asked for it to be over. This time around, I didn't want to be the limiting factor for the success of the shoot. This time, friends, if you can imagine it, I wanted an A grade in submissive masochism.

Having decided on a plan of action, I thought that I felt a little better. I sat up, and then noticed that my hands were shaking. I wished, far too late, that I hadn't read the script – knowing what we were about to shoot was making everything worse. It was 11.45 a.m. I decided that the best thing to do was to knit. I was knitting a simple knit-five purl-five pattern, and I thought I could just about count to five, even in my shaky state. But somehow, I couldn't remember how the stitches worked. I unpicked and reworked the mistakes, wondering how I could possibly have forgotten how to do something I'd been doing since I was eight years old.

I jumped, stupidly, when the front door opened, but managed not to scream. Eric was ready to shoot. We walked over to the studio together, and I fought down an urge to just run away, down the track and into the woods. The studio seemed like a very dangerous place to be walking towards.

'I'm okay doing all of it,' I said suddenly to Eric, worried that my responses were going to alarm him. 'I'm bruised, but it's okay, I just think my reactions might be quite *dramatic*.' Eric looked relatively amused. He deals with screaming, crying models on a regular basis; I probably didn't need to worry about scaring him. Only one of us was a highly strung, hyperventilating

submissive who had temporarily lost her taste for masochism, and it wasn't him.

When we arrived in the studio, the set was already
brightly lit, and I averted my eyes from the table with
BDSM equipment on it. There was no point knowing
the details of which implements Eric was planning to
use; knowing would only make me more scared. But for
God's sake, I thought. I was kinky, I liked doing this
kind of thing. When, I wondered, was my body going to
kindly remember that?

Then I was lying on my back on a table, and Eric was
binding my hands together above my head, in preparation for tying them to a post, which would begin the
task of immobilising me. I tried and failed to stop my
hands shaking. And I concentrated on trying to take
deep breaths. I wanted to start. Surely I couldn't remain
this frightened when I had the immediacy of pain to
manage? Eric tied my feet next, securing them to the
table so that I was stretched out, on my back, dressed in
nothing but a tiny, shiny silver thong, which I suspected
wouldn't make it very far into the movie.

Eric picked up a leather strap. It was a spanking
implement – how could he use that on me when I was
lying face up? I'd barely had time to wonder, when he
swung it down, and it landed across my left breast.
Breast-strapping was new to me. I gasped as the pain of
the impact reached me, but as I did so, the second stroke
landed over my right nipple.

Impact play often, for the first few strokes, feels absolutely intolerable; I feel as though I'm going to vomit
from the sheer pain, and I can't catch my breath. I struggled to control my reactions as more strokes rained

down on my breasts. Eric was pacing them carefully, giving me time to adjust, and this knowledge made me *want* to adjust. This was, after all, only the beginning, the warm-up, and the sooner I could make peace with the sensations, the sooner (I hoped) I'd reach a mental state that would take the panicky edge off my pain and fear. If there was enjoyment to be found, I'd find it once I'd calmed down.

The way I see it, the skill of the best Tops is in their ability to work incrementally. There's nothing sexy to me about someone trying to hurt me as much as they can, as quickly as they can. Anyone can do that, and there's no particular skill in it. Watching Eric's film back in order to write this chapter, I've noticed things that I was in no condition to observe at the time. The pace, for example. The way in which, if my reaction to one stroke was particularly dramatic, Eric placed the next stroke somewhere else while the pain from the first subsided. And when he added the nipple clamps, and attached twine pulled up towards the ceiling to increase the tension on the clamps themselves, he worked carefully and precisely, so that while the pain certainly increased on a steep trajectory, it wasn't beyond what I could bear. It was the feeling that Eric was being careful with me, that he was entirely in control of what he was doing, and wasn't going to hurt me by mistake, that started, finally, to make me glad that we were shooting this scene.

The shoot progressed. Eric added a crotch rope attached to an overhead hoist, then snipped my panties off and added labia clamps, which he tied off to nails he'd driven into the table. The pain climbed steeply upward, seemed to come from everywhere at once, and with it came the beginnings of a sense of peace. I could breathe, Eric's rig was working, and I was a long way from wanting to safe-word. Quite the opposite: I wanted to know what was going to happen next.

Nothing happened next, for quite some time. Between the ropes and the clamps, I was close to being totally immobilised, and the pain from the clamps rose, slowly but inexorably, over the next few minutes. As it did so, I started to feel disoriented as I stopped being able to judge how much time had passed, and ceased to really think clearly at all. It's a wonderful feeling, like a holiday from my own brain. But the pain from the clamps continued to build as the two sides of each one crushed the flesh between.

The problem with clamps of all kinds, wherever they're attached, is that the worst pain comes when they're taken off. I knew this from previous experience, and so when Eric eventually came back from where he'd been adjusting the cameras, and I suspected what he was about to do, I'd probably have tried to stop him if I'd been able to. He removed the labia clamps first. I screamed. Working up my body, he unhitched the crotch rope from the overhead hoist, taking the tension out of it temporarily. 'Thank you,' I murmured through the ballgag. It had been excruciating. And then Eric removed the first of my nipple clamps. The first flare of white-hot pain radiated out from my nipple to instantly encapsulate my whole breast. And before it had even peaked, he removed the second.

The incendiary sensation flooded me. I screamed and thrashed, trying to somehow evade the burning feeling that had settled across my entire chest. My eyes were still shut and I'd not had time to register Eric's left hand reaching around my throat to keep me still, when his open right hand connected hard with the side of my face.

It had been six whole months ago when we'd had a conversation about my ridiculous attempts to incorporate face slapping into all my stage-fight routines back when I was at drama school. And he'd remembered, or maybe he kept notes. He really was extraordinary at this.

He slapped the other side of my face, and then the first. I'd entirely forgotten the pain in my nipples and pussy. I looked up at him, and an angry stranger returned my gaze. My moon-water drinking, dog-rescuing, kindly friend was temporarily absent.

'I loosened your crotch rope. I took *all four* clamps off. And I did not get *one thank you*,' Eric reproached me, slapping my face again.

I was sure I'd said thank you at least once. But actually, being punished unfairly was, if anything, even hotter than if it was entirely justified.

'Thank you!' I gasped. And, since my mind really wasn't functioning very well anymore, and because, however much I liked being slapped, it was still genuinely terrifying when there was no way to stop it, I got kind of stuck, saying 'thank you' over and over again like some kind of breathless, broken robot doll. It was more or less the only thing I said for the rest of the video. Except for swearing; I swore quite a lot.

Eric untied me, retied me with my hands twisted way up behind my back in a reverse-prayer position, then ungagged me. 'Thank you!' I repeated three more times, in the manner of a semi-conscious Stepford Wife. He immediately re-gagged me with the panties he'd removed from my body earlier in the shoot. He retied me face down on the table, and it was in this position, with my feet tied to a vertical post, and my hands so far out of commission that I couldn't begin to use them to protect myself, that he began the extended spanking and belt-whipping sequence that I'd known was in the schedule.

Years before, I'd read an erotic short story about a woman sentenced to being strapped every day. In the book it had been described as mind-bendingly awful, and I'd been sceptical. Obviously, being hit on top of existing bruising would *hurt*, but I didn't see why it'd be that much worse.

Now I saw. All the tolerance I'd built up over my years as a spanking model seemed to have been washed away. Strokes landed over bruising, in burning agony, and I had no way of escape. With unrestrained spanking scenes (and the vast majority of them *are* unrestrained) I'm always in control of the pace to some extent. If I move out of position, the Top waits until I'm back in place. If I reach back, the Top has to either wait, or take the time to reposition my hand out of the way again. But, entirely immobilised as I was, I had no control over any of it, and the pace was fast. I screamed and screamed through the panty-gag, and as I'd promised myself, my reactions were honest, because my mind was auto-piloting. I couldn't think about anything but the pain.

Eric had directed me to keep my face away from him, towards the cameras. I'd done so for most of the spanking. But my thoughts were unravelling; I was only aware

of the overwhelming pain, and my own desire for comfort. I felt lost and exposed and lonely, and craved
physical contact. I couldn't move towards Eric; all I
could do was turn my head in his direction. As a substi-
tute for a hug it was a poor one, but I wasn't thinking
at all. I turned my face towards him.

Eric noticed it immediately. 'Didn't I tell you to
keep your head facing *that* way?' He grasped my head
and turned me back to look towards the cameras. He
had told me that. I'd forgotten because my instincts
were taking over from my conscious thinking brain, the
one that remembered things like professionalism, and
cameras, and movie-making. But the spanking continued, and my brain didn't switch back on. I seemed to
be made up entirely of feelings. It was frightening, and
it was wonderful.

When he finally stopped spanking me, Eric added a
rope behind the back of my neck and pulled me up into
an arched position, so that my nipples were clear of the
table. I guessed that nipple clamps were going to make
a reappearance. My nipples were throbbing in time
with my heartbeat; the idea of more clamps seemed
utterly impossible, but first, Eric was ungagging me
again. Then, from a table, he produced the giant cock
gag. At least ten centimetres long, it was the one that I'd
choked on during my last visit. I'd been so disappointed
that I'd spent the last six months making a video diary
about learning to control my gag reflex, and I thought
that I'd maybe achieved it. I'd not tried it on while tied,
though, and I was suspicious that panic might make me
choke again. Time seemed to suddenly be moving very
slowly. Eric held the gag in front of my face; I opened

my mouth. And he pushed it right to the back of my throat, before retracting it and slamming it back in repeatedly. I started to gag on it, my eyes beginning to tear up. And he thrust it down my throat one more time before fastening the strap behind my head, keeping the silicone protrusion lodged deep, where my body could not eject it.

I continued to gag for a few seconds, before successfully pushing down my rising panic and remembering that by breathing shallowly, I could easily keep getting air. And, realising that I'd stopped gagging, I felt blessed, grateful relief. I might not get an A grade for this production, but I was better at it than I'd been six months ago.

There wasn't much time to enjoy the sense of achievement. Eric added hooks in my nostrils, which he attached via elastic bands to the back of my head. These distorted my face and hurt immensely. But I nearly forgot about them altogether when he re-clamped my nipples and tied them to a nail he'd driven into the table in front of me, before a few minutes later, removing the giant cock gag and attaching another clamp to my tongue and securing it, with twine, to the same nail. Pain seemed to be radiating from all the most sensitive parts of me, and my whole body was shaking in reaction, which only served to put more tension through the various clamps. And when Eric started spanking me again, it was impossible to keep absolutely still, however much I tried. The plethora of sensations was overwhelming.

Finally, he stopped, quite unexpectedly, and asked me if I'd had enough. I'd completely lost any ability to assess how much time had passed. It didn't feel as though anything like an hour had gone by. Surely the movie wouldn't be long enough? And I remembered, faintly, the promise I'd made to myself: that when the shoot ended, it wouldn't be because I'd asked. I wanted the movie to be as long as Eric wanted it to be. I wanted to have submitted as thoroughly as possible.

Expressing this sentiment around a tongue clamp was challenging. It was hard to form words, and it was hard to think clearly enough to make a sentence.

'I want whatever you want,' I tried to say. He knew what I meant. And the enormity of what that could potentially involve (another hour of clamps? More spanking? An even bigger gag?) overwhelmed me. I did want to have done the best possible job. But *everything* hurt. I wanted it to stop. I couldn't bear the idea of it stopping. As Eric walked back behind the cameras, the confusion of feelings was too much, and finally, I started crying. What courage I'd had was used up, along with my physical resilience. I knew we were making a movie, but it didn't feel like a movie. Nothing felt real except for all the pain. *I* didn't feel real. And I couldn't remember where I was.

I don't remember Eric cutting the ropes or untying me. I don't remember the clamps or crotch rope being removed, and I don't remember going back to the house. What I *do* remember is the heavenly feeling of lying curled up on Eric's couch, in my pyjamas, with my face resting against the cool leather of the sofa. I opened my eyes. Eric was across the room, in his armchair. His eyes were also closed. He looked exhausted, but very peaceful. He looked the way I felt, which was wonderful: boneless, relaxed, tranquil, warm. He'd done that to me, and I hoped that I'd had a hand in making him feel the same way. Because good BDSM is a two-way form of communication, but as a submissive, the person who's experiencing all the sensations, it's hard to comprehend what the dominant is getting out of the whole thing. Nothing is actually happening to them. To me, it feels like the poor side of the bargain, but I have to hope that it doesn't feel that way to them. And I hoped that Eric knew how really extraordinarily skilled he was at his job. It crossed my mind to hope that my friend Busby might get some of this experience too, from watching the movie he'd commissioned. I wanted him to; he hadn't physically been there, but it was his idea, and all the blissful, peaceful happiness that I now felt was because of it. I love BDSM as a recreational activity, but I also, for different reasons, love BDSM film production, due to its power to bring pleasure to people who weren't physically on set, but were there in spirit. I hoped that's what this movie would do.

We still had another video to shoot that day. My makeup had been washed off by my sweat and tears, my body was covered in rope marks, and my hair had turned into a crazy mess of tangles stuck to the side of my face. I got up quietly, made my way towards the bathroom, and felt lucky, as I do every day, that my sixteen-year-old self's worries about being the only kinky person in the world were so entirely unfounded. There were many wonderful kinky people in the world. And by great good fortune, I not only knew some of the best ones, but I got to make movies with them too.

At the end of his novella *The Body*, Stephen King writes:

'I never had any friends later on like the ones I had when I was twelve. Jesus, does anyone?'

It's a beautiful line, but it made me sad when I read it as a teenager. And I'm glad to say it's not been my experience. For me, it would read:

'I never had friends earlier on like the ones I found when I became a BDSM model. And I wish the same for you.'

Chapter Twenty-seven

Captain Anal Hook

With Hywel, Dallas, Alistair, Drago, Eric and a small number of other excellent producers and co-performers worldwide I was regularly making movies that I was proud of. Not that they'd be to everyone's taste, but they were to mine, and all I wanted was to speak to people like me through my work. And, though making movies for other people to enjoy will make me happy for as long as I have the privilege of doing it, the personal pleasure I get from doing the very best BDSM that my friends and I are capable of producing is a multifaceted delight. And I realise, I've not really explained how it feels. So: this is how it feels.

I think that what I was *expecting* to feel, when I started seeking out opportunities to experience pain and submission, was vulnerability. I wanted to be scared, and to be hurt, and to feel like a victim. It seemed romantic to me, and as someone who's always been tall, and who as an adult mostly appears to be quite confident and probably noisy, I crave feeling the opposite. Finding subspace makes me feel smaller, more fragile. More feminine too. Like the version of myself that I was trying to find back when I was taller than all the other kids in my class at school, and was experimenting with talking differently. 'Immi? Am I shweeet?' I never felt small, or fragile. BDSM makes me feel that way, and I treasure it.

And in the aftermath, once the scene is over, I experience something far more unexpected, and something I wasn't looking for at all, because it's so counterintuitive. I feel better about myself. Whether it's been a hard, sadomasochistic scene with heavy corporal punishment, or a gentler, romantic dom/sub scene, or even a pure rope-bondage experience, I emerge from subspace feeling clear-headed, more peaceful, and with a sense of self-esteem that I'm rarely aware of in day-to-day life. That's not to say that I feel bad about myself under normal circumstances, but in the aftermath of any good BDSM experience, I feel a sense of fulfilment; as though I've been doing what I was made for.

I feel powerful too; I like knowing that I've had an emotional effect on the other participants in the scene, just as they have on me. I may be playing the submissive role, but in reality every scene is a collaboration, and each of us is responsible for giving the other person what they need. BDSM *is* a sexual experience for me, which is what I was expecting when I first tried it. But what I hadn't expected was the spiritual dimension. The feeling that I'm in the right place, doing the right thing, and with the right people. The sense of peace and happiness is profound.

But to develop the working relationships that made me feel all of these splendid things, of course I have to accept first shoots. When shooting alongside people I ended up working well with, even our first collaborations were a pleasure. But of course, I can't be lucky every time. When I'm not lucky, this is the kind of thing that ensues.

I was contacted in 2015 by an amateur spanking filmmaker who wrote to me via FetLife, which is like Facebook for kinky people. He reassured me that although he was planning to do the spanking himself, he was hiring a camera operator and another model. This would ensure that a potentially intimate situation would be diffused by having lots of people around. I accepted the shoot.

The location turned out to be a flat where the other model lived with her boyfriend, who was to be the camera operator that day. They had another temporary flatmate, who was sleeping in their kitchen. There was barely any furniture, the kitchen was full of dirty pots and pans as well as the camp bed, and the entire place felt a curiously down-at-heel environment to have chosen to shoot in. The producer (we'll call him William) was a tall gentleman in his sixties, with white hair and an autocratic manner. He seemed quite well-to-do, which made his low-budget choice of location seem even more peculiar. But stranger things have happened, and I wasn't yet perturbed.

The other model had worked often with him before, so I, reassured, followed her lead. We were to play two hitchhikers caught out in the rain, who ask if they may stay in the grand country home they find themselves on the doorstep of. Indeed, the 'country house' was going to be represented by the cramped and grubby bedroom that we were shooting in. It might make the movie a less than fantastic one, but it wouldn't really affect my experience of the day, I thought.

Most BDSM players with enough confidence to appear in movies are reasonably good actors who are happy to throw themselves into a role play relatively skilfully. Once we started shooting, I certainly did my best, and the other model did a good job. William did not. He seemed disinterested in setting the scene, and the story almost immediately arrived at the moment of William spanking the hitchhikers to introduce them to his way of life.

It was a silly story, but it's hard to come up with plausible reasons for two adult women to allow a stranger to spank them, and I couldn't have come up with a better story at short notice. But the spanking was rather odd. Once I was over William's knee, he ceased to try to engage in any kind of role-play conversation at all. The smacks he gave me were perfunctory, barely hard enough to redden my skin, and they were accompanied by an awful lot of unwelcome rubbing of my bottom. Personally, I think over-the-knee spanking is quite intimate enough, and do not appreciate having my bottom stroked by a stranger. The entire scene seemed to last forever, and I was unusually relieved when we finally got it done and we took a break.

I was just leaning over, picking up my water bottle, when a hand landed, hard, on my bottom. This is almost unheard of. It might seem unlikely, but every legitimate producer knows that the more intimate/painful/sexual a shoot is, the more important it is that none of the action continues when the cameras aren't running. Being spanked when not in character at a shoot is as weird as it would be if a mainstream film director casually started dry-humping Jennifer Lawrence just because there'd been a sex scene in the script that day. When 'cut' is called, I cease to be Amelia Jane, spankee, and become Joceline, a happily married professional model who doesn't offer private play sessions.

Consequently, Joceline took control. 'You can't do that when we're not shooting,' I said to William (naturally, when I turned around I discovered that the hand had been his).

'Oh ho!' he said roguishly, leering at me. 'Now I've found your pain threshold!'

I do not like being smacked at random times, and I do not like having my pain threshold insulted. I would not tolerate having this man thinking that one stupid hand smack had hurt me more than I could bear. 'No,' I contradicted, attempting calm. 'It's not that it was too hard; my point is that you can't spank me when we're not filming.'

'I see. I *am* a hard spanker!'

I wasn't pleased. '*No*,' I said (less calmly), and was about to explain it *again* when the temporary flatmate suddenly came unexpectedly to my rescue.

'She doesn't want to be spanked when you're not filming,' she chimed in. I loved her.

'Well, it's not *sexual*,' he replied, a little petulantly. If he was telling the truth, what an odd thing to be doing with your afternoon, at considerable personal expense. If it *wasn't* sexual, why on earth was he doing a spanking movie at all?

The shoot limped onwards. We were spanked for not

dusting our room properly. On a break from shooting while the camera was being moved, William suddenly ran the prop feather duster up between my legs. 'Ticklish?' he grinned at me.

'You can't do that,' I said, feeling repetitive and prudish and guilty. I try not to say 'no' to too many things at any one shoot; it feels disobliging.

'Oh, it's not *sexual*!' he insisted again. I'd not, actually, said that it was, though obviously it *was*, given that he'd deliberately used a foreign object to make contact with my genitalia. And his response showed the lie for what it was. If someone refuses a biscuit you offer them, you don't feel the need to assure them that the biscuit isn't sexual. Biscuits aren't sexual. Pussies are.

Wearily, I resumed filming. It was difficult. I don't require sexual chemistry between my co-stars and myself, but it's hard to let someone spank you if you don't even respect them. However, there was less than an hour to go, and in a room full of people he could hardly try anything more inappropriate than he already had.

I was wrong. During breaks throughout the shoot, he'd been rather wearingly testing my knowledge about various subjects. 'Do you know who the Victorians were?' he asked. 'Do you know what "duplicitous" means?' 'Have you heard of Chaucer?' None of these questions were relevant to the hitchhiker storyline; I think he just believed himself extremely knowledgeable, and was looking for ways of demonstrating this wealth of information upon ignorant me. If he'd only known, the most rudimentary physics question would have achieved this, but he persisted with arts subjects. Idiot. 'Victorians?' I rejoined. 'Of course I've heard of the

Victorians. I've known about them since I was nine, and have been fantasising about their corsets and birches ever since.' I didn't. I was tired of William and had no interest in trying to demonstrate my intellect, knowledge, or sexual interests.

But just when I thought that he'd run out of ridiculous questions to ask me, he suddenly reached into his suitcase and produced an anal hook. 'Do you know what *this* is?' I hadn't seen one before in real life, but in the context of this ludicrous shoot, I was pretty sure of what it was.

'It's an anal hook,' I replied, dead-eyed like Wednesday Addams.

'But do you know how it's *used*?' he replied.

Well, friends. Could you possibly figure out what a hook might do, and, given that it's called an *anal* hook, can you possibly work out where you might use it?

So could I. 'Yes,' I said, still being Wednesday Addams as hard as I could, raising an eyebrow disagreeably.

'I'll show you!' he continued, having, naturally, not listened to Wednesday. And then, he tried to *actually bend me over.* I don't know if he planned to insert it; it seems unlikely since I was clothed, but really, who knows? I'd had quite enough.

'You can't do that,' I recited loudly, finally beyond worrying about how disobliging I was being. The rest of the room chorused their support. Somehow, we finished the last scene. I felt as though I'd survived Dunkirk. 'Ah, but do you know what I *mean* by Dunkirk?' I'd have liked to ask him.

I drove home, furious. I waited until his funds had cleared in my account. I wrote him a calm email, and in it, I typed a sentence I never thought I'd need to write. 'Your behaviour with the feather duster,' I wrote, 'was completely unacceptable.'

His response, perhaps unsurprisingly, was absurd. 'I'm sorry. Actually I'm not sorry. You were very cunning at finding things out; I hope you're not going to blackmail me.'

It seems to me that if you don't want to be blackmailed, then hiring young women, spanking them, boasting about how rich you are and then continually ignoring their protests about your behaviour is probably best avoided. I do hope that he manages to do that in future. 'But do you know what sexual offender *means*?' I replied by email.

I didn't really. But I still think about mean things I could have said to him. Fortunately for him, my only revenge is this chapter.

Chapter Twenty-eight

Danger Money

I have a scar, small, round and faded, just above my Achilles tendon on my right ankle. Would you like to know how I got it? It's my book and I'm going to tell you, but I'll endeavour to make the topic entertaining.

Although many people who find out about my work are most shocked by the fact that I let people spank me, it's actually bondage that has more potential to do serious harm. After all, it'd be hard to kill someone with a cane. It's easy to do with a rope. And while I've enjoyed telling you about some absurd and predatory photographers, the most dangerous experiences I've had at work have been with perfectly well-intentioned people who just got carried away with the excitement of creating BDSM art, and didn't consider the consequences of something going unexpectedly wrong mid-shoot.

So, the scar. It was 2007, and I was working with a professional producer I'd not shot with before. He was relatively new to the business, and was full of ambitious, creative ideas. In the scene, I was going to be tied up on the floor, attached to anchor points and facing upwards. Above me was a metal frame. To it, a forest of long slender candles were attached with plastic cable ties. The candles would be lit, and as they melted in the heat, I would be showered with molten wax. I was unperturbed by this; hot wax is only painful for a couple of seconds, after which it cools enough to become solid again and causes no lasting damage to the skin.

We started filming. At first, each wax droplet was brief agony, but as the scene progressed and more wax fell, many of the drops started to land on existing wax, which made it easier to endure. I relaxed a little, and the scene progressed well past five minutes, and closer to ten as the candles diminished in length.

Then, unexpectedly, a candle fell, landing near my head and rolling away from me. Before I had time to react, another fell, snuffing out on the floor below. And then, a third. This one fell near my right leg, and rolled directly under my ankle. The flaring pain was immediate, but I found that I couldn't move my foot out of harm's way – the restraints were too tight, and my leg was burning.

As more candles plunged down towards me, I screamed, struggled to get away, and inarticulately attempted to explain what was wrong through my panic. One of the challenges of a BDSM shoot is that real distress can just look like a very realistic bit of acting, but fortunately the producer understood, and knocked the candle out from under my leg.

I was shaken up, realising that while this had been unpleasant, it could have been much worse. What if a candle had landed in my hair? What if it had been my face that had been burned? The reason the candles had begun to fall all at once was that they'd all burned at a similar rate, and therefore the flame of each reached the cable tie attaching it to the frame at more or less the same moment. The plastic ties, of course, also melted. A proper test of the setup would have showed the producer that this wasn't safe, but I understand why he didn't test it; it's hard to think through every eventuality. I hadn't anticipated it either.

As it was, the scar faded, and now, fifteen years later, it's barely noticeable. But I try to stay more switched on to danger at work than when I was a beginner. It's all too easy to abdicate responsibility when playing a submissive role. These days I'm more likely to ask things like 'What's going to stop this rope from strangling me?' than I would have previously, and I try to suggest the same to newer models. It feels rude, but helps everyone in the long term, the producer included.

I needed all of my assertiveness in 2015, while touring the Netherlands. I'd been hired by a new bondage production company run by two male producers. The first, a young and garrulous fellow, picked me up from the airport and drove me to their studio, where we'd all be staying the night before filming the next day. I was a little surprised to discover that the studio was a tall, narrow house on a residential street, but I was unconcerned. There'd definitely be heating, and a proper shower, I thought.

Indoors, I met the other half of the production team, a small, serious man with a rather disquieting stare. He showed me round the house, leading me eventually to the third floor, where the studio space was set up. 'Here's your room!' he said, with great pride. I was standing in front of a cupboard. Its floor space was roughly the size of a door frame, and the floor was covered in water-proof padding, like a crash mat, as were the walls and the ceiling. There were no windows. I was looking at a padded cell, and one which was smaller than a single bed. 'This is where you'll sleep,' he expanded. 'We can lock you in overnight and film you.' Indeed, there was a camera set up in one corner where wall met ceiling. I had not signed up to shoot content while I slept, and I had certainly not agreed to be locked into an upstairs room of an old, timber-framed house overnight. What if there was a fire?

'I don't think that'll work for me,' I began, trying to be gentle. 'I might need to pee in the night, you see.'

The disquieting little man smiled broadly. 'It's okay, you can wear a diaper,' he replied brightly. 'I sleep in here in a diaper all the time. I lock myself in with a time-lock 'til morning.' That explained the faint, unpleasant smell coming from the padded floor. It made me anxious to think of him locking himself in, alone in this house, with a time-lock on the door. But short term, I was more anxious for myself.

'Thank you, but I don't want to wear a diaper,' I continued, trying to sound reasonable. 'I'm a bit too tall for this room, I think. I'll need to lie with my head in the doorway, so I won't want to shut the door.' Really, I should have left – perhaps I wasn't at risk of actual murder, but accidental death certainly seemed like a possibility. It was late at night, though, I was at the next day's shoot location, and I thought I'd prob-ably be safe. Probably. When I went to 'bed', I put the pillow on the landing outside the cell, and my head firmly on the pillow, to ensure I'd wake up if anyone tried to shut the door on me in the night. For extra assurance, I wedged my phone and a pair of panties into the hinge. I also texted Hywel and asked him to send someone to the address if he didn't hear from me by 8 a.m. the next day.

In situations like these, I try not to assume that I'm modelling for an individual with bad intentions, but experiences of this nature have taught me that people sometimes let their sexual appetites override their ability to make wise professional choices on behalf of their model. In those instances, I've discovered that I need to be especially vigilant, and assertive about discussing my safety concerns. I'm no longer eager to volunteer as anyone's experimental human goalpost the way that I was when I was ten.

Producers tend to be primarily concerned with the safety of their kit, but many of the risks they take come not from using their bondage equipment wrongly, but from not taking time to attempt a basic understanding of the physics of the human body, and not considering the worst-case scenario if equipment fails. Here are some things I'd love every bondage producer to know:

- Legs only bend at the knee – you can't make the thigh bone bend just because it'd be convenient for your picture. Similarly, they only bend in one direction. If you want to experiment with this theory, do so on your own leg, not a model's.
- Models can't breathe through their ears. Either her mouth or nose has to be uncovered at any one time.

- If you wrap rope tightly enough around a limb, you'll eventually cut off circulation. Blaming your model's weird body is not the solution. Learn to tie securely without tying too tightly, or learn to shoot fast.

- Not even the best models can be dangled by their wrists from metal handcuffs. That's because even light models do weigh something, as you will discover if she steps on your foot in her stilettos. By mistake or otherwise.

- Hair will stick to duct tape. It won't detach itself effortlessly at the end of a shoot just because that'd be convenient for you. You can blame the model's hair (someone once claimed the reason for a tape-in-hair debacle was because my hair was blonde), but she will remember, and tell people about your cluelessness forever. Models will compare notes about you. We need our hair.

- You usually can't suspend people by only their nipples. Or only their hair. They will break. And then that broken model will drag herself online and will tell everyone. Similarly, you can't suspend people from ordinary light fittings. Please, please believe me on this.

- Naked flames burn people, and human beings thrive best when not set on fire. Don't take risks with candles around a tied-up person.

- Finally, hearts don't necessarily respond well to electrical current. Unless they've already stopped, in which case you have my blessing to try, if I'm the casualty. I don't mention this at

> random; I mention it because once, as a new
> model, I allowed myself to be attached to a
> homemade electro play device. As a result, I
> developed an irregular heartbeat that took
> eighteen months to resolve.

I can understand the excitement of tying up a bond-age model for the first time: as a submissive I've sometimes not paid much attention to my own safety because I've been so eager to experience something. I can see how this could be true of a dominant fetish pho-tographer too. But when you're planning to use BDSM equipment on another human being, you have a respon-sibility to figure out not only how *it* works, but how your model's body works.

That sounds boring, I know, and I'm sorry to be the killjoy to say it. But here's a thing that maybe the people who're skipping the safety briefings are missing. Com-petence is so fucking sexy. And I'm telling you, from a submissive model's perspective, nothing makes me feel more inclined to let you go to extremes with me than your demonstrating a high level of competence.

One of the very sexiest things about Hywel, to me, is how capable he is. From my first shoots with him, I always felt safe. I knew he'd have thought through any-thing he planned to do with me, and that he'd have the equipment to do it safely, even if something unforeseen happened. At his studio, Hywel always has fire extin-guishers, crash mats, spare sets of handcuff keys, bolt cutters and the like. This makes me feel safe, and willing to do things I wouldn't say yes to under less favourable circumstances. Competence is arousing; of course it's not the only reason I love my husband, but it was certainly a reason for my early attraction to him.

The opposite is true for people who burn me, mistakenly hit me in the eye with rope ends, lose their handcuff keys, try to cut rope off me with kitchen knives, tie me to furniture that collapses, or forget to wash gags they've used before on someone else. To those people, listen up: we, the submissive models of this world, are warning each other about you. Learn to be safe and competent. It's going to help you in the end, and as a bonus, you won't kill anyone. You might even get to marry a fetish model; a thing you may or may not enjoy.

Chapter Twenty-nine

Fantasies, Fans and Friendship

Some of the highs of being a BDSM model have been high enough to give me months of happiness; an especially good shoot can give me a sense of satisfaction that never entirely fades. Some of the lows have made me occasionally question whether being a professional BDSM model is a good idea. My chosen career certainly developed its challenges as the years went by and I became increasingly busy. I tended to tour away from home for two weeks out of four. During tours, I didn't come home at all; I travelled to a different part of the UK, or to a different country, and stayed there. Then, for a minimum of ten and a maximum of twenty days, I'd shoot for an average of eight hours a day. Between shoots, I'd drive from one location to another. And then, from various hotel rooms around the world, I'd do my work-related administration: all the shoot-related emails, and messages from fans; all the purchasing of flights, car rental, nights in hotels, airport parking, train tickets, costumes and makeup happened during this time too. I worked out in my hotel rooms, and ate meals made up from dehydrated packets I kept in the back of my car, unless the hotel had a restaurant, in which case I sometimes took my laptop there and ate with one hand while typing with the other.

Sometimes I missed Hywel very much. Occasionally I wondered what the point of having a beautiful house was, when I was only there half the time. And regularly, the unpredictability of my life on the road made it impossible for me to relax well enough to sleep properly. I found myself awake at midnight still answering emails, and I often woke up at 3 a.m., scared of sleeping through my alarm. I'm not complaining, but touring hasn't always been the best thing for my health, which is why, in 2016, I made a small change that ended up having a huge impact on my life, and made me feel even more connected with other kinky people from around the world. Let me tell you all about it.

Up until 2016, I worked only with photographers and fetish producers. I loved it, whether I was working with full-time professionals or first-time amateurs with shaky hands and no idea of how to direct a model. As long as I was working with nice people (and I don't take a second shoot with anyone who I think *isn't* nice), I was content. But what I didn't do was work directly with fans. I knew I *had* some fans – over the years people have been very generous in emailing me with feedback for productions they've particularly enjoyed. But I was late to realise that there's a whole market for shooting pictures and videos especially *for* fans, in the form of privately commissioned work.

Assuming that shooting, editing and delivering my own productions would conflict too much with my life as a touring model, I initially turned down any requests for custom videos that I received. But my various model friends were shooting their own content, and I started to wonder if it would give me the chance to stay home a little more often if I *did* start doing some more work that could be done from my house. I think I'll always love touring, but I liked the idea of producing things myself too. I built a little website, and wondered, just as I had in 2003 when I put my model portfolio online, whether anyone would be interested.

What a remarkable education it has been. I'd thought I had a comprehensive understanding of the variety of things people fantasise about. But as requests from customers came in, I realised that even with all the pornography available online, there are many people with interests that are underrepresented. *So* underrepresented, in fact, that there appeared to be many people who were prepared to underwrite the entire cost of having a movie made that'd appeal to their sexual tastes. My first order was from someone who wanted me to get into a cold bath and spend five minutes complaining about it. I was happy to – I love complaining. Another customer sent me some beautiful Wolford tights and wanted me to make a video in which I seduced him into giving me a job by flirting outrageously with my legs and feet during an interview. This was the sort of improvisation that I'd excelled at when I was at drama school; I love playing sexually manipulative characters.

Soon, customers were ordering sequels too. A customer who'd wanted a video depicting his aunt teasing him with glimpses up her skirt asked for another video of the same character. I discovered that I loved playing Upskirt Aunt, and she turned into my best-selling, long-running series when I began uploading my videos for sale to the public. She sometimes feels so real to me that I like to think she's *my* aunt, and I'm grateful to her for her efforts in paying off my mortgage.

Released from having any responsibility towards a co-performer, since my videos were mostly monologues shot point-of-view style, as though the camera was the viewer, I found that there was almost no limit to how badly I was prepared to behave towards a camera. I didn't mind being emotionally manipulative, abusive, inappropriately flirtatious or downright threatening when my performance was directed at a camera lens, not a co-performer. And finally, after over ten years of avoiding dominant roles at shoots because it made me too unhappy, I discovered a way of playing dominant characters that was not only tolerable for me, but a pleasure.

Despite knowing many, many submissives and masochists, and knowing from my own perspective what a pleasure it can be to be dominated, I've never coped well in situations where I've been asked to play an aggressor. I can tie models up at Hywel's shoots, but I don't enjoy doing it on camera. And the couple of times I've spanked another model, it's made me cry. Both times left me feeling unhappy and shaken up, and disappointed with myself; many people who are mostly submissive are happy playing dominants from time to time, but it just felt distressing to me. Perhaps, having had to fight to be seen as a submissive at the beginning of my career, and because it took me a long time to discover that I could live as a submissive at all, I'm particularly protective of my right to be one, even if I look like some people's idea of a perfect dominant.

But I discovered that I adored playing dominant roles straight to camera. When I didn't have to actually carry out any of my threats, I discovered that I could be inventive, cruel and unpleasant. Or teasing, patronising and seductive. Or just authoritative, firm and very strict about discipline. As a submissive, I had a wealth of experience of working with the very best dominants in the business, and I knew how *I* liked them to behave. It turned out to be a useful launching pad for playing dominant characters of my own.

I made videos where I shamed a customer for getting turned on by looking at me in a rollneck sweater. I played a boxing champion who deliberately knocked out a journalist who was interviewing her. I threatened a student with a caning he'd never forget. I refused to let a customer have an orgasm, while teasing him with my leotard-clad body. I played an ancient Roman aristocrat, cruelly flaunting my bare feet at my slave boy, who longed to touch them but would never be allowed. I played a nurse, a werewolf, a hypnotist, a babysitter, a demon. And I loved every character, except for the time I had to eat an apple and a banana, while Hywel, off-screen, did the voices of the fruits, pleading for their lives. This was a step too far for me. I don't want to *really* dominate anyone, even a talking banana with an unlikely Birmingham accent.

I was, and continue to be, both touched and impressed by the people who trust me with their most private fantasies. Often their kinks are not mine, but knowing that I was born this way, I understand that none of us choose our sexual identity, and I never judge anyone, even if their fantasy is not something I can shoot. Sometimes a customer's request introduces me to something I'd never thought of, but which turns out to be hotter than expected to shoot, like the time someone paid me to kneel facing the wall for half an hour. I eventually almost fainted (try it, it's hard), but I loved the challenge and couldn't help weaving a story in my mind to explain why I was there. Making my own custom videos has been a sexual education for me that I've appreciated immeasurably.

And it's helped me to get some things clear in my mind about my own sexuality. I'd shot a series of videos for a customer who wanted me to play a dominant role. His fantasy appeared to be for female superiority; I had to be smarter, stronger, more sexually experienced, more popular, more attractive, and altogether a more impressive individual than he. And in the process of explaining how he wanted me to play the character, he said something that struck a chord with me.

'It's not that I want to be a complete loser; my character has done their *very best* to compete with you, and has eventually lost, despite his best efforts. He tried, but he failed. And he has to acknowledge your superiority.'

It fascinated me. This was exactly what I wanted sometimes too. In almost every scene I do, either at work or in private, I want to have done my best to try to win the game, and to play it to the best of my ability. But I want, ultimately, to lose. I'm playing to lose, but giving every appearance of wanting to win.

So I understood exactly what my customer was looking for, and it delighted me to give it to him. There's something especially rewarding for me about producing work for other subs, albeit mostly male ones. I feel an affinity with them, and if I can help them by being the dominant of their dreams through a camera lens, I'll always be happy to be of service, like the submissive that I actually am. It's complicated.

In producing my own work, I soon discovered that I couldn't do everything on my own. Sometimes my customers wanted to see me tied up. So, after years and years of our financial relationship being rather one-sided, with Hywel paying me to model for him, I've finally been able to reciprocate by hiring him as my bad guy and camera operator. I can't pretend this always goes especially smoothly:

'Now tie a rope around my neck, and pretend you're strangling me.'

'No. I don't want to. It isn't safe. I'll put a rope around your chest instead.'

'*No*. It has to be around my neck. My *customer* said so. Tie it off so it can't tighten and just *pretend* to be pulling it. I'll just act like I can't breathe.'

It's tremendous fun. I am a very *bossy* boss when I'm trying to please my customers, and Hywel doesn't tolerate it especially well. I often accuse him of having a can't/won't attitude. He rolls his eyes at my disinterest in lighting and lens choice.

Sometimes my custom-video storylines require a larger cast. Five years ago, Hywel and I moved from near London to mid-Wales, having realised that one of the things that made us happiest was walking in the mountains, and that the southeast of England didn't have any mountains. Hywel worked from home and didn't need to live anywhere in particular. I, conversely, worked everywhere, and so it hardly mattered where our house was – I'd only be there half the time in any case. So we decided to move out of the crowded south-east. While house hunting, we found a property online that had been on the market for eighteen months already. It was massive, according to the floor plan, and it looked beautiful – a brick-built, three-storey Georgian house, with a big kitchen, lots of storage, and, bafflingly, a large empty space right in the middle of the ground floor. Hywel and I didn't know what to make of the floor plan; it looked as though there was a great big *nothing* where a room should have been, and we were intrigued. So off we went to the Welsh borders to have a look.

The property was empty and cold but so beautiful. It had two formal sitting rooms at the front of the house, both with big fireplaces, and one with a lovely wooden floor. The kitchen had a bright yellow AGA oven and enough space for an eight-seater kitchen table. There was a Victorian conservatory, a long barrel-vaulted corridor. A dining room with delicate paintings of birds adorning the walls. A huge utility room with three floors. And, in the middle of the house . . .

The estate agent showing us around looked a little ashamed. 'This is a bit of an unusual feature,' he apologised, gesturing to the empty space on the floor plan. 'It's through here; it's a bit strange . . .'

And he led us through the utility-room door into a dungeon. A stone cell with a high ceiling and rough-hewn walls. Around the cell itself was a horseshoe-shaped corridor, also stone-walled. It was absolutely perfect. We couldn't help it – Hywel and I started laughing. The estate agent looked quite baffled.

'Have you got any ideas about what you'd use this space for?' he asked, hopefully, picking up on our delight but unsure as to the reason for it.

Oh my.

'Well, we're fetish photographers. This would make a great set,' Hywel explained, recovering himself.

And we were suddenly quite sure that this was the house for us. I tried to make an offer then and there. Hywel shot me a scandalised look. We made our offer half an hour later instead. We were buying a dungeon with a house attached.

We didn't have any friends or family in mid-Wales; it seemed like a big move. However, we wondered if we could change that. Michael Stamp, who used to run a spanking website called Bars and Stripes set in a women's prison, had been a friend of mine for over a decade, since I'd first worked with him as a new spanking model. A couple of years before, he'd married a professional model and dominatrix called Zoe, who shoots with us for Restrained Elegance. They made a fabulously unlikely couple: Michael, a calm, kindly, retired shipbuilder and fearsomely excellent on-screen dominant, and Zoe, small, innocent-looking, cute like a kitten, but just as liable to suddenly pounce on you with her claws out. 'Be more Zoe,' I sometimes say to myself, when I'm in a situation where ruthlessness that I do not possess is required. And they were looking to move house now that Michael had retired from his day job.

We recommended mid-Wales. And barely two weeks before we moved, Michael and Zoe moved into a house only ten minutes' drive away from our new house. We didn't even live in Wales yet, and we already had kinky neighbours.

The kinky neighbours became our invaluable collaborators in both our personal and our professional lives. Michael played a ruthless capturer of women who trained them to behave like ponies in one of Hywel's epic feature-length movies. He was scary, awesome and believable as an uncompromising pony-girl master. And Zoe can do everything. A highly skilled dominatrix and Top, she also makes a perfect damsel-in-distress. I hired her over and over again. Together, for my custom videos, we tormented our butler, played college girls planning to spank our much-fancied male fellow student, tied each other up with silk scarves, worshipped each other's feet, and screamed hysterically together while being menaced by an invisible, ghostly spirit who tied us up with enchanted ropes.

Michael couldn't get used to living in Wales. After a couple of years of the relentless rain and cold, he decided that for the sake of his health, they needed to move to Spain. Hywel and I were sorry to see them go; we'd loved having kinky neighbours, and we loved them both. However, Zoe wasn't ready to retire, and soon, she was coming back to the UK on a regular basis to work. She sometimes came to stay with us, but mostly she stayed down south, with our mutual friend David.

Everyone calls David 'Dodgy Dave'. It's a joke – he's the least dodgy man you could possibly meet. Small, neat and polite, and very English, he lives in Surrey in a large, ivy-covered house with a big garden. Being part of the British spanking scene, David has over the years offered his home as a location for countless fetish film productions. Many producers shoot almost all their content there. Partly this is because he has a lovely house and a private garden. But mostly it's because of David himself. I'd only met him a couple of times when I decided to go to Shadow Lane, a big spanking convention in Las Vegas. I wanted a roommate for moral support, and although I knew many of the people who'd be attending, it was David, who I hardly knew, that I decided I'd feel most comfortable sharing a room with. Since then, he's become my regular roomie when I go to spanking conventions. I love waking up to see him in the bed next to mine, dressed in his cute tartan pyjamas, looking like one of my long-ago cuddly toys come to life. I always want him to wake up immediately and start entertaining me with his understated wit and endlessly acute social observations. I've found that if I make him coffee, he is far more obliging than Hywel is when it comes to long conversations first thing in the morning. Sometimes I call him my spare husband.

But I have to share him with Zoe. Being away from home a lot herself, she *also* needs a spare husband. And she stays with David more than I do. I think of her as his main wife, even though she's Michael's actual main wife. And I think of her as my *porn* wife. So many wives and husbands. It's very confusing, and wholly wonderful. When Zoe and I are both at David's house, we often make custom movies that involve corporal punishment; it makes sense since we all like it. My favourite thing of all is when they both gang up to punish me. Zoe can play everything from a businesslike, authoritative Top right through to a theatrically crazy sadist. And David is marvellously, Britishly, icily authoritative in roles that require him to be so. It is such a treat to work with them both.

In 2018, my porn wife Zoe, her real husband Michael, our spare husband David and I all found ourselves at a spanking convention in Houston, hosted by our American spanking model-turned-producer friend Sarah Gregory, and her dashing British fiancé John Osborne, who, in my head, always wears a tuxedo. We had adjoining rooms: David and me in one bedroom, Zoe and Michael in the other. We left our connecting door open all day. In gaps between official activities, we shot spanking movies for our respective online video stores, with David and Michael swapping between spanking me and spanking Zoe, in a haphazard and joyful fashion.

And as we finished shooting for the day and started getting dressed for the evening's formal dinner, ambling in and out of each other's rooms to help fasten cufflinks, adjust ties and zip up our dresses, I realised that I had, beyond any doubt, found my place in this world. These weren't just my friends. These cheerful, creative, entertaining, kinky people felt like my family. And back home, I had a husband who trusted me enough to let me fly around the world to enjoy these events, even though the idea of a hotel full of noisy people who all knew each other was his idea of actual hell. I loved him for that, just as I loved them. And if I could have sent a snapshot back to my teenage self as we posed together for selfies in our room before heading down to the formal dinner to meet up joyfully with Sarah and John, I'd have done so. And I'd have written on the back:

You're going to be okay. In 2018, these are your

friends. You've slept in their beds, told them your fantasies, and been spanked by all of them. You've never had to keep a secret from any one of them. You'll work with them often, and it won't feel like work. So, while you wait to find friends like these, don't be impatient. All the ridiculous and unpleasant things that happen to you along the way will one day just be funny stories to tell these friends. And you'll laugh along with them, because you'll feel safe and understood. And all your anxiety about being a sadomasochist will feel as though it was experienced by another person. You'll have arrived at a place where you know your kinkiness is okay. And you'll know this because your friends share your kink, and they are much, much more than okay.

Chapter Thirty

Covid and Kink

In early February 2020, I was shooting with Drago again, in another grand room with another four-poster bed. It was late at night after a long day of filming multiple stories, and I'd reached the happy state of disinhibition I associated with the combination of subspace and sleepiness. This made me curious, and unapologetic about it. 'If you had to be locked in a room for a year with only one person, who would you choose?' I asked him suddenly. He laughed. It seemed a funny hypothetical question at the time. A month later, it was no longer hypothetical. In the UK we watched the Covid news from Wuhan, then from Italy, and as March began, we started to talk about locking down too. Hywel and I celebrated my birthday on 15 March with afternoon tea in a deserted hotel lounge, and then drove nervously home, wondering if we'd been irresponsible not to cancel. We didn't drive anywhere again for four months.

Like millions of other people, Hywel and I were suddenly faced with working exclusively from home, with only each other for company. I cancelled my planned UK tour, followed by my trip to Munich; the bondage convention I'd been due to appear at was cancelled too. I cancelled my flights to the USA, where I'd planned to be Sarah Gregory's bridesmaid, and to visit Eric Cain for another week of limit-pushing BDSM. And, like many other self-employed people, I got ready to see my income drop substantially as the world around us locked down too. It didn't seem important; people were dying, and we had savings. I just hoped that being together 24/7 for an extended period for the first time in our relationship wouldn't be a disaster – Hywel and I had never spent more than two weeks at a time together before, and we weren't sure how to do it.

Friends, it was not a disaster. Hywel was a delight. I discovered I was a much nicer person when I wasn't constantly either packing or unpacking. We lit candles and watched movies. We listened worriedly to the news together. I took up line dancing and wrecked the slate patio in the back garden with my cowboy boots before Hywel noticed and put a stop to my wearing them to dance in. Hywel ordered an orangutan glove puppet called Gareth, and insisted that Gareth had told him he only spoke Welsh. So we learned Welsh, and sat in the garden with Gareth, looking at the slates I'd wrecked by stamping on them and pretending to be an American. We were scared, and we loved each other extra, united against the unseen enemy that threatened us all.

But as the fear began to abate and we learned to live with the continued lockdown, I discovered two things. Firstly, that people in lockdown buy a *lot* of porn. In April 2020 I earned more than in any other month of my entire career. May was even better. My income suddenly seemed to have a doubling time only slightly longer than that of the Covid cases sweeping across the globe. It was the last thing I'd expected, but it told me that other people were experiencing what I'd discovered for myself: that porn can make you feel less alone. It might be an atypical way to connect with other humans, but it was what we had.

The second thing I discovered was that *I* was lonely in lockdown too, and that making porn helped me stay connected to other kinky people. I'd been in the immensely privileged position of travelling the world like a snooty sommelier, sampling the very best quality BDSM experiences with the very best producers over the last decade. Now that was over, and I missed my kinky friends, and the variety of activities we filmed together. And the fact that Hywel didn't want to do anywhere near as much BDSM as I did became an issue for the first time in our relationship. I didn't blame Hywel – I knew I was greedy, and exhausting, and probably a bit unbalanced for wanting to be kinky the entire time. And Hywel didn't blame me; he just patted me kindly and apologised for not being as insatiable as I was, before gently disentangling himself from another of my desperate, clinging hugs. It wasn't his fault; he was only one fetish producer, not twenty. And I couldn't expect him to provide all the experiences that my collaborators had, pre-Covid. I realised that I had to find the answer on my own, and as had happened often in my life, I found that answer in my imagination.

What if, by exploring my fantasies by myself, on-screen, I could make BDSM movies that would make people feel like they were here with me? Could I make myself feel like *I* was there with *them*? I thought it was

worth trying. There were many activities that I loved
but had never filmed, either because I was too shy, or
because I'd been worried that other producers would
pressurise me to shoot harder sexual contact with them
if they saw me doing it elsewhere. Mid-lockdown, that
concern no longer seemed pressing – were we ever going
to see actual people again? I wouldn't have to look anyone in the eye for a while if I made a mess of things and
created films that no one liked.

I had another reason too for wanting to produce
some more personal, sexually frank work. A few months
before, I'd made a passing comment on Twitter about
shooting with butt plugs. A fan had replied. 'I'm glad
you don't shoot porn,' he said. 'You're too classy for
that.' He meant it kindly, I was sure, but it made me
uncomfortable. It was true that I didn't shoot hardcore,
penetrative work. But I knew that people masturbated
to my videos, just as they did when they watched more
explicit content from other models. The intention was
surely the same, which meant my work *was* also pornographic, even if not explicitly so. I knew why I didn't
shoot hardcore, and it wasn't because I was *classy*. It
was because I was *scared*. I didn't want people to judge
my work as crude or distasteful. And I didn't want anyone to think I was desperate for money. But I wanted to
stand beside all my peers, including the ones who shot
more sexual stuff than me – if they weren't classy then
neither was I, and I didn't want to be congratulated for
it. I thought that perhaps it was time to be braver. And
no one could pretend I was doing it for emergency
cash – in my industry everyone can see how well others'
products are selling because of the multiple sales charts

published every day, and I was already near the top. It felt like a good time to experiment.

My new series was called *My Favourite Things*, and I decided to dedicate one video to each activity that I wanted to explore. Everyone knew I liked being tied up, spanked and caned, and I assumed that plenty of people would be able to accurately guess at least some of my other sexual interests. But shooting my first episode still gave me nightmares in the few days leading up to it. I shot *My Favourite Things 1 – Blow Jobs* on 28 May 2020. I stuck a dildo to a mirror, set up my lights, got dressed into cord dungarees and a plaid shirt (to look less pornographic? I don't know), and pressed Record on my camera. And then I started to talk about how much I liked giving blow jobs. It felt necessary to demonstrate various techniques as I discussed them. I introduced the subject of deep-throating and decided to demo that too. Several minutes later I was still doing it. Somewhere along the way I'd lost sight of the fact that the dildo on the mirror didn't belong to a real person, and was sinking deeply into a dom/sub fantasy that I was enjoying very much. Fifteen minutes later, I realised the movie was longer than I'd intended, that I was feeling rather light-headed, and that I might have wasted my time on a video that was too emotionally exposing for me to publish. Breathlessly, I hunched over my laptop, waiting for the footage to load. Watching it back wasn't comfortable, though it was certainly honest, and I felt proud of that. So, before I could lose my courage altogether, I exported it and put it up for sale on my stores. Then I realised that there was no point making it available if I was too embarrassed to tell anyone it existed, so I anxiously tweeted a screen-grab, and waited for my fan base to desert me, en masse, in favour of a classier performer.

I watched my inbox nervously, like a head chef watching their soufflé rise. Someone bought my movie. Then two more did the same. Appreciative comments started coming in on Twitter, and people began reviewing the video online. 'If there was a university with a programme teaching women submissive skills,' wrote one customer, 'this would be a video from its tenured professor.' I felt rather proud. And since it's hard to feel proud and embarrassed at the same time, my embarrassment lost the battle. I went to bed still feeling proud, had nightmares about people calling me a whore, and woke up to more sales than I'd ever seen for a single video. It was nice to be earning money but more important was the feeling of being accepted. My fans, who'd been watching me shoot movies that danced around my sexual tastes in a shy, elliptical fashion for the last few years, weren't disgusted with me for being so coarse as to admit to enjoying oral sex. On the contrary, they seemed almost as pleased as I was. Armed with this knowledge and new confidence, I began planning my next episode.

Over the following weeks, I shot everything my heart desired. I had an on-screen orgasm for the first time, shortly followed by several more. I shot butt plugs, double penetration, nose hooks, cock gags, electric shocks and bound orgasms. A kind fan bought me a fucking machine, another bought me a Sybian vibrator. And just as I'd found when I first shot tougher BDSM with Eric Cain, my customers were mostly respectful and appreciative of my attempts to stretch my limits. My custom-video orders began to reflect my newly expressed interests, and the messages people sent me were as honest and emotionally exposing as my new work. As I shared more of my fantasies, my customers felt safe to share more of theirs. And as I'd hoped, I felt more connected to them than ever. Nothing would stop me missing my BDSM friends and collaborators, but shooting everything I fantasised about, and knowing I was giving my customers pleasure, felt a bit like having an orgy with the whole world. In a very classy and non-slutty way, obviously. Obviously.

Though I hadn't been wrong to be afraid of how my pre-Covid photographers and producers might respond. I'd long been aware that some more old-school employers of models considered us to belong to them in some way. I'd lost count of the number of photographers I'd heard complain about models with 'secret levels', such as there being pictures that they would only pose for with selected photographers, or types of content for which they didn't advertise their availability. At the start of my career I'd been very concerned about being even-handed and shooting the same genres for everyone at the same price. But with more maturity, I no longer felt that was necessary or reasonable. Why shouldn't models vary their work depending on how comfortable they felt with any given photographer? I didn't want to shoot foot torture with anyone except Hywel, because he especially loved it, and was sufficiently safety conscious to do it carefully. I did my toughest bondage with Eric because I trusted him not to let me die. I did my most sexual-looking movies with Drago because I loved his romantic style and he made me feel comfortable. And I shot my sexual experiments on my own, with my own cameras, and with power over my own edit. I didn't owe any of that to anyone – it was my body, and my career. I'd made sure to be as open as possible about my new *Favourite Things* project, and had shared my reasons for beginning it. I hoped that would stop any of my employers getting overly territorial or judgemental.

Dear friends, it did not. To be fair, most people were lovely, but a few were absolute idiots. One particular producer took to Twitter, like the fine citizen of Wankerage that he is, to slut-shame me for shooting penetrative content, after working with me for the entire previous decade. He'd also been shooting sexual penetration for that whole time, and it had never occurred to me to judge him for it; I just hadn't wanted to shoot it with him myself. Being met with a backlash from fans, he deleted his comments, but guaranteed I'll never work with him again under any circumstances, penetrative or not. I'd love to say this was a one-off, but it wasn't. I heard the 'she's shooting stuff she'd never have done with *me*' complaint several times more, and I found it both annoying and bewildering. As a model, I'd never expected producers or photographers to give me the exact same treatment they gave to other models in terms of fee, accommodation, publicity or anything else. And the idea that anyone would feel insulted because I'd not granted them sufficient commercial access to my vagina made me feel a bit sick. Who were these people I'd been working with all this time? Was that really how they saw models' bodies – as things they felt deserving of control over? And did their definition of what was acceptable to shoot extend only as far as to their own fantasies, not to models' own tastes? It was a shock and a disappointment. I'd thought we were all better than that, in an industry that faces so much discrimination and judgement from outside.

Mostly, though, people *are* better than that. I apologised to Immi, worried that the new content on my Twitter feed might be a bit much for her. 'It's fine, I can scroll past it fast if I need to,' she said, reassuringly. My nephew laughed, and did a horribly accurate impression of my special sexy-video voice. Sam, always my best friend, messaged me: 'WOW, you're getting brave!' I was certainly trying. Drago emailed. 'Excellent BJ on the dildo stuck to the mirror. You'll be hearing from my lawyers.' It's true that I'd stolen the idea from him; we eventually settled out of court. By which I mean we visited another lovely hotel between lockdowns, and did another heavenly shoot, which is the way everyone should settle legal disputes, especially if there's a dildo involved. And Hywel, who has always, always supported me in everything (except Botox, but whatever), told me he was proud of me, as my profits soared and my fans sent dildos to the house in a never-ending multicoloured supply. He did eventually take exception to an almost life-sized headless torso dildo that a customer sent to me – even Hywel has limits. Hywel named him, unflatteringly, 'Clammy Dead Boy', and developed a theatrical phobia of touching him. I retaliated by staging Clammy Dead Boy in alarming locations around the house. Currently, he's reclining, silent, headless and sinister, under a duvet in Hywel's library, awaiting rediscovery.

Since all the people I actually cared about were kind

about my new work, I continued to try to film every fantasy that I had in my head, while taking note of the most poisonous reactions from former employers and shrinking my post-Covid client list accordingly.

Interestingly, slut-shaming appeared to be the activity of choice for many locked-down journalists too. When Covid struck, many models in my acquaintance, including me, had already been using sites like OnlyFans for several years to generate extra income. Essentially a monetised version of a social media platform, we used it to upload selfies and videos, and subscribers could pay to see our daily updates. It had been paying my mortgage but not much more for about four years when the first lockdown hit. With more time on my hands, and more sex toys at my disposal, I began updating multiple times a day, talking to my members more, and doing live shows from my bedroom. People who'd only been vaguely familiar usernames pre-Covid became friends I spoke to every day. In our new, socially atomised world, we needed each other as far more than orgasm inspiration. But all of a sudden, it wasn't only models who were using OnlyFans. New creators flooded onto the platform as people lost their jobs due to Covid, were furloughed, or simply wanted to be appreciated sexually while stuck at home alone. I loved seeing it – with so many people who previously hadn't considered doing sex work entering the industry (albeit in a relatively low-risk, gentrified way), surely some of the social stigma surrounding getting naked for money would begin to break down, I thought.

In the short term at least, I was wrong. The explosion of users and creators on OnlyFans and similar platforms created the beginnings of a widespread moral panic. Sex work was suddenly big news, and lots of people didn't like it. Documentaries and newspaper articles began to appear, and many of them seemed to be a desperate attempt to discourage 'normal' women from becoming like us, their fallen sisters. The right-wing press largely vilified us for what they appeared to view as our being able to make more money than we deserved from a standing start. The left-wing press indulged in hand-wringing about how we were destroying our future opportunities to be employees, mothers, et cetera.

It was very annoying to witness. So much so that, armed with all my locked-down extra time, I decided to write some articles of my own. Since the journalists writing about OnlyFans all appeared to have discovered online sex work about half an hour ago, I thought my two decades of experience as a nude model, plus my five years of using that specific platform, might count for something. So I wrote three articles altogether: one for HuffPost, and two for a couple of quasi-intellectual publications. All three were published. And I started to receive hate mail.

I'd been lucky, I suppose, not to have received much in the way of online hate before. I have had a couple of stalkers, a few BDSM practitioners who accused me of doing submission 'wrong' over the years, and the occasional individual who took exception to BDSM altogether and wrote to blame me for it. But the volume, and fury, of this response was a little unsettling, not least because people seemed angry that a sex worker had dared to write anything *at all*. Having spent my entire career working in theatre, film and pornography,

I've been surrounded by liberal-minded souls for my whole adult life, so it was quite a discovery to be the recipient of so many hateful messages. 'Your parents must be so ashamed,' they wrote. 'Good luck finding a husband now.' 'You've ruined your chance to be a mother.' 'You're just a whore, though, and *so is your father*,' wrote one particularly passionate (and entirely incorrect) individual.

Daughter, wife, mother, whore. Taken as a whole, the comments betrayed an interesting preoccupation with what a woman should be. And as I read the comments, I realised that I should not have been surprised. This is how my profession has traditionally been spoken of. This is what people are taught to think about us, and many have neither the perspicacity nor inclination to think for themselves on the topic of sex work.

It was tiring, and it made me sad, and then it made me angry. I was a professional with twenty years' experience in my field, but when I shared my knowledge in written form, I was met by people telling me I was naive to love my job, too stupid to do anything else, and too rich to be allowed an opinion on an industry that some entered out of desperation. 'Enjoy your money and SHUT UP,' wrote one furious reader.

I didn't want to shut up. I wanted to enjoy my money very loudly, since it seemed to bother them. The experience of being published had made me aware that plenty of people hated it when sex workers and pornographers were allowed a voice in a non-pornographic arena. I wondered what they'd feel if I wrote an entire book. Volcanic fury, I could only assume. So, friends, I decided to find out.

Chapter Thirty-one

The Feminists, the Famous and the Publishing Giant

I wrote my book, and I loved every bit of it. To be sure, occasionally Hywel found me curled up with my laptop, crying over a particularly horrible memory, but nevertheless it was a pleasure. I walked to the tearoom of our local castle and wrote there. I walked up the canal path to our nearest garden centre and made notes in the café, among the plants. I'd never been able to tell anyone the whole story of the time that sixteen-year-old me thought she'd discovered a vocation as a nun, but instead discovered that she was a sadomasochist. But I managed to hand my manuscript over to Hywel, and to finally share the last secret piece of my life with him. He read it, and hugged me for a long time. And once I'd finished my first draft, I sent the chapters that made reference to other people to them so that I could get their consent. 'It's absolutely lovely,' said James, my ex-media studies teacher, 'but yes, I'd like you to change my name.' Ditto Scott, my fight master. Reconnecting with people from so far back in my life, and being honest with them about who I'd really been, and who I was now, felt cathartic in itself. It was uncomfortable, but to be fully understood is precious. And in reciprocation, people shared things about themselves that I'd not known. Altogether, it was a beautiful experience.

Eventually, my book was finished. And I couldn't see why everyone made such a fuss about how hard it was to write one. It hadn't been hard at all, and now all I needed to do was to find an agent and then a publisher. No problem: there were loads of literary agents and they all had websites. I'd find a few who represented non-fiction, and one of them would surely like my book. I started doing my research.

To begin with, I felt immensely encouraged. Literary agents, it seemed, were almost all young, middle-class women with arts degrees, living in London, just as I had been a few years before. Many of them said they were particularly looking for books written by women, feminist writing, and books covering women's sexuality. I was delighted – I was a woman, I was a feminist, and I'd written about my sexuality. Furthermore, I liked reading the same sorts of books they were looking for. This was perfect, I thought. Not only that, but I found several agents specifically interested in hearing from 'marginalised voices', sexual minorities and people from religious cults. I *was* in a sexual minority, sex workers are routinely discriminated against, and, thankfully, I had cult-related trauma to share too. What a jackpot.

So I wrote to my shortlist of agents, these young, feminist Londoners who sounded so much like me; these seekers of feminist non-fiction about sexuality and religion. I couldn't wait to meet some of them. I sent my covering letter and synopsis, and I waited for requests for my full manuscript.

These did not come. No one wanted to read my manuscript. No one appeared to want to hear from a professional BDSM model. 'It's a shame it's not fiction,' replied one. *Not for me it's not*, I thought. I was quite glad to be alive and factual. 'It'd perhaps be more compelling if you were trans,' replied another. I could see that it might be convenient for them if I could neatly encapsulate every single attribute anyone could discriminate against but perhaps, if I did, I wouldn't have had the confidence or leisure to write the thing in the first place. 'It's a shame you don't have a bigger Twitter following,' said a third agent, from an agency who specialised in working with authors from groups under-represented in publishing, and LGBTQ+ stories. My Twitter following was three times the size of theirs, despite the discrimination adult performers experience on social media platforms, which routinely 'shadowban' us, making us invisible in searches. If an agent who was specifically looking for stories from people who weren't often represented in publishing *still* wouldn't consider my manuscript, I thought I might be out of luck. I sensed that it was perhaps the fact that I made a living from my kink that was the issue; there were memoirs by other submissive women in existence, but none of them were professionals in the field. I wondered if the women of publishing I'd contacted saw me as somehow tainted by my job.

Then, mid-lockdown, a surprise package arrived for me, sent from a private members' club in Pall Mall, central London. A well-known political author had gifted me a signed copy of his most recent book, and a letter in which he expressed his admiration for my BDSM work.

This was a most unusual situation. Ever since the horrible press coverage I'd seen of Stephen Milligan's death, back in 1994 when I was a frightened sixteen-year-old, I'd been aware that anyone in a prominent position, especially in the political sphere, tended to be extremely guarded when it came to any marginal sexual interests. And here was a man with plenty to lose, trusting me with his real name, his sexual identity and his address.

Courage, I felt, should be answered with respect. I wrote back to him. He replied, and soon we were pen friends. Realising he lived alone and was probably lonely as a result of the intermittent lockdowns, I suggested a Skype call. We did so and he delighted me – he was funny, and audacious, and deeply knowledgeable. I'd never met anyone so thoroughly of the British Establishment before, and I wouldn't have expected to have anything in common with a person who had prime ministers, TV producers and newspaper editors on speed dial. But kinkiness is a great leveller, and we had lots to talk about. Knowing that he'd trusted me, I felt like I could trust him, so when he asked to read my manuscript, I sent it to him.

When the country opened up again for a brief respite between Covid waves, my new friend, who I'd begun to call The Famous, invited me for lunch at his club. And, feeling like Eliza Doolittle off to meet Henry Higgins, I anxiously put together an outfit that I hoped didn't look too porny and which ended up looking very much like a school uniform. I cycled from my cheap hotel in Docklands on a silly hired bike all the way to Pall Mall.

In a huge hall with marble pillars, an open fire and highly polished furniture, we sat and drank cocktails.

He told me he loved my book, and would like to help me get it published. 'Aww lawd love-a-duck!' I replied. 'Wouldn't that be loverly?' I didn't. I was trying very hard not to be Eliza Doolittle. I asked him what I needed to do. And over lunch, he told me.

Back home in Wales, I made myself a short white Mary Quant-style shift dress with matching blazer. I embellished the dress with dark red velvet ribbon at the neckline and hem, and I took myself back to London, where The Famous had secured an invitation for us both to a most remarkable Christmas party being held by a glamorous and extremely well-connected friend of his who I'd already met at lunch. The party was in a beautiful ornate library with low, golden lighting, and was full of people I recognised. I clutched desperately at a glass of white wine, and willed The Famous not to leave my side. I had no idea how to network in this terrifying room. I thought more wine might help.

A short while later, a newspaper editor whose name I knew was introducing himself to me. I began to stammer my own name, preparing to skate over what I did for a living and why I was there. The Famous was having none of it. 'This,' he began, loudly and clearly, 'is my dear friend Joceline. She is a top international porn star.' I'd never have described myself like that, but I had to respect his courage. He'd gone for the least apologetic description of my profession possible; I thought China Hamilton would have been proud of him. And for the rest of the evening, The Famous stayed by my side and repeated this introduction over and over again.

Some people, I think, thought he was joking. But many more asked interested, respectful questions. A gorgeous architect wasn't sure what a BDSM model was; it turned out she hadn't heard of BDSM at all. I got as far as explaining bondage and masochism when she erupted in excitement, 'I like pain too! And whips! And you can do this as a *job*? Could I?' I assured her that she could, and began to feel a little braver.

A while later I found myself in a corner, mid-conversation with a political film-maker I also recognised. He leaned closer. 'Do you ever have *normal* sex?' he asked, regarding me closely as though I were a rare, exotic creature. I wasn't sure if it was an invitation. 'Not really, no,' I replied, having considered the question, and wondering if I should ask him the same thing. Perhaps this was something one should ask everyone in polite society.

I bumped into a politician, was introduced as charmingly and clearly as ever by The Famous, and found myself in a conversation about the laws relating to porn. Everyone was polite and accepting; maybe we're kinder to individuals that we meet face to face than we are to groups of people we don't know personally. Or maybe it's just a question of being introduced by someone who knows what they're doing.

There were literary agents in that room too. Not perhaps the young, feminist ones who I'd expected to be new BFFs with by now, but older, established agents with friends in high places. One of them approached me and told me he'd like to read my book. After all the emailed rejections, I was briefly worried that he was joking. By the end of the night, I'd collected a clutch bag full of business cards, and The Famous took me to the club's dining room for fish pie and mutual congratulations. I wasn't sure, but it felt like the beginning of something. Perhaps my book would get an agent after all. And whatever happened, I had a new friend. He'd introduced me to his world, and I hoped I could introduce him to mine. He'd led a full, exciting life, but he'd never acted on his kinky instincts until he'd written to me. I might not be able to personally provide him with the experiences he desired, but I certainly knew people who could, and I could absolutely provide him with his first kinky friendship. Just as China Hamilton had opened up a whole world for me when I walked into the art gallery under Waterloo, I'd try to do the same for The Famous. I thought he deserved it. We stayed overnight in two little bedrooms upstairs at his club. It felt like being at boarding school: the rooms were charming and old-fashioned, but had no locks on the doors, presumably in order to allow Matron access to check no one was doing forbidden things after lights out. It was bizarre, and wonderful, to be introduced to the world of the political elite, not in spite of my strange, kinky job, but *because* of it.

Two weeks later, I was back in my boarding-school room for the night, with The Famous next door. He'd arranged a lunch meeting with one of the very best literary agents in the business, a giant in the publishing world, who'd expressed an interest in meeting me. But tonight, he was taking me to the Savoy Hotel for dinner. We talked, and laughed, and The Famous asked if I'd cane him one day. 'Only if you don't mind me crying the entire time,' I replied, but I promised to introduce him to my porn wife Zoe, who'd have no such inhibitions. And as dinner ended and we walked back to his club together through a quiet Trafalgar Square, he said a thing that explained everything. 'When you're old,' he said, 'take someone young and talented to the Savoy for dinner, and help them with their career like this.' The Famous hadn't come from a privileged background – he'd achieved his success through his own hard work and courage. And now he was helping me, by lending me his respectability and contacts, to get my story heard. I promised him, and myself, that I would do as he said.

Lunch with the Publishing Giant was a success. I liked him immediately, in part because he clearly had no discomfort with discussing BDSM, sexuality and pornography, or being seen in public with Eliza Doolittle, the Top International Porn Star. The Famous persisted in his efforts to make me sound interesting ('Joceline's father worked at Chernobyl, and she interviewed him for her YouTube channel!' 'Joceline has been shooting a caning movie this week!') and the Publishing Giant confirmed my worries about the current culture in publishing. But over dessert (The Famous was having port; Eliza Doolittle was eating a huge chocolate swiss roll) he said that he thought he could help. I sent him my manuscript that evening, and two days later we were working together. My book was perhaps going to take flight, after all. This submissive, inconveniently non-fictional, inconveniently cisgender BDSM model was going to have her story read. I was going to have my chance to make the people who'd hated my OnlyFans articles even more incandescent. I looked forward to it.

Chapter Thirty-two

Pornotopia

Back when I was a member of the Campaign Against Pornography, and hadn't seen any porn yet, I was willing to take others' word for it that porn served to do nothing but turn people (men) on and turn sex into commerce. Now, seeing what the existence of porn has done for my life, I am ashamed of my sixteen-year-old self's ignorance.

Pornography told me that I was not alone. It educated me about activities and relationships that I wanted to try. Porn gave me a community to belong to, and friends to cherish. It was the community of kinky porn producers who helped me get back on my feet after bad shoot experiences. Porn has given me my house. The car I'm driving, the watch I'm wearing, the rock I'm rocking. In the movie *Pretty Woman*, Richard Gere's character shouts at his lawyer, 'I've made you a VERY rich man, doing EXACTLY what you love.' As a teenager, it stuck in my head because it sounded so nice. And I still think about it often. I'm not *very* rich, but I'm far richer than I ever had any expectation of being. And I'm certainly doing *exactly* what I love.

Pornography gave me that, along with my husband, and my sex life.

The UK, at present, is in the grip of various attempts to make pornography harder to access. I don't want young children to view pornography any more than the next sane, rational human being does. But I think back to my guilty teenage self. If *only* I'd known I wasn't alone, and wasn't dirty or broken. If I'd been able to see my sexuality depicted in artwork, the way I eventually did when I entered the gallery under Waterloo station when I was twenty-five, then years of denial, guilt and bad relationships need never have happened. I don't regret it anymore, but those experiences took a serious toll on my mental health. And I was lucky that I had enough support around me to have survived the experience. If things had been just a little different for me – if I hadn't had my kind older sister to confide in, and parents who I thought would miss me – it's easy for me to imagine having killed myself back when I was sixteen and thought I was a danger to society. I know that many teenagers go through feeling that things are so wrong in their lives that suicide seems a viable option. I know I wasn't unusual in that. But the fact that the thing I was suicidal over turned out to be one of the very best things in my entire life makes me determined that I must do everything I can to stop other people feeling that way. Because discovering your sexual identity should be cause for happiness and anticipation, not guilt.

So, I try to be brave, on behalf of my sixteen-year-old self and everyone like her. I try to be like China Hamilton, who once told a twenty-five-year-old stranger that he was a sexual sadist with no sense of reticence or shame, and made her wonder if she'd ever be able to do the same. For years, I've had separate vanilla and kinky email accounts; but what, I wondered four years ago, would really happen if I used kinkyarielanderssen@gmail.com for everything? Would my accountant refuse to represent me? Would my financial adviser cease to want my business? I decided to find out. I'd been buying properties to rent out, so I was dealing with estate agents, solicitors and brokers on an almost daily basis. I sent out a message to them all, explaining that since my vanilla address was becoming unreliable, I was switching to my work email. I apologised for the NSFW (not safe for work) email address, and said that I hoped they'd still be happy to work with me. My charming Welsh solicitor wrote back immediately. 'None of us in the office knew what NSFW stood for!' she replied. 'We had to look it up, but we're all feeling quite educated now...' Everyone was fine. Kinky Ariel Anderssen still has a good relationship with her local mortgage broker. Kinky Ariel Anderssen has taken on a new accountant who doesn't even have her original email address on file. All of Ariel Anderssen's properties are looked after by agents who know how she earned the money to buy them in the first place.

Recently, I went to meet one of them for the first time, having only spoken previously by email. Before I had time to introduce myself, he said my name. 'How did you know?' I asked, briefly puzzled; I'd not even spoken yet. And as we looked into each other's eyes, I realised what it meant. He'd looked me up. We didn't talk about whatever he'd seen in his Google search, but I was suddenly aware of the fresh cane marks under my clothes – I'd come straight from a shoot. It felt a little awkward, but it was okay. He still let me have the keys to my new property, and he still shook my hand. And as I left his office and started my journey home, I hoped for a future in which no one would think they had to hide their sexuality or profession like a guilty secret. Maybe by letting the people I work with as a property investor in on what had once been *my* secret, I could do my bit to change perceptions of what a sadomasochist, or a sex worker, might be like.

I continue to love the career that I discovered almost by accident in 2003. When I turned thirty, I expected work to slow down for me. Numerous photographers had told me that this would be the case: that models over the age of thirty find themselves in less and less demand. At that point, I'd only been a model for five years, and was frightened that my dream job was about to evaporate. It didn't. Over the last eleven years, I've seen myself get busier and busier, booked up further and further ahead, and I've been the grateful recipient of more and more fan mail. Furthermore, I've become aware of plenty of fetish models in their forties, fifties and beyond. Injury or illness could end my career, but I'm no longer especially frightened that my age will automatically take it from me. So if you're a model or a prospective model and you're reading this, try not to be frightened either. Take the jobs you love and the ones that you can do well. Look after your health. Put savings aside. And enjoy the trip – this career has brought me more joy than I have the facility to describe adequately. I wish the same for you.

And I want to be honest with you, so I will tell you

this too. I know that when you read someone else's story, especially if they've done things that you would like to do, it's easy to feel envious. It's tempting to see their life as a charmed one, and to feel as though you'll never have the luck to be so happy yourself, or to enjoy such career satisfaction. If you, like me, are tempted to feel that way, I want you to know this, though it's not especially easy to say.

Since the morning I woke up with back pain, aged eighteen, I've not experienced a single pain-free day. My back injury turned out to be just the first manifestation of a suite of physical problems lying in wait for my adult life. I'm hypermobile, and while my flexibility makes me a good bondage model, it's made me injury-prone, and my body is always painful. My feet, always highly arched and made more so by training in classical ballet, hurt all the time; many activities are unsustainable for me as a result. And, as is common for people with hypermobility, I'm susceptible to other conditions. After ten years of suspicious and unpleasant symptoms, I was finally diagnosed with an incurable autoimmune disease that is at times debilitatingly painful. The pain makes it hard to sleep, which means it's responsible for my managing to finish this book at all. And when I tell you that my adult life has nevertheless been an absolute joy up to this point, and that while the chronic pain has sometimes been hard to face, I've still been happier than I'd have dared believe as a teenager, I hope that it will maybe give you courage to live your life as fully as you can through your own problems too. You probably don't need me to tell you this – you very likely already are.

I don't have a charmed life, and I think that perhaps,

when you look closely, no one actually does. But there is such happiness to be found in friendship, and love, and creativity, and in good sex. And, if you're wired that way, in BDSM with a partner or friends you trust. In case you, like me, are dealing with chronic pain on a daily basis, I'll say this too. If BDSM appeals to you, you should still try it. For me, it's the very best way of escaping the inconvenient realities of the world, including my chronic pain. Be careful with yourself; perhaps some activities will be too risky for you, or your recovery period might be too long. But I never feel more whole, healthy and comfortable in my own skin than when I've shared a high-quality BDSM experience with someone I care about. And if it should do the same for you, why, I would be delighted.

As I started writing this chapter, by happy chance, I found myself back on the other side of the world, shooting again with one of the producers who started this adventure for me. Dallas, who still spanks as hard as ever, whose work still scares and excites me, and who is now married to the sweetest Southern belle I've ever had the good fortune to meet. 'You've never had chicken for breakfast?' Sabrina asked incredulously. 'You don't have Taco Bell?' 'Would you like some iced tea?' I love her. With her influence over Dallas's work, he's diversified from the straight disciplinary spankings he used to produce, and we've done increasingly far-fetched, fabulous theatrical movies in the last few years, culminating in 2013 in a spanking hitman storyline, in which Dallas is sent to discourage my character from marrying into British royalty, by – well, I'm sure you can imagine.

But this shoot was going to be different. He wanted

to circle back to our first shoot and do a disciplinary spanking again with us playing ourselves. This meant that I had to find some things I felt guilty about with only a few hours' notice.

During a massage that morning, I sifted through my memories of my recent behaviour. Was I feeling guilty? I'd not spent my three weeks abroad drink-driving, swearing at people, being rude to waiters or shoplifting. But I'd also not written any of this book. Perhaps that'd do. I felt a little shy; always star-struck by one of my early industry influences and having not seen Dallas or Sabrina for almost five years, I felt embarrassed about confessing any real-life things to them. I wished I could take refuge in a far-fetched character.

But I was certainly not going to deny him the request, and I wasn't going to cheat. If not for him I might never have shot spanking movies at all. He's like my spanking godfather, which sounds like a storyline in itself.

So Dallas and I sat together on the sofa in their hotel suite with hot video lights trained on us along with their three video cameras, all being operated by Sabrina with patient precision. And it became evident that Dallas was not looking for *one* bit of bad behaviour to punish me for. He wanted to shoot *six* punishments, for six different reasons. And I did, after a fair amount of prompting, manage to come up with six things I'd done wrong (getting into fights on social media, taking so many bookings that I didn't get enough sleep. . .).

But, in a brief break between spankings, while Dallas and Sabrina were moving lights, I had a startling small epiphany. Of course I'd done things wrong, and recently. We all do, all the time.

But I don't feel so guilty anymore. Which, for an ex-Jehovah's Witness, ex-fundamentalist Christian and self-diagnosed sexual deviant, is a remarkable point to have reached. I feel happy, and peaceful, and accepted. My life is better now that I don't have secrets from my friends and family, and becoming open about my sexual identity has washed away the guilt I used to feel about being sexually atypical. When I make choices that aren't the best, I try to learn from them, rather than endlessly obsessing about what I've done wrong. So here's some of what I've learned in the process of writing this book – I do hope that you'll find some useful advice:

- Working to get A grades is something worth aiming for, irrespective of the hotness of your teachers.
- Being a nun is possibly not the best career choice for you if the main things you think about are hot men, sex, bondage and spanking.
- Writing feminist poetry is best left to people who've figured out their feelings about BDSM.
- Avoiding all contact with teenagers makes life safer.
- Performing rap should never be attempted if you're a white, middle-class twenty-two-year-old dressed in a tutu and Doc Martens. Even if you *are* backed up by a crew of other white, middle-class twenty-two-year-olds. Perhaps especially then.
- Trying to live out your sexual fantasies through performing in Shakespeare plays is a frustrating and incomplete way to get sexual satisfaction.

- It's dangerous to assume that people are dominant just because they're good-looking or tall. It's a really great idea to ask people. The ones you'll probably want a relationship with are the ones who'll a) know, and b) be honest about what they are.
- If you're invited to an art gallery, go. It might change your life.
- If you find yourself in a romantic relationship that makes you unhappy, make changes or leave. Don't wait for things to get worse.
- If you feel the deep desire and need to do something (like spanking, or bondage, or knitting, or golf), don't worry about what other people will think of you. It is your life – do what delights you.
- If someone (like your future husband) turns you down for something you think you could do well, ask again. And then pay attention to their opinions about woolly socks.
- Most photographers aren't murderers, although some of them might kill you by accident if you let them get ambitious.
- When you have a chance to make a new friend, take it. Those opportunities, and those friends, are precious.
- The happiest kind of life is one in which you're honest with yourself. I've tried the dishonest kind and the honest sort. The second type is by far the happiest and most peaceful.

Epilogue

It's May 2022. I hug a newlywed Sarah Gregory good-bye and drive myself back to Boston for my flight home. I've spent the last two weeks reacquainting myself with old friends I last saw pre-pandemic, before finally attending Sarah and John's wedding after the years of postponements. Early the next morning, I arrive in Bir-mingham and test myself for Covid (negative) before catching a train to mid-Wales and home. Hywel meets me on the platform, and we hug for a long time. We go out for dinner and I tell him everything. About the hap-piness of visiting author and bondage producer CJ, one of my oldest BDSM friends, and the first person outside my family to read my manuscript back when it was a first draft and my publishing struggles were still ahead of me. About staying with Eric Cain again, our discus-sions regarding whether or not the world is real (I think it is), and about the day Eric said he wasn't feeling sadistic, so we'd spent the afternoon watching birds and frogs in his backyard instead of filming anything. About the unfamiliar glories of American wedding cake, and about the kinky post-wedding afterparty.

Back at home, we wander together into our garden overlooking the canal and sit in deckchairs in the warm twilight. Hywel tells me about a woman from one of his online role-playing games, how she turns out to be into BDSM too, and about a sexting role play they did together the week before. I am proud of him for being able to merge his *Dungeons & Dragons* interests with BDSM successfully, and for giving her a good experience – I tell him so. I show him the dramatic bruises from my shoots with Eric; my bridesmaid's dress had barely covered them, and I'm proud of the evidence that I can still do the hardest BDSM after a long, Covid-enforced break. He laughs at me a little as I describe how much I love the bruises. He tells me he will award me a Grade A in submissive masochism; he understands my need for approval, while persisting in gently mocking it.

Hywel and I are pornographers, and we are kinky. Hywel fancies submissive women; I like dominant men. To an ungenerous feminist (like, for example, a confused sixteen-year-old member of the Campaign Against Pornography), our respective sexual orientations may make me appear disempowered. Our career choice may seem frivolous and irresponsible, and my role within it unliberated and even objectifying.

As a feminist myself, I reject this viewpoint because I cannot see how trying to censor any woman's sexual expression can possibly be good for us. None of us can choose our sexual identities, or who and what we love. The best we can do is to confront these desires honestly, and respect ourselves and others when we engage with them. In a society which is currently reassessing the historical treatment of women by men, with the #MeToo and #TimesUp movements, it is not always comfortable to produce work that features images of women in submissive roles. Occasionally, people have mistaken my sexual tastes for my worldview, but I don't think any group of people should ever have to be submissive towards another, least of all women towards men. I want everyone to have equal rights, opportunities and responsibilities, including within the sexual arena.

What, I wonder, could be more feminist than casting off the norms of a patriarchal religion that taught me that being a woman should limit my opportunities, in order to do a job that I love? What could be more empowered than learning to enjoy my sexual tastes without shame, despite their atypical nature? And if, having done these things and found happiness myself, I have told the world about it as loudly as I can through my work, is that not a responsible decision? Enjoying my proclivities in private changes nothing, and helps no one. BDSM practitioners still face routine discrimination from media, financial institutions and employers to name a few, and I don't blame anyone for staying private. But I cannot, because I want future confused kinky people like the teenager I was to find representations of their fantasies in art. Perhaps my work can form part of the trail of breadcrumbs that they will follow through the dark forest of self-discovery to the warm castle full of other kinky people waiting to welcome them home. That is why I do my job, and that is what I hope for, every time I press Record on my video camera. I'm sexually submissive, but I'm not an object. I'm a woman, and these are my desires. I will not be quiet about them, because they are legitimate.

It is almost dark in the garden, and Hywel and I have told each other everything we can remember about our time apart. We are holding hands; I have missed him. We have been married for eleven years, and nothing is a fairy tale, but I don't want one. I want this: honesty, and understanding, and love, and mutual respect. Equality, and the ability to put equality aside for a while when we both want to enjoy a pretence of something else. I'm tired, and coughing a little. I kiss Hywel goodnight and go to bed.

I don't know it yet, but I have given him Covid. Of course.

Acknowledgements

Well, friends, I wrote a list of people I wanted to thank before I actually researched what the acknowledgements page is meant to be for. You're not just allowed to start promiscuously naming your friends willy-nilly, after all. You have to mention people who specifically helped you write your book. This shrunk my oversized, vulgar list considerably because I don't like asking for help, so I did it as little as possible. Here are the people who were most indispensable.

Hywel, of course and always. You not only let me repeatedly invade your privacy within these pages, but you have also read every word that I've written, and have been unfailingly supportive as I've wobbled anxiously around, trying to figure out how to be a writer. *Dw i'n caru ti, mêt.*

Gareth, our small Welsh orangutan glove puppet. He says he's helping me write the acknowledgments, which he believes qualifies him to be in them. And I cannot argue with his big, optimistic face. IDK, he is determined, and I'm poor at enforcing boundaries.

Immi, my favourite storyteller. You have rescued me from many things in my life (falling downstairs, bad boyfriends, makeup disasters and all) but your generosity in helping me trail loudly after you into your professional field, just when you probably thought you'd finally escaped me, has been remarkable. Immi, I love you always. Can I come and sleep in *your* bed?

My parents, with love. If not for you and your determined acceptance of nudity, perhaps this story would never have been mine at all. Thank you for your positive attitudes to the human body, which gave me not only a lack of shame about mine, but a career that I love. In thanks, I'm going to cross out all the sex bits in this book, so you can have a nice non-BDSM copy.

Pippa, for bringing your friends to stay, and in doing so providing me with a prologue that gave me such joy to write. Your lack of shame about your noisy aunt and her peculiar career makes me happy every day, and gives me hope for the future of THE WHOLE WORLD.

Also Ely. Your shamelessness is similarly much noted and appreciated. I trust you both to do your bit in making the world a kinder place for kinky people.

Busby, for your detailed early feedback at a point when I was maximally insecure about what I'd written. It was invaluable.

Coed-y-Dynas, for having the best coffee cake, and for letting me occupy corner tables as I furtively typed up a great deal of non-garden-centre-appropriate memories.

The Royal Oak, Welshpool, with the kind manager who always asked how my writing was going, but tactfully never asked me specifically *what* I was writing.

CJ, for being the best friend a newbie writer could wish for. For reading the first three chapters with a kindly, uncritical eye, and for persevering with the whole of the first draft. The fact that you liked it comforted me many times during the long rejection process.

Thank you; in gratitude I insist that you must continue to tie me up as often as possible.

Eric, thank you for furnishing me with Chapter Twenty-six, and for trusting that my writing won't scare off prospective models from working with you. In thanks, I shall persist in making you cups of strange British tea.

Sam, for your courageous part in doing what real friends do, and changing the direction of my story. With love and gratitude, and in everlasting friendship.

Drago, for giving me the precious material for a chapter that I'll probably never be able to read aloud without hiding my face in my sweater, and for giving me feedback that was so reassuring I basically memorised it. Thanks for the dances, my lovely friend.

Tom, my darling fake nephew for entering my friendship circle unexpectedly mid-pandemic, and becoming so indispensable, so quickly. Our writerly discussions continue to be illuminating and delightful, and I shall hope one day to see your work in print too.

D, for your remarkable kindness and expertise, for treating me like a writer right from the beginning, and for making me believe that I was one. Thank you for introducing me to your world, and for one of the most unexpected friendship adventures of my life.

Andrew Lownie, for your wisdom, support and company. Thank you.

Katy Guest, who originally commissioned my manuscript at Unbound, for your kindness and patience, and to everyone else I worked with during the publication process. Cassie, Kate, Imogen, Mark, Hayley and Tamsin; I kept expecting you to send me angry notes to tell me I'd done things wrong, and I hugely appreciated your positivity, which I shall always remember.

And finally, always, to my international kinky family, for your part in creating a world where people like us can find friendship, self-expression and, sometimes, book deals.

A Note on the Author

Ariel Anderssen is a BDSM model with a lifetime's interest in submission and masochism. The daughter of a nuclear physicist, Ariel was brought up as Jehovah's Witness by her devoutly religious mother, and to a lesser extent by her father, who was busy with the Chernobyl nuclear reactor in the wake of the 1986 disaster.

She has a YouTube channel about 'How to be a Really, Really, Really Old Model', and tweets daily about her kinky life. She lives in Wales with her husband. Her hobbies include dressmaking and collecting antique swords. *Playing to Lose* is her first book.

Unbound is the world's first crowdfunding publisher, established in 2011.

We believe that wonderful things can happen when you clear a path for people who share a passion. That's why we've built a platform that brings together readers and authors to crowdfund books they believe in – and give fresh ideas that don't fit the traditional mould the chance they deserve.

This book is in your hands because readers made it possible. Everyone who pledged their support is listed below. Join them by visiting unbound.com and supporting a book today.

Scott A
Andrew Abbott
Niall Adams
P K Admirer
Paul Aguilar
James Ahearne
Kent Akselsen
Amanda
Adrian Anderson
Trevor Anderson
Andy
Anton
Jack Archer
Giovanoli Arturo
Sabrina Artus

Arty163
Ash
Ashrarn
Lord Allan Aspinall
Class Asset
Tim Atkinson
Paul B
Stuart B
Nicholas B.
Jim Baker
Jason Ballinger
John Bannergram
Brian Barlow
Chris (Sarge)
    Barratt

Oksana
    Bartosiewicz-
    Callaghan
Michael Bast
Alan Bastinado
Bear&bird
Mr Beas
Drago Bee
Richard Beek
Thom Bell
Katherine Belt
John Benford
John Benson
Amy Binns
Rodney Birch

Dean Bisseker
Angela Black
Kenneth N. Bladon
Timon Blok
Mark Bloor
@bonddom14
Emma Jane Bonham
Joshua Bonnici
Matt Booth
Ulysse Bourdeau
Chad Boykin
Sam Brackenbury
Graham Bradley
Samuel Brannan
Leah Brett
Mick Bricknell
Paul Broderick
Mark Brookes
Ben Brown
Jeremy Brown
Scott Brown
Richard E Brown
    - RBPhotographic
Brian Browne
Jeremy Browning
James Bubear
Anthony Bucknall
Christian Burrell
Erica Bussey
George Butch
Byrnwiga
Catherine C
Ian C
Mike C
Steve C
C.P.
Niall Calder
Bert Calis
Casey Calvert
Camillo
Ian Campbell
Ramsey Campbell
Lynn Cane
Alistair Canlin
Peter Canning

David Cano
Chris Carman
CarmineWorx
Christina Carter
Stephanie Carter
David Carty
Carumbad & Chazzna
Elia Catena
CBP
Peter Cechowitz
Sissy Cecile
Emma Celeste
Chai (he/him)
Dan Chalmers
Andrew Chandra
@chastitynchains
Martyn Cheney
Sam Chipperfield
Andrew James
    Chisholm
Emma Christie
Andrew Clarke
John Clarke
Jen Cleator
Richard Cohen
Rachel Colley
Philippe Collin
Stuart Collins
Kevin Connery
Sarah Cook
Imma Coomer
Rachel Cooper
Ness Cooper
    Sexologist Therapist
Barry Coppock
Tracy Cottis
Malcolm Craik
Royston Craven
Nicholas Crepea
Keith Cross
N. Crotty
Maria Crutchley
CSR
Finn Cullen
CycoMania

D.F.
Aaron D'Avalon
Ian Daere Produc-
    tions, LLC
Emily Olivia Dalton
Marc John Bordier
    Dam
Anthony Daniell
Teann Daorsa
D.R. Darke
Dodgy Dave
Ben Davies
Simon Davies
DazzaB - subrugbylad
Mark de Bretton
    Gordon
André de Cordes
Quinte de Vreeze
Christophe Debacq
Nicholas Devenish
Lisa Devillers
Yvano Di Michele
John Dick
Michael Dinerman
Patrick Dixon
dojolife.style
Adrian Donohue
Snidley DoRight
Andrew Doyle
Andy Doyle
Scott R. Driver
John Duder
Matthew Dunn
Steven Dyson
Ingrida Dzonsone
Paul Eagle
Darren East
Samantha Eastman
Stephen Edbury
Blaise Egan
Eli
Ashley Elsdon
ELY
Lee Engemoen
Steven English

Gary Evans
John Evens
Ollie Everitt
Shelley Eversole
Val F
David Fabijan
Karl Fagan
Jack Fair
Jason Farina
FatSuitGuy88
Fenrir 247
Brent Feller
Jack Fisher
Brad Fitzgerald
Molly Fletcher
Fondofgags
Lynsey Forbes
Stuart Forbes
John Forest
Charlotte Forrest
Andy Fortytwo
Ove Fosså
Paul Foster
Ned Fowden
Noel Fox
Scarlett Foxett
Martin Francis
Shelley Frayja
Charles Fritzen
Freddy Fun
Uncle G
Gaby
Laura Gale
David Gallagher
Pedro Gallegos
Peter Gamez
Tom Gannon
Andrew Gardiner
Sean Garvey
Niall Garvie
Bradley Gass
Awesome Gazz
Gerhard
Mark Gerrard
ggreyphoto

Malcolm Gibson
David Giffin
Cyntha Gioia-Puel
Mary Pat Godigkeit
Dr Gonzo
Peter Gordon
Joshua Graham
Dominic Granello
Leslie Granzo
GrassyBreakfast
James D Green
Rachel Green
David Greene
Lydia Greentree
Steven Greer
Sarah Gregory
Phillip Griffith
Tracey Griffiths
Grinning Wolf Games
    Games
Minx Grrl
Marshall Gruskin
@GTeaPea
Katy Guest
Arturs Gulbis
Slackerwith Gusto
Ben H
Marcus H
Nick H
Steve H
Elizabeth Hackford
Ken Hadley
James Hage
John Haines
Thomas Hamilton
Ray Harano
Paul Harbour
Kelvin Hard
Kevin Harding
Hardyman
Neil Harper
Mark Harris
Nicola Harrison
Harrison A
Tom Harwood

Carsten Hauck
Sam Hawcroft
Andrew Hawkins
John Hay
Saffron Hayes
Jonathan Haynes
Rob Haynes
Stu Haynes
Max Headroom
Geoffrey Hedger
Felix Helianthus
Stuart Hennings
Iain Hepburn
George Hildred
Joe Hill
Lyndell Hockersmith
Peter Holenstein
Mark Hood
Thomas Horne
Neil Horsburgh
Dave Houghton
David Hoult
Abbie Howson
Ely Howson
Imogen Howson
Philippa Howson
Jerry Hughes
Richard Hurst
I love you Sarah
    Beaton - Stu x
Jen Ibbs
James Iles
Russell Iles
Shin Inaho
Irish Mistress Lucy
Kirsten Irving
Jessica Ive
Martin Jaba
Neal Jackman
JackPinkie
Jeff Jackson
Rodney Jackson
George J. Jacobi
Frank Jacobs
Max Jaffe

Edward James
Miss Jay
Amelia Jayne
Ross Jenkins
Simon Jenkins
Danielle Jenner
William Jessop
John & Jenny
Davida Johns
Lucy Johnson
Dr Jon
M Jones
@jpinter4
Kai & Sarah
John Kailofer
Matthew Kane
Phil Karn
Malcolm Karpeta
Leonard Kearon MSc
Sean Kelly
Kelvin
Paul Kemna
Dan Kieran
Lauren Kiley
John Killingback
Kilroy
Jon King
James Kingston
KinkyWriter
Ian Kirk
Wendy Kirk
Kiwi
Bernd Kleinert
Kevin Knippa
Eeku Koponen
Christopher
    Kozlowski
Clifford Kruger
Sam Kurd
Kye
Matthew L
Pierre L'Allier
Lottie La Belle
Ashley Lane
Richard Langton

Stewart Larking
Bjørn Egil Larsen
Stig Larsson
Lark LaTroy
Laura Beth Donna
    Laura
Michael Lawrence
Alan Lawson
Jenet Le Lacheur
Ray Leaning
Roz Allyson Leclair
Gary Lee
Zara Lee
@Lefty564
James Leggott
Mhairi Leishman
Laurence Leng
Leon & Mariëlle
Adrian G C Y Leong
Dave Levingston
Jessica Lewis
Kenneth Leyden
Lilith
Lisette
Owen Lloyd
Sub London (M)
Peter Loose
Mike Lord
Stuart Lorraine
Kat Love
Andrew Lovenstein
Lex Lucas
    (Entrancement)
Lunar Caustic
    Photography
Jeff Lynes
Bill M
Dean M
James M
Sean M.
Andy Mac
JJ MacCrimmon
Nondeterministic
    Machine
Alasdair Mackenzie

Araneae Mactans
Dan Maher
Sidney Mail
Susan Main
Malbon
Mark Margetts
Drew and Ann Marie
Kat Marie
AJ Marion
Matt Markland
Ian Marks
Richard Marqua
Carl Marsden
Rebecca Marshall
Dan Masciarelli
MasonGrogu
C.J. Masters
Stuart Mather
Thomas Matsui
Lex Matthews
Roger Mavity
MaW
Paul Mc Nally
Shaun McGarry
Grant McGill
Katie McGuire
Gary McIver
John McNairn
Adrian Meissner
Tobias Memnet
Carl-Eric Menzel
Chris Meredith
Desmond Merga
Donald Meyer
MidgePhoto
Joe Miglionico
Alex Miller
Ben Miller
Hans Miller
John Miller
R Bruce Miller
Sue Mills
Lorelei Mission
Steve Mitchell
John Mitchinson

Paul Mlynarski
Ken Monaghan
Stephen Monaghan
Colin Mondesir
Martin Moon
Moraxian
Tom Morgan
Mark Moss
Jason Motbey
Neil Munro
Wm Darius (Bill)
    Myers
MG n clover
Kaoru Emi
    Nakashima
Carlo Navato
Donald Necessary
Nic
David Nicholls
Martyn Nichols
Duna Nichs
Wolfgang Noack
noodledoodle
Simon Norcott
Norman Normal
Joe Nuttman
Pearl O'Leslie
Mikey O'Neill
Mark O'Reilly
Laken Oikle
Rob Oliver
David E. Olvera
Oniros
Osbaldeston
Michael Österlund
Paul Ottey
Chris Pace
John Palmer
Steph Parker
Shaun Parkes
John Parkhill
George Partridge
Alex Paterson
Ray Paterson
Mark Patten

Alex Paul
Darren Pearce
Matthew Pearson
Scott Pearson
Tim Pease
Stephen Pellow
Peter
Jason Petit
Claudia Phillips
Heather Phillips
Hywel Phillips
Pief
Caroline Pierce
Mister Pink
Joel Pinkston
David Piper
John Pirrie
Justin Pollard
Richard Powell
Ford Prefect
Andrew Priestly
Carl Proffit
Mistress Puissance
Laura Quin
Mike Quinn
Kitty Quinzell
Bob R
Ja Ra
RA
Elena Ramos
Dan Ramsden
Keith Ramsey
Miss Tara Red
Frank Reding
RedTeamLeaderoo
Jens Reichel
Alan Reilly
Steve Reinmuth
Jean-Philippe Rey
Robert Reyer
Tim Rich
Laura Richmond
Jon Rickard
David Rickman
Rimmer

Izzabella Robbins
Richard Robertson
Stephen Robins
Kevin Roche
Martin Roche
Joshua Rodgers
David Rogers
Laurence Rogers
Roland @
    naughtymediauk
Bodo Roloff
Rommel
James Romney
Craig Rose
Elizabeth Rose
Olivia Rose
Christian Rövekamp
Paul Rowlands
Oddvar Rugland
Dominik S
S
Rainer S.
Steven S.
S.B
Heidi Salander
Chris Sandalls
Jake Sanderson
Juan Sanmiguel
Ray Sawhill
Philippe Schaeffer
Keith Schuerholz
Wolfgang Schwarz
Thorsten
    Schweinsberg
David Scott
Gemma Scott
Scott
Soles Scream
@SecretAdrianShh
Paul Senior
John Serbin
Paul Shanley
Richard Sharman
Tim Sheerman-Chase
BIG DICK Akira Shell

Len Shenker
Jeroen Sijsling
Giordano Silvestri
Simon & Cheryl
Bryan Simpson
Craig Simpson
sleepyhead
Russell Sloan
Brian Small
Harry Smart
John Smet
Chris Smith
Lee Smith
Robert Smith
Fred Sned
Ian Snowley
JP Solignac
Ted Sone
Andrew Southern
Barrie Spence
Valerie Spencer
Tania Sperlonga
Carl Spicer
Geoff Spink
Square2Lark
Blank Stare
Neil Starfruit
Helen Stephens
Sarah Stern
Martin Stevens
Carole Stone
Jeff Stratford
Damian Streets
Sue & Justin
Dr Paul Summers
Rich Sumner
S Surf
Nick Sutton
Sheldon Sutton
Blair Switch
Paul T
Tasha Tarte
Faye Taylor
Helen Taylor
J Taylor

Mark Taylor
Niall Taylor
David Tazzyman
The Dacey Harlot
The Havering
  Collection
The_Neon_God
Tom Theunissen
Catherine Thomas
Mark Thomas
Stuart Thomas
Philip Thompson
Mike Thorne
Susan Thorne
John Thornhill
Hrafn Thorvaldsson
Christopher Tibble
Alfred Timberlake
Joanna Tindall
Phiriya
  Tingthanathikul
John Tisbury
Melissa Todd
Chris Tolkien
TolstoyTony
Tony and Beverley
Hans Torslett
Benjamin Toth
William Treadwell
Mark Tregent
Stephen True
Jay Turnock
Tyher
Alan Urie
Dean Vanderkolk
Craig Vaughton
Adam Velez
Mark Vent
George W
Peter W. Frey
James Waddell
Valentino Wagner
Paul Walker
william walker
Aalen Wall

William Wallace
Chris Walsh
Cole Ward
John Ward
warmachinet
Bethany Watson
Richard Webb
William Webber
Ingela Savborn
  Weidsten
Malcolm Weir and
  Marlowe
Mark Wells-Pestell
Sascha Wendler
Wes
Alex West
Becky White
JT White
Paul White
Stephen White
Bill Who ???
Mog Wilde
Busby Wilder
Isaac Wilkins
Dee Williams
Jodi Williams
Mark Williams
Theo Williams
Don Wilson
Lisa Wilson
Mark Wilson
David Wiltshire
Guy Windsor
Zoe Wiseman
D. Gene Witmer
Nigel Worrall
Andy Wright
Penelope York
Alan Young
Dr. Zee
Zena & Leigh
Terence Zhang
James Zimmerman